THE MEANING OF MODERN POETRY

A TutorText

THE MEANING OF

PUBLISHED BY

DOUBLEDAY & COMPANY, INC., GARDEN CITY, N.Y.

1962

Modern Poetry

by John Clark Pratt

PREPARED UNDER THE DIRECTION OF

EDUCATIONAL SCIENCE DIVISION

U.S. Industries, Inc.

Library of Congress Catalog Card Number: 62-8102

Printed in the United States of America

Grateful acknowledgment is made for permission to use the following copyrighted material: "On Dwelling" from *Collected Poems, 1914–1947* by Robert Graves. Copyright © 1955 by Roturman S. A. Reprinted by permission of Doubleday & Company, Inc.

"Buffalo Bill's" from *Poems 1923–1954* by E. E. Cummings. Copyright, 1923, 1951 by E. E. Cummings. Reprinted by permission of Harcourt, Brace & World, Inc. and Faber & Faber Ltd.

"Return to Ritual" from *Selected Poems* by Mark Van Doren. Copyright 1939, 1944, 1948, 1953, 1954 by Mark Van Doren. "The Oven Bird" from *Complete Poems of Robert Frost*. Copyright 1916, 1921 by Holt, Rinehart and Winston, Inc. Copyright renewed 1944 by Robert Frost. "Limited" from *Chicago Poems* by Carl Sandburg. Copyright 1916 by Holt, Rinehart and Winston, Inc. Copyright renewed 1944 by Carl Sandburg. All reprinted by permission of Holt, Rinehart and Winston, Inc.

"Night Clouds" from *The Complete Poetical Works of Amy Lowell.* Reprinted by permission of Houghton Mifflin Company.

"The Death of the Ball Turret Gunner" by Randall Jarrell. From *Little Friend, Little Friend,* copyright 1945 by Dial Press, Inc. Reprinted by permission of the author.

"I Saw a Man Pursuing the Horizon" from *Collected Poems of Stephen Crane,* copyright 1930 by Alfred A. Knopf, Inc. Reprinted by permission of the publisher.

"The Oxen" from *Collected Poems of Thomas Hardy*. Copyright 1925 by The Macmillan Company. "Leda and the Swan" from *The Collected Poems of W. B. Yeats,* Definitive Edition, 1956, copyright 1928 by The Macmillan Company, renewed 1956 by Georgie Yeats. "General Salute" from *Angel of Accidence* by Peter Kane Dufault. Copyright 1954 by Peter Kane Dufault. All used by permission of The Macmillan Company.

"Arms and the Boy" from *Poems of Wilfred Owen*. All rights reserved. "Sarolla's Women . . ." from *Pictures of the Gone World,* copyright 1955 by Lawrence Ferlinghetti. Copyright © 1958 by Lawrence Ferlinghetti. "Not From This Anger" from *Dylan Thomas, Collected Poems*. Copyright © 1957 by New Directions. All reprinted by permission of New Directions.

"God's Grandeur" from *Poems of Gerard Manley Hopkins,* copyright 1948 by Oxford University Press. Reprinted by permission of the publisher.

"Musee des Beaux Arts" from *Another Time* by W. H. Auden. Copyright 1940 by W. H. Auden. Reprinted from *The Collected Poetry of W. H. Auden* by permission of Random House, Inc. and Faber & Faber Ltd.

"The Timid Future" (copyright © 1958 The Atlantic Monthly Company) is reprinted with the permission of Charles Scribner's Sons from *The Gardener and Other Poems* by John Hall Wheelock. "A Woman Too Well Remembered" (copyright 1955 Louis Simpson) which first appeared in Discovery #5 is reprinted with the permission of Charles Scribner's Sons from *Poets of Today II: Good News of Death and Other Poems* by Louis Simpson. All reprinted by permission of Charles Scribner's Sons.

"The Virgin Mary" from *The Form of Loss* by Edgar Bowers. Copyright © 1956 by Edgar Bowers. "And What is Love" from *The Exclusions of a Rhyme: Poems and Epigrams* by J. V. Cunningham. Copyright © 1960 by J. V. Cunningham. All reprinted by permission of the publisher, Alan Swallow.

Preface

The average modern adult, apparently content with advertising doggerel, newspaperese, and business jargon, is wholly indifferent to the attitudes, opinions, and beliefs of the more serious-minded poets of his Age.

This indifference, usually based on honest ignorance, should not exist. Poetry characterizes Ages, and any person who ignores poetry risks isolation from the most important ideas of his time. But once introduced to the poetry of his Age, he begins to investigate the vital questions of all time: what and where he as an individual really is — and why.

This book is not merely an attempt to demonstrate my own feelings about the chosen poems. Realizing that dissection of any poem often results in chuckles from the poet and the bored indifference of the reader, I have tried to help the reader in creating his own attitude toward and appreciation of a particular poem.

In addition, few poems are glitteringly perfect. To say that a poem is good or bad is not enough; the reader must justify his attitude, and in order to do so, he must realize not only what poetry says but what it can do for him.

A teacher cannot show anyone what a poem *really* means, but he can help a student learn for himself. No single interpretation of a poem is absolutely, incontestably correct. A poem which is instantly clear to one man is gibberish to another. This book should help the reader resolve the difference.

I have selected the contemporary period (1885 to the present) because the subjects of most contemporary poems fall within the reader's own experience, thus linking the substance of poetry to familiar surroundings, things, and ideas. This book should give the reader the basic equipment to work with any poem he might read.

I wish to thank the poets for permission to comment (not always favorably) on their works, and especially to thank Harold Dennis Gray, Leighton Steele II, and Kellogg Smith for their editorial assistance.

J. C. P.

Contents

NOTE TO THE READER

This is not an ordinary book. Although the pages are numbered in the ordinary way, you must not try to read them consecutively. You must follow the directions at the bottom of each page.

You will find that reading this book is like having an individual tutor. The book will continually ask you questions and correct errors as well as give you information.

Your progress through this course will depend entirely on your ability to choose right answers instead of wrong ones. It is recommended that you not try to go through this course in one sitting, or even two or three. As a rule, several short sessions are more productive than a few long ones.

You should have a good dictionary at hand so that you may look up whatever unfamiliar words and poetic terms you encounter.

Follow the instructions, and you will reach the final page with increased knowledge and understanding of contemporary poetry.

CHAPTER I

What Is a Poem?

What is a poem? Few writers are in complete agreement, but no matter what differences arise, poets seem to agree in one area: a poem must at least be honest, consistent, and complete. A group of words in verse is not good poetry simply because it expresses an idea or emotion. The idea or emotion must be expressed as a fused unity. No good poem has ever been written because the author *had* to express his feelings; nor is a fragment a poem. However weary the author, he must not give up halfway through. No good poem is dishonest, inconsistent, or incomplete.

Almost everyone has read some poetry, and we can all recognize a poem when we see one. Or can we?

Which of the following statements is true?

I?
Why?
    is not a poem. **page 7**

abcdefg
hijklmnop
qrs and tuv
w and xyz
    is not a poem. **page 9**

Both of the above are poems. **page 11**

Neither of the above is a poem. **page 13**

You have reached this page by mistake, for you could not have arrived here by following directions. To repeat: This book is not put together like ordinary books. Although the pages are numbered serially (1, 2, 3, and so on), you must not try to read them serially. On each page there are clear instructions directing you to the next page you are to read.

Many pages contain questions, and you indicate your answer by turning to specific pages as directed. Sometimes the directions will refer you to a page you have already seen; other times you will be sent on to new material.

Now go back to the page you just came from, and follow directions.

[*from page 11*]

YOUR ANSWER:

abcdefg
hijklmnop

is dishonest.

Wrong. The use of part of the alphabet is entirely honest. There is no attempt by the author to put something over on the reader, no use of language just for its own sake, no unjustified words or emotion — any of which offenses would signify a dishonest poem.

Honesty implies adherence to a standard, and this implication applies to poetry. An honest poem is one in which there is *justified treatment* of the subject of the poem: no hysterics, no editorializing, and no digressions.

The letters *a* through *p* arranged as above constitute an honest attempt at writing a poem.

Return to page 11 and select another answer.

[*from page 8*]

YOUR ANSWER:

abc
Woe is me

violates honesty.

You are right, but only partially so. The poem is obviously dishonest, for there are no demonstrable grounds for the author's woe. But aren't there other violations? How about consistency and completeness? We must not, when reading a poem, fasten upon one flaw or good point and let all other qualities go unnoticed. Wouldn't this be dishonest criticism?

Not only must the emotion and content of a poem be honest, consistent, and complete, but so must the reader's approach. Look at the above poem again. Can you see all three requirements — honesty, consistency, and completeness — being violated?

Yes, all three are violated. **page 12**

No, I cannot see all three being violated. **page 14**

[*from page 11*]

YOUR ANSWER:

abcdefg
hijklmnop

is inconsistent.

Think. What is inconsistent about the letters as arranged in this example? They progress as they should, from *a* to *p*.

Is there anything unnecessary added? Anything taken for granted or omitted which leaves the reader unsatisfied? These are the questions to consider when discussing the consistency of a poem, and in regard to the fragment of the alphabet, you have to answer "no" to all of them.

Consistency means that the poem has a logical progression from beginning to end. You will encounter poems which at first appear to lack structure, but if a poem is good, its structure will become apparent at closer reading. In the example above, the main virtue of the poem is its consistency.

Return to page 11 and choose another answer.

[*from page 8*]

YOUR ANSWER:

abc
Woe is me

violates consistency.

Yes it does, but that is not all. The poem is made inconsistent by the unjustified jump from the first three letters of the alphabet to an expression of the author's woe. But aren't there other violations? What about honesty and completeness? We must not, when reading a poem, fasten upon one flaw or good point and allow all other qualities to go unnoticed. Wouldn't this be inconsistent criticism?

Not only must the content and the emotion of a poem be honest, consistent, and complete, but so must the reader's approach. Look at the above poem again. Can you see all three requirements — honesty, consistency, and completeness — being violated?

Yes, all three are violated. **page 12**

No, I cannot see all three being violated. **page 14**

[*from page 1*]

YOUR ANSWER:

I?
Why?

is not a poem.

Why not? Do you think that a poem must have a specific number of lines or look regular or contain a certain amount of material? If so, you are wrong. "I? Why?" has been called the shortest poem in the English language because its two words rhythmically express a complete thought. It asks a question that has plagued men since the beginning of time: "Why do I exist?"

During this century poetry has undergone a period of experimentation. Changes in approach, style, and subject matter have sometimes produced oddities. But the English language is flexible, and you must expect poets to utilize its versatility. However, all poems must still meet the three requirements mentioned earlier: honesty, consistency, and completeness.

Return to page 1 and select another answer.

[*from page 11*]

YOUR ANSWER:

abcdefg
hijklmnop

is incomplete.

Right. The alphabet, as presented above, is fragmentary. The poem is far from finished. If the arrangement were

abcdefg
w and xyz

it would also be incomplete, because a familiar and important section is omitted. Though the reader may disagree with me, I do not believe that a fragment can be called a poem.

Any arrangement of letters is both honest and consistent. In its own terms, such a poem would contain no material, no references, no subject matter which exceeded the poem's limited intention. Within the poem the letters would progress consistently, from one to the other. We can see here that the letter *a* is to be taken as the first letter of the alphabet, *b* the second, and so on. Even if the arranger were to scramble the letters, their disorder could be construed as consistency, as long as the author intended to create chaos.

So far we have talked mainly about the subject and the material used in the poem. But what about the attitude of the poet? Shouldn't it also be honest, consistent, and complete? Yes, it should. Emotion, too, must be limited by honesty, consistency, and completeness.

Consider the expression of emotion in poetry, and apply the tests to the following poem.

abc
Woe is me

The poem violates honesty. **page 4**

The poem violates consistency. **page 6**

The poem violates completeness. **page 10**

The poem violates all three. **page 12**

[*from page 1*]

YOUR ANSWER:

abcdefg
hijklmnop
qrs and tuv
w and xyz

is not a poem.

Careful. It is a poem, for it well exemplifies the requirements of honesty, consistency, and completeness set forth earlier. The alphabet, although commonplace, is not an unfit subject for poetry, even though its poetic possibilities are limited. In fact, the alphabet, in its normal order, was actually used in the 1920's as a poem entitled "Suicide."

Poets often experiment, and you should be willing to accept variances from what you might consider traditional forms. But remember the requirements for good poetry: honesty, consistency, and completeness. If the poem violates one or more of these requirements, you are likely to have a difficult time understanding its author's intentions.

Return to page 1 and select another answer.

[*from page 8*]

YOUR ANSWER:

abc
Woe is me

violates completeness.

Yes, it does. But is this the only violation? The poem is incomplete because it appears unfinished, fragmentary, implying that there should be more to it: more letters, for instance, or at least some evidence for the author's woe. What about honesty and consistency, however? We should not, when reading a poem, fasten upon one flaw or good point and let all other qualities go unnoticed. Wouldn't this be incomplete criticism?

Not only must the content and emotion of a poem be honest, consistent, and complete, but so must the reader's approach. Look at the above poem again. Can you see all three requirements — honesty, consistency, and completeness — being violated?

Yes, all three are violated. **page 12**

No, I cannot see all three being violated. **page 14**

[*from page 1*]

YOUR ANSWER: Both are poems.

Yes, you are right. "I? Why?" could be entitled "A Metaphysical Introspection of Myself in Terms of the Universal." The alphabet, so presented, is complete within itself, honestly portraying all that the arranger (he can't really be called an author) meant.

You would have a difficult time justifying to a scholar your view that the two examples are poetry unless you defined your terms. Most disagreements about poetry stem from a failure to do just this. One reader might object to the language of a poem while praising the subject; another might not understand the subject but be delighted with the language; a third would disapprove of both subject and choice of words, and so on. Always insist on a clear definition of the terms used in a discussion; otherwise you can expect only meaningless argument.

Consider the three terms: honesty, consistency, and completeness. If we have a poem

abcdefg
hijklmnop

which of the three principles is most obviously violated?

The poem is dishonest. **page 3**

The poem is inconsistent. **page 5**

The poem is incomplete. **page 8**

[*from page 4, 6, 8, 10, or 14*]

YOUR ANSWER: The poem violates all three requirements: honesty, consistency, and completeness.

Right. We now have an adequate basis for further discussion.

We shall soon start looking at specific poems. Before we do, however, here is why the lines

abc
Woe is me

violate the three requirements of a poem. The reader can obtain no idea why the poet is upset. Is the poet distressed because the alphabet is unfinished, or because he cannot go any further? His expression of emotion is dishonest, for he makes no effort to tell why he is reacting thus to the three letters. The reader is left dangling, wondering what the fuss is about.

Contemporary poetry often calls for rereading because authors commonly obscure their intentions. Only by going over a poem again and again can the reader grasp its meaning. A good poem does not ramble. Every word, line, and stanza is packed with as much meaning as possible.

Poetry differs from other forms of writing, not only because it intensifies language and ideas, but also because it appeals to the eye and ear. To comprehend fully what the poet means, you should read the poem aloud, thus drawing on the sensuous appeal of poetry.

Now you should know what a poem is: appealing first by appearance and sound, it is an arrangement of words which, in terms of its occasion, subject, and the author's emotion, is honest, consistent, and complete. Now go to page 15 and we will discuss the language of poetry.

[*from page 1*]

YOUR ANSWER: Neither is a poem.

Are you willing to back up this belief with evidence? Can you define for yourself what a poem is? Try it. In 25 words or less, complete the following statement: "A poem is . . . ."

Could you do it? If so, didn't your definition contain references to rhyme, rhythm, and sound? The alphabet as presented on page 1 certainly rhymes, doesn't it? And aren't the lines about the same length? Finally, if this arrangement of the alphabet is not a poem, what else is it? You should be able to apply any of the above questions to "I? Why?"

Just because a group of words does not appear to mean anything at first glance does not preclude its being called a poem. Basically, a poem is a composition in verse, a group of words which appeals to the ear as well as the eye. For the moment, let us not be any more specific than this.

Accept both of these examples as poems. From now on, we will attempt to determine why some poems are better than others.

Return to page 1 and select another answer.

[*from page 4, 6, or 10*]

YOUR ANSWER: No, I cannot see all three being violated.

We have a problem.

In order to understand poetry, you must accept some of the conventions, and you must not quibble over minor points before you have sound basis for discussion. If you honestly could not see that the poem violates honesty, consistency, and completeness in terms of both subject and emotion, then return to page 1 and start again. Take the nonsense poems as aids to the definition of terms, and then go on to page 12. If you still can't agree, then I suggest that you:

(1) Burn the book and go through life thinking poetry is a waste of time, thereby shutting yourself off from a field of culture which is enlightening and enjoyable.

(2) Go on to page 12 anyway, just because you are good-natured and are willing to accept some of the author's views for the sake of argument.

CHAPTER II

Metaphor: The Language of Poetry

Here are some lines from "To His Coy Mistress," by the seventeenth-century English poet Andrew Marvell:

> Let us roll our strength and all
> Our sweetness up into one ball,
> And tear our pleasures with rough strife
> Through the iron gates of life.

Though this poem was written three hundred years ago, its metaphorical language strongly resembles the language of many poets writing today. Note the poem's title, "To His Coy Mistress." The poet addresses a young woman in the hope of seducing her. Does he ask her bluntly or directly? Does he expect her (and the reader) to take what he says literally? Can you imagine anyone's actually taking a handful of strength and a handful of sweetness and rolling them into a sort of snowball? No, of course not. What is the device that enables Marvell to state simple, even commonplace, ideas in this exciting and lively form? The answer to my question is metaphor, the language of poetry. Marvell speaks in metaphor, and by his use of metaphorical language, he transforms an ordinary proposition into an appealing and lively poem.

For the purposes of this study, please disregard the definition of metaphor you may already be familiar with; we are discussing not grammar but poetry. I will show that *all* comparisons made in poetry fall into the general category of metaphor and that they can further be divided into simile, image, and symbol. By reading this section you should obtain a clear understanding of what I mean by metaphor, the language of poetry, as found in specific poems.

First, what is metaphor? It is little more than the comparison between two elements, an implied equality between objects or ideas which are not ordinarily compared. A poet uses metaphor much as a chemist uses a weight and balance to make the material on one side of the scale correspond in weight with that on the other side. When we say of a word or a group of words, "This is metaphor," all we mean is that there is a metaphorical equals-sign present.

Please go on to page 16.

[*from page 15*]

A *simile* is a metaphor which uses the words *like* or *as*. "George looks like Joe," we might say, using a simile, but in order to recognize George, don't we first have to know what Joe looks like? Certainly. If we do not know what Joe looks like, the comparison is meaningless. A simile must have a *referent* (the basis for the comparison; in this example, Joe) which is either familiar or can be made precisely identifiable. The referent, the thing being compared *to*, must be stated.

If we were to say, for example, that a particular tree is like life, we would be making an odd simile which would require explanation. A simile properly compares something which a reader might find strange or new to something which is readily understood.

Read the following epigram by J. V. Cunningham and identify the referent used in the simile.

> And what is love? Misunderstanding, pain,
> Delusion, or retreat? It is in truth
> Like an old brandy after a long rain,
> Distinguished, and familiar, and aloof.

What is the referent used in the simile?

Love. **page 19**

Brandy. **page 24**

[*from page 24*]

YOUR ANSWER: The world is on fire.

How can this be? Read the lines again.

> The world is charged with the grandeur of God.
> It will flame out, like shining from shook foil;

What will *flame out*? The world? Not at all. Hopkins meant *it* to refer to the grandeur of God, flaming out "like shining from shook foil."

Perhaps you read the lines hastily, or perhaps you were confused by the metaphoric language. Here, Hopkins asks the reader to visualize the product of a physical act, the shaking of a sheet of foil. Take a sheet of foil yourself; hold it up before a light, and shake it. What do you see? Nothing, if you hold the foil between you and the light. But if you hold the foil so it catches the light and then shake it, you will see a glittering reflection. This visual image is what Hopkins uses in the poem to represent the grandeur of God.

The world, says Hopkins, is charged with this grandeur. What are the implications of the word *charged*? Do you not feel a sense of latent power as in a charged battery? God's grandeur, charging the world, *will* flame out, the poet asserts.

Read these lines not only to perceive the image, but also to discover what causes you to sense what you do.

Return to page 24 and choose another answer.

[*from page 25*]

YOUR ANSWER: *Speed* is being symbolized.

I'm afraid not. Certainly there is motion: a man pursues the horizon; and in the second line Crane states that "round and round they sped." But the questions concerned the *symbol* in the first line, not the action taking place in the poem. Remember, that which is being symbolized is shown in terms of something we can apprehend with our senses. The symbol itself may be an object, an action, an animal, or a human being. With our intellect we then make the connection between the symbol and what is being symbolized.

At the beginning of this chapter, you read four lines of Marvell's poem "To His Coy Mistress." Marvell lived three hundred years ago, but poets of the twentieth century have used literary symbol in much the same manner Marvell used it. Here are the four lines you saw earlier:

Let us roll our strength and all
Our sweetness up into one ball,
And tear our pleasures with rough strife
Through the iron gates of life.

Look at the last line. *Iron gates of life* is a symbol. Note how the phrase can be defined first as an implied simile (certain features of life are *like* iron gates), then as an image (we can *see* what iron gates are), and finally as a symbol of restraint.

Return to page 25, reread the poem, and choose the correct answer.

[*from page 16*]

YOUR ANSWER: *Love* is the referent used in the simile.

Wrong. You have misunderstood the meaning of the word *referent.* In using a simile, a poet compares a specific notion to something recognizable or familiar. The basis for the comparison — the familiar object, sight, or feeling — is the referent. For us to understand a simile, we must understand the referent. Only then can we see the point of the author's comparison. For example:

The sky was as blue as a robin's egg.

The referent here is *robin's egg*, and because we presumably know the color of a robin's egg, we know the particular shade of the sky. The simile is

color of sky = color of robin's egg

and the word *as* is a substitute for the equals-sign of the metaphor. Note how the sentence can be rephrased to use the word *like*:

The sky was blue, like a robin's egg.

In both examples, the referent remains the same.

Return to page 16 and choose the right answer.

[*from page 24*]

YOUR ANSWER: God's grandeur is shimmering.

Correct. Hopkins sees the grandeur of God in every created thing, and the shimmering reflections from a shaken piece of foil represent to him God's magnificence.

Don't be misled, however, into thinking that an image must always be a picture. An image may appeal to any or all of the senses: sight, hearing, smell, taste, and touch. Remember Cunningham's brandy? The image he creates is the taste of old brandy, sipped after a long rain.

Here is a poem by Amy Lowell, an early champion of the Imagist school, a group of poets who sought to express their emotions and ideas through clear, precise images. Her poem creates a sense of frantic motion, futile movement. Within the poem is a series of images which produce the total result.

Night Clouds

The white mares of the moon rush along the sky
Beating their golden hoofs along the glass Heavens;
The white mares of the moon are all standing on their hind legs
Pawing at the green porcelain doors of the remote Heavens.
Fly, mares!
Strain your utmost,
Scatter the milky dust of stars,
Or the tiger sun will leap upon you and destroy you
With one lick of his vermilion tongue.

Read the poem again, carefully noting individual images. Is there anything disturbing in the poem? Is each image clear? Is each of the three requirements for a good poem met? Or is there something dishonest and inconsistent in the series of visual images?

Which of the following is most appropriate?

There is nothing dishonest or inconsistent in the poem. **page 23**

White mares never gallop in the sky. **page 27**

Golden hoofs and green porcelain doors are out of place here. **page 30**

[*from page 30*]

YOUR ANSWER: *Glass heavens* is not an implied simile.

Wrong. The phrase above *is* an implied simile. Lowell is saying that the heavens are translucent; in other words, the heavens are *like* glass.

Return to page 30 and select the phrase which does not have a separate, identifiable referent.

22

[*from page 29*]

YOUR ANSWER: *Weapons of war* is the subject of the predominant series of images.

Wrong. Although the bullet heads, the bayonet blades, and the cartridges may be construed as traditional symbols, they are certainly *not* the predominant series of images in the poem.

An image appeals to one of the five senses. Remember the "shining from shook foil" in the Hopkins poem "God's Grandeur." It was not the foil but the *shining* which was the image. Weapons of war may be traditional symbols, but they are not images.

In "Arms and the Boy," Owen fastens onto a particular quality of the weapons. He looks at each type of weapon from a particular point of view. Is Owen's image of a bayonet blade an image of death? or of hunger for blood? What sights, sounds, tastes, smells, and feelings is he trying to arouse in your imagination?

Return to page 29 and reread the poem again. Obviously the poem concerns weapons of war, but you must decide on the particular use Owen makes of them.

[*from page 20*]

YOUR ANSWER: There is nothing dishonest or inconsistent in the poem.

All right. Read the poem again, this time remembering the definitions of honesty and consistency.

Night Clouds

The white mares of the moon rush along the sky
Beating their golden hoofs along the glass Heavens;
The white mares of the moon are all standing on their hind legs
Pawing at the green porcelain doors of the remote Heavens.
Fly, mares!
Strain your utmost,
Scatter the milky dust of stars,
Or the tiger sun will leap upon you and destroy you
With one lick of his vermilion tongue.

Each image must have a logical connection with the poem's subject, in this example the image of white clouds against a night sky. Visualize this sight. One of the favorite devices of the Imagists is the broad use of color, but I, as a reader, demand that these colors be used honestly. Perhaps if you could ask Miss Lowell what she means by some of her extraordinary images, she might answer, "Nothing; that's how I see it." But such an attitude does not justify calling "Night Clouds" a good poem.

Once again, visualize the night sky, the stars, the clouds, the moon; then reread the poem and determine which images are dishonest and inconsistent with such a sight.

Return to page 20 and select another answer.

[*from page 16*]

YOUR ANSWER: *Brandy* is the referent used in the simile.

Right. This answer seems like the obvious one, even though perhaps everyone has not tasted old brandy. Does unfamiliarity with old brandy impair understanding of the poetry? No, the poet cannot be concerned about everyone who reads his work; he writes from his own experience. He can use Greek phrases, Latin echoes, or Sanskrit sentences, as long as he uses them honestly, consistently, and completely. If a reader does not understand a poem, the burden is on him to perform the research and find the answer. Not all research, however, is so pleasant as that in old brandy.

A simile, then, is a metaphor which always uses *like* or *as* in place of the implied equals-sign.

For now, though, let us go one step further. The second type of metaphor is the *image*, roughly defined as an impression created by words which appeal to the senses. Often a simile is used to build a desired image, as can be seen in the opening lines of Gerard Manley Hopkins' poem "God's Grandeur."

> The world is charged with the grandeur of God.
> It will flame out, like shining from shook foil;

Notice here that the referent, *shining from shook foil*, has an immediate appeal to the sense of sight. The foil (to Hopkins, a thin sheet of beaten silver or gold, like that used in church decoration) is not standing still or lying crumpled in a corner; it is being shaken. The comparison of the *shining from shook foil* to God's grandeur produces an image.

What picture or image is created by the use of the simile?

The world is on fire. **page 17**

God's grandeur is shimmering. **page 20**

I'm not certain. **page 32**

[*from page 30*]

YOUR ANSWER: *Remote heavens* is not an implied simile.

Right. This phrase is merely descriptive, as are *white mares* and *vermilion tongue*. There is, however, implied simile in the phrases *glass heavens* (heavens like glass), *tiger sun* (sun like a tiger), and *milky dust of stars* (stars like milky dust).

Now, what about symbol? It differs from the other types of metaphor by its appeal to the intellect. Here's an elementary example. To a young child, a burning match is *like* the fire in the fireplace, and even a one-year-old can usually recognize a picture of fire. He responds to images through his sense of sight. What happens when he touches fire? Suddenly the fire takes on a new quality — pain. The fire as a symbol is not *like* pain; it does not stand for pain; it *is* pain.

Thus it is with the symbol as used in contemporary poetry. A symbol (an action, object, animal, person) does not stand for something else; it *is* that usually abstract concept which it symbolizes. Take Lowell's *tiger sun*, for instance, which we first saw as an image. By use of our intellect we can make this a symbol of fierceness and destructiveness, both of which are qualities of a tiger. We are told that the sun will not gently chase away the clouds but will leap upon them and devour them. Our sense of sight has yoked tiger and sun together; our intellect has responded to the symbol.

Let's investigate the use of symbol in this poem by Stephen Crane.

> I saw a man pursuing the horizon;
> Round and round they sped.
> I was disturbed at this;
> I accosted the man.
> "It is futile," I said,
> "You can never — "
>
> "You lie," he cried,
> And ran on.

What is being symbolized in the first line of the poem above?

Speed. **page 18**

Futile determination. **page 28**

Pursuit. **page 35**

26
[*from page 37*]

YOUR ANSWER: *War's killing of boys* is symbolized in the predominant series of images.

No, your answer concerns one of the great tragedies of war, to be sure, but in terms of this poem this view is not of major importance.

Owen is concerned with a *particular* aspect of war. What is it, he is asking, that makes war so necessarily terrifying?

We all know that war is horrible; yet we have difficulty in honestly pinning down the reasons and translating our result into words. Often, war poetry is designed either to shock or disgust the reader. Owen, however, provides an original and memorable answer to the question of war.

Return to page 37 and reread the poem, this time isolating every word or phrase which, according to our previous discussion, is an image. Notice how each of them is honest, consistent, and complete.

[*from page 20*]

YOUR ANSWER: White mares never gallop in the sky.

Metaphorically speaking, they can. Remember the discussion of the language of poetry and allow yourself to admit that anything can happen within a poem as long as the result is honest, consistent, and complete.

You might look at a specific woman and say that to you she represents the Ideal Woman. The poet, however, looks at the ideal, the universal, and then tries to show not this universal quality but its representation *as he sees it*. A painter might represent the water as a stable, unchanging body, and the land as a muddy, shifting mass. Why? He might wish to depict the changelessness of the sea and the changeability of land, a process that to him reveals the evolution of nature. Just because most persons see the land as stable and the sea as mobile is no reason to deny the painter his right to paint the world as he sees it. We don't have to like his painting, but we must admit his right to paint as he pleases.

So please let mares gallop in the poet's sky. Cirrus clouds, often present at night as vestiges of more turbulent daytime clouds, are called by meteorologists "mares' tails," because of their wispiness and movement. You must demand, however, that a poet's use of imagery be honest, consistent, and complete. Would elephants' tails fit here? Or beavers' tails?

Return to page 20, reread the poem, and attempt to identify any images which are not honest results of the sight of night clouds.

[*from page 25*]

YOUR ANSWER: *Futile determination* is being symbolized.

Correct. The man pursuing the continuously receding horizon symbolizes futile determination. Though flying machines may occasionally steal a march on the sun, the horizon can never be caught, for it is only the apparent line between the sky and earth.

Some symbols have meaning apart from poems in which they occur. For example, a rock can symbolize hardness; the moon, woman; the sun, man. But even these are often altered within a specific poem. For instance, a rock, though hard, can be drilled with a diamond-headed tool.

If you are still uncertain about the meaning of symbol, go back to page 25 and read the definition. Then return to this page.

Read the following poem by Wilfred Owen as many times as necessary to recognize Owen's use of simile, image, and symbol.

Arms and the Boy

Let the boy try along this bayonet-blade
How cold steel is, and keen with hunger of blood;
Blue with all malice, like a madman's flash;
And thinly drawn with famishing for flesh.

Lend him to stroke these blind, blunt bullet-heads
Which long to nuzzle in the hearts of lads,
Or give him cartridges of fine zinc teeth,
Sharp with the sharpness of grief and death.

For his teeth seem for laughing round an apple.
There lurk no claws behind his fingers supple;
And God will grow no talons at his heels,
Nor antlers through the thickness of his curls.

Please go on to page 29.

[*from page 28*]

Now read the poem two more times, the second time aloud. Look for the series of images which, when taken together, create a symbol of the particular aspect of war which Owen is concerned with in this poem.

Arms and the Boy

Let the boy try along this bayonet-blade
How cold steel is, and keen with hunger of blood;
Blue with all malice, like a madman's flash;
And thinly drawn with famishing for flesh.

Lend him to stroke these blind, blunt bullet-heads
Which long to nuzzle in the hearts of lads,
Or give him cartridges of fine zinc teeth,
Sharp with the sharpness of grief and death.

For his teeth seem for laughing round an apple.
There lurk no claws behind his fingers supple;
And God will grow no talons at his heels,
Nor antlers through the thickness of his curls.

What is the subject of the predominant series of images?

Weapons of war. **page 22**

Death. **page 33**

Desire for food. **page 37**

[*from page 20*]

YOUR ANSWER: Golden hoofs and green porcelain doors are out of place here.

Correct. Perhaps silver hoofs would be acceptable, but even so, the image of green porcelain doors is disturbing to me. Some of the Imagists used images indiscriminately, only because they liked a certain sight, sound, or smell; for this reason much of their poetry is meaningless. The Imagists' effect on other poets was, however, significant, and much of the sensuous appeal of contemporary poetry is derived from this group of poets of the early twentieth century.

Another term we should know is *implied simile*, a type of metaphor which exhibits all the properties of a simile without using the words *like* or *as*. In all similes we must sense both the referent and the other term simultaneously; in effect, we place both elements of the comparison side by side, then observe.

Both parts of a simile must appeal to the senses, whether the words *like* or *as* are present or implied. The symbol, as we shall see, differs considerably.

If you have difficulty identifying implied simile, simply ask yourself, "Can I see both sides of the equals sign?" If you can, you should then be able to insert *like* or *as* into the comparison with no change in meaning.

Which of the following phrases is not an implied simile?

Glass heavens. **page 21**

Remote heavens. **page 25**

Milky dust of stars. **page 36**

[*from page 37*]

YOUR ANSWER: *War's predatory hunger* is symbolized in the predominant series of images.

Right. Owen consistently introduces hunger imagery, becoming more subtle and more specific as the poem develops. In stanza 2 he compares cartridges to sharp teeth, setting up the contrast with the boy's teeth in stanza 3, teeth which "seem for laughing round an apple." So far, however, he has used only the hungry, *man-made* weapons which are *tried by* the boy (line 1) or *lent* to him (line 5). But notice the transition to the inevitable, primordial hunger when Owen introduces the true predatory nature of war. The lurking claws, the "talons at his heels," and the antlers are all images of the weapons of wild animals which must fight or prey for survival. Taken together, these images are a symbol of the predatory nature of war, stated ironically by reference to weapons which are lent to a boy, as toys.

Finally, is the poem complete? Within the limits stated in the title, "Arms and the Boy" is a complete poem. It is concerned only with war; Owen introduces no material which does not bear directly on his subject.

Can we now say that we are through with this poem? Not at all. There is much more to it. What, for instance, is the significance of the title? Does it echo any well-known, often quoted piece of literature? Would knowing the source of the original expression "arms and the man" add to our knowledge of the poem's meaning? Of course it would. See if you can find the origin of this phrase; if you can't, continue reading, and you will be told the origin later.

Proceed to page 38.

[*from page 24*]

YOUR ANSWER: I'm not certain.

All right. A poet's use of metaphor is often difficult to understand, so let's review. You did, did you not, notice the simile in these lines?

The world is charged with the grandeur of God.
It will flame out like shining from shook foil;

Let's start with the referent, the *shining from shook foil*. What is the foil the poet refers to? Aluminum foil? No, but something much like it. Hopkins actually means gold or silver leaf, that is, metal hammered into very thin sheets and used to decorate churches, statuary, and the like. But is *foil* the referent? No, it is the *shining* upon which Hopkins bases his comparison:

grandeur of God — flames out — (like, i.e. =) shining

What do you see? If you were to take a sheet of foil and hold it up so you could see light reflected, what would occur when you shake the sheet? Try it and see.

This shining is what Hopkins is trying to project on the mind of the reader, the sight of "shining from shook foil." This sight is an image.

Here we are concerned with one visual image which is contained in two lines of a poem. As you will see, a poem usually contains many images, each one of which contributes to the over-all unity of the poem. An image may appeal to any or all of the five senses; it may make you imagine that you feel wetness, for example, or smell a particular odor, or hear a certain sound. Be alert for these images in poems you will read later.

Return to page 24 and select another answer.

[*from page 29*]

YOUR ANSWER: *Death* is the subject of the predominant series of images.

No, this is not entirely true, but you have noticed some of the less significant imagery. The cold steel bayonet-blade and the blind, blunt bullet-heads create pictures which could be construed as images of death, but you have failed to recognize the predominant series of images.

Here is the poem again. Note the underlined images.

Arms and the Boy

Let the boy try along this bayonet-blade
How cold steel is, and <u>keen with hunger of blood;</u>
Blue with all malice, like a madman's flash;
And <u>thinly drawn with famishing for flesh.</u>

Lend him to stroke these blind, blunt bullet-heads
Which long to nuzzle in the hearts of lads,
Or give him cartridges of <u>fine zinc teeth,</u>
Sharp with the sharpness of grief and death.

For his <u>teeth seem for laughing round an apple.</u>
There <u>lurk no claws</u> behind his fingers supple;
And God will grow no <u>talons at his heels,</u>
Nor <u>antlers</u> through the thickness of his curls.

When you have decided what elements these images have in common, return to page 29 and select another answer.

[*from page 37*]

YOUR ANSWER: *War's inhumanity* is symbolized in the predominant series of images.

Sorry. You have selected an answer which is the substance of almost every war poem ever written, but you have not examined *this* poem closely enough. You could, from the first few lines, decide that Owen considers war inhuman, and in a sense you could say that everything about the poem points to this fact. I'll not argue the point. You are right, but you have missed seeing *how* Owen goes about treating a particular facet of war's inhumanity. You have overlooked what it is that makes this poem a good one. You should read each poem for its own sake.

You must try to read "Arms and the Boy" as if you had never heard of the subject under discussion, and you must give the poem undivided attention.

Return to page 37, read the poem again while considering only the material within it, and select another answer.

[*from page 25*]

YOUR ANSWER: *Pursuit* is being symbolized.

Wrong. You have failed to see the significance of the pursued object. The man is not chasing just anything; he is bent upon catching the *horizon*.

To interpret a symbol, you should understand all parts of it. In the line "I saw a man pursuing the horizon," the symbol consists of three parts:

man — pursuing — horizon

Determine first what visual image is being used; then allow your intellect to tell you what this image symbolizes.

Return to page 25, reread the poem, and try again.

[*from page 30*]

YOUR ANSWER: *Milky dust of stars* is not an implied simile.

Wrong. Think of the Milky Way on a clear night. Its very name is an implied simile: clusters of stars create a milky-looking path across the night sky. On an exceptionally clear night, *all* the stars appear *like* a gigantic Milky Way, *as* a milky dust.

A simile is any comparison in which one thing, action, or relation is compared to another with the words *like* or *as* expressed or implied.

Return to page 30 and select the phrase which does not have a separate, identifiable referent.

[*from page 29*]

YOUR ANSWER: *Desire for food* is the subject of the predominant series of images.

Right. The images "keen with hunger," "famishing for flesh," "fine zinc teeth," and "laughing round an apple" are all concerned with eating.

Here is the poem again with the predominant series of images underlined.

Arms and the Boy

Let the boy try along this bayonet-blade
How cold steel is, and keen with hunger of blood;
Blue with all malice, like a madman's flash;
And thinly drawn with famishing for flesh.

Lend him to stroke these blind, blunt bullet-heads
Which long to nuzzle in the hearts of lads,
Or give him cartridges of fine zinc teeth,
Sharp with the sharpness of grief and death.

For his teeth seem for laughing round an apple.
There lurk no claws behind his fingers supple;
And God will grow no talons at his heels,
Nor antlers through the thickness of his curls.

Note the wild beasts? Is their presence inconsistent? Hardly. Try to associate the images of hunger, of the wild beasts, of claws, talons, and antlers. Then answer the following question:

What is symbolized in the predominant series of images?

War's killing of boys. **page 26**

War's predatory hunger. **page 31**

War's inhumanity. **page 34**

CHAPTER III

Form, Metrics, and Rhythm: The Tools of Poetry

Mankind in this era of history appears more concerned with the concepts of design and function than ever before. Buildings, aircraft, furniture, automobiles all reflect our interest in the relationship between how things look and how they work, and even man himself is undergoing study from every angle to discover how he operates. These days we approach everything with the questions: "Is it functional? Does it work?" If assured that "it" does work, we then ask:

"Will it survive a New England winter?"
"Is it economical with gasoline?"
"Is it washable?"
"Will it stand the test of time?"

And so on. Although such questions are not unique to this era, the frequency with which they are asked show our concern with function in this scientific century.

Poetry always has been functional. In order to succeed, a poem must appeal first to the ear, then to the intellect. A poem is made to succeed by the skillful use of the tools of poetry available to the poet. By the end of this chapter, you should have gained a basic understanding of the tools of poetry: form, metrics, and rhythm.

Please go on to page 39.

[*from page 38*]

Here is "Arms and the Boy" again. Read it aloud and then answer the following question.

Arms and the Boy

Let the boy try along this bayonet-blade
How cold steel is, and keen with hunger of blood;
Blue with all malice, like a madman's flash;
And thinly drawn with famishing for flesh.

Lend him to stroke these blind, blunt bullet-heads
Which long to nuzzle in the hearts of lads,
Or give him cartridges of fine zinc teeth,
Sharp with the sharpness of grief and death.

For his teeth seem for laughing round an apple.
There lurk no claws behind his fingers supple;
And God will grow no talons at his heels,
Nor antlers through the thickness of his curls.

How would you classify this poem?

It is a dramatic poem. **page 42**

It is a lyric poem. **page 46**

It is a sonnet. **page 49**

I don't know. **page 52**

[*from page 46*]

YOUR ANSWER: It is an ode.

Now I am in for trouble, because you are not entirely wrong. Certainly, though, it is not a regular Pindaric ode, consisting of three-stanza units of strophe, antistrophe, and epode. There is no chorus, and the poem has none of the other features of a Pindaric ode. (If you wish definitions of these terms, see the guide for further study at the end of this book.)

There are, however, grounds for calling this poem an *irregular* ode, primarily because no one knows exactly what the term means. Historically, poets have entitled certain lyric poems odes, either because they thought erroneously that the poems really were odes, or because they just liked the word in the title. Literally, *ode* means "song," and the early Greek odes were written to be sung, accompanied by the seven-string lyre.

Let us not call this poem an ode, for two reasons: first, it is obviously not written to be sung or chanted, and second, the term "irregular" is useless. Most modern poetry defies classification into any but the most general categories.

From this brief discussion you should now be able to select the right answer on page 46. Return and do so.

[*from page 53*]

YOUR ANSWER: Free verse.

Wrong. The rhythm of each line conforms to a recognizable pattern. Free verse is entirely informal and irregular, and the standard metrical patterns, if they appear, do so only accidentally. Here is an example of free verse:

I am going
to write
a very short poem
                    about
free verse.

Free verse is unrhymed, irregular verse. If you can identify a regular, repeated rhyme, then the poem is not written in free verse.

Return to page 53 and select another answer.

[*from page 39*]

YOUR ANSWER: It is a dramatic poem.

Wrong. Don't be afraid of saying "I don't know." Guessing will only cause trouble for you later on.

A dramatic poem is usually long, and the personality of the poet is rarely present in the poem itself. In past centuries plays were written in verse. The Greek tragedians, as well as Shakespeare, Marlowe, Jonson, Racine, and others, wrote dramatic poems. Most modern plays are, of course, written in prose, but Maxwell Anderson, T. S. Eliot, Christopher Fry, and other writers in this century have written plays in verse.

Under the heading of dramatic poetry fall epic poems and long narratives. Chaucer's *Canterbury Tales*, Spenser's *Faerie Queene*, Milton's *Paradise Lost* are dramatic poems, as are Homer's *Odyssey* and *Iliad*.

Return to page 39 and select another answer.

[*from page 46*]

YOUR ANSWER: It is a sonnet.

You are guessing. Shame on you.
A sonnet has *fourteen* lines; this poem has only *twelve*.
Return to page 46 and start again.

[*from page 53*]

YOUR ANSWER: Blank verse.

Not at all. Blank verse is written in iambic pentameter *without* rhyme. But *apple* and *supple* do rhyme; therefore "Arms and the Boy" is not written in blank verse.

If you are not satisfied that the lines rhyme, please read on, and perhaps I can convince you that they do.

Return to page 53 and select another answer.

[*from page 55*]

For his teeth seem for laughing round an apple.
There lurk no claws behind his fingers supple;

YOUR ANSWER: Masculine.

Wrong. Masculine rhyme refers to the rhyming of final accented syllables.

I saw the cat.
He ate the rat.

Here, the words *cat* and *rat* are a masculine rhyme.

Feminine rhyme, as defined on page 55, consists of a rhyme between words which have *two* beats, the first accented and the second unaccented. Example:

Victory which is painless
Is also quite gainless.

See the difference between the rhyme of *cat . . . rat* and *painless . . . gainless*?

Return to page 55 and select another answer.

[*from page 39*]

YOUR ANSWER: It is a lyric poem.

Right. The poet says what he personally thinks, presenting a situation as he sees it. All of the poems in this book are lyric poems, for this era seems to produce mainly lyric poetry. Few good dramatic poems have been written in this century, and it is not our purpose in this book to discuss them. Most lyric poems are short in comparison with dramatic poems, which are generally long.

Let's further limit the classification. In which of the following traditional lyric forms would you place "Arms and the Boy"?

It is an ode. **page 40**

It is a sonnet. **page 43**

It is an elegy. **page 50**

It does not fit into any of these categories. **page 53**

I don't know. **page 56**

[*from page 53 or 69*]

YOUR ANSWER: Neither free nor blank verse.

Right, and this answer applies not only to this poem but to most contemporary poems. Since World War II, however, the trend has been toward a form of free verse which poets call "projective verse," in which they attempt to use the human voice, the sound of the words, and the required stops for breathing as devices in themselves.

Remember, if a poem has regular rhyme or any other than five-beat meter, it is not written in blank verse, and if it has no regular rhyme *or* meter, it is written in free verse.

Let us analyze these two lines further.

> For his teeth seem for laughing round an apple.
> There lurk no claws behind his fingers supple;

How would you describe these two lines?

They are both iambic pentameter. **page 54**

The first is irregular; the second is iambic pentameter. **page 58**

I don't know. **page 62**

[*from page 51*]

YOUR ANSWER: Assonance.

Wrong.

For assonance, one or more of the vowels of the rhyming words must sound alike. An example would be a rhyme between *moaned* and *gloaming*, where the *oa* sound appears in both words.

Return to page 51 and select the correct answer.

[*from page 39*]

YOUR ANSWER: It is a sonnet.

Wrong. A sonnet must have fourteen lines. There is no such thing as a twelve-line sonnet, despite the terms you may have seen such as "augmented sonnet," "diminished sonnet," and the like.

Although the rhyme schemes of sonnets vary, there are only two regular forms, Petrarchan and Shakespearean. The Petrarchan sonnet is divided into an *octave* (eight lines) and a *sestet* (six lines) which may or may not be presented as two separate stanzas (poetic paragraphs).

The Shakespearean sonnet is made up of three *quatrains* (four lines), each with its own set of two rhymes, and a couplet (two lines which rhyme) at the end.

You should see now why "Arms and the Boy" is not a sonnet. We will study some sonnets later. For now, return to page 39 and select another answer.

[*from page 46*]

YOUR ANSWER: It is an elegy.

I almost wish I had not asked this question, because we are likely to embark upon one of the most pointless arguments connected with poetry:

Question: When is an elegiac poem not an elegy?
Answer: In the poem "Arms and the Boy" (and many others).

I won't push this answer too far, however, because there are more important items to discuss. Basing your answer on the poet's discussion of death, you assumed the poem to be an elegy.

But is it really? The best definition of an elegy I know is: "a short poem of lamentation or regret, on the death of a beloved or revered person, . . . or on the pathos of mortality." With respect to the subject of "Arms and the Boy," we cannot rule out much of this definition; a young man is certainly beloved, and it is pathetic that in war the young must die. But does Owen express lamentation or regret? Does he imply that the world will be forever changed, or rather suggest that war is war, and we must sadly accept it? Usually an elegy is mournful and meditative; this poem is not. And actually the poem is not about death at all, but about a particular quality of war: its predatory hunger.

Therefore, I would not consider this an elegy, but I would not dismiss other points of view supported by fact. This discussion points out the futility of trying to pin specific labels on contemporary poems. So, unless you are prepared to back up an opinion with proof, be careful about saying of a contemporary poem, "This *is* . . ." or "This is *not* . . . ."

Please accept this poem as *not* being an elegy, return to page 46, and select another answer.

[*from page 55*]

YOUR ANSWER: Feminine.

You are right. Notice, however, that the words do not sound exactly alike, even though they have something in common. In contemporary poetry, appeal to the ear is often made by words that sound *almost* the same, but not quite. Just as modern music uses dissonant harmonies, so modern poetry tries to please the ear by more sophisticated means than words which rhyme in the traditional manner.

Few sounds, as the linguists have shown, are identical, but to all intents and purposes certain rhymes are close enough to be called "true" rhymes. *Ring . . . sing, I . . . why, even . . . steven*, exemplify "true" rhymes because the sounds are as similar as two separate words can make them, but the differences are obvious when a minute inspection is made of each word. The *r* and *s* sounds of the first two are dissimilar, as are the *e* and the *ste* of the last. But in "true" rhyme, the sounds are *almost* identical.

Let us discuss half or slant rhyme, in which the *differences* in sound predominate, while the similarities serve only to link apparently different sounds. *Other . . . tether*, *doom . . . glum*, *wind . . . mind*, are examples of half or slant rhyme.

Sometimes you will see even more disparate examples, like *mind . . . mud*, *thing . . . thought*, *glum . . . glad*, and so on. If this use of slant rhyme is consistent with the purpose of the poem, it may be successful. But if slant rhyme is used for lack of a better word, then the poet has not worked hard enough and has produced a sloppy poem.

The two main types of slant rhyme are *assonance* (in which the *vowel* sounds are similar) and *consonance* (in which the *consonant* sounds are similar). Which type is found in the last words of the following lines?

> And God will grow no talons at his heels,
> Nor antlers through the thickness of his curls.

Assonance. **page 48**

Consonance. **page 64**

[*from page 39*]

YOUR ANSWER: I don't know.

Good, you are honest. One of the great impediments to learning is the refusal to admit ignorance.

All right. I divide poetry into two categories: dramatic and lyric. A dramatic poem is usually long, taking the form of a narrative or of a play to be acted by actors. Dramatic poetry is intended to show the views of the poet by example rather than by stating them. Shakespeare's plays are dramatic poetry, as are Milton's *Paradise Lost*, Chaucer's *Canterbury Tales*, and T. S. Eliot's *The Wasteland*.

Shorter and more personal than dramatic poems, the lyric usually has the poet as its main character. The poet tells us honestly: "This is what *I* think." All the poems discussed in this book are lyric poems.

My categories are open to challenge by those who prefer other divisions, but please accept these two terms for the purposes of this book.
Return to page 39 and select another answer.

[*from page 46*]

YOUR ANSWER: It does not fit into any of these categories.

Right, and I recommend this approach to contemporary poetry mainly because poets today are not generally concerned with traditional forms. Actually, this poem has characteristics of the sonnet, the elegy, and the ode. "Arms and the Boy" is not a true sonnet (the poem has twelve instead of fourteen lines), but it might well be called either an elegy or an ode.* As is common in poems of this century, the accepted forms have been discarded in favor of new, individual structures. About all we can say of "Arms and the Boy," then, is that it is a lyric poem which does not fit into any regular, traditional form.

There are three *stanzas*, each roughly equal to a paragraph in prose, and within each stanza the lines are about the same length. Here are the first two lines of stanza 3.

> For his teeth seem for laughing round an apple.
> There lurk no claws behind his fingers supple;

Using these two lines as an example, what kind of versification is evident in this poem?

Free verse. **page 41**

Blank verse. **page 44**

Neither free nor blank verse. **page 47**

I don't know. **page 57**

---

* If you are interested in precise definitions, see pages 40, 49, 50, and consult the Appendix.

[*from page 47*]

YOUR ANSWER: They are both iambic pentameter.

You are right. The lines

> For hís | teeth séem | for laúgh|ing roúnd | an ápple.
>
> There lúrk | no cláws | behínd | his fín|gers súpple;

contain five feet (pentameter) and are composed predominantly of *iambs* (unaccented syllables followed by accented ones). If you feel that you are familiar with all the other kinds of feet, read on. If not, then read or review the sequence starting on page 71.

We could run this business of meter into the ground, but let's not. Why measure poems in the first place? For two reasons. First, we understand a little more about the nuts and bolts, the make-up of a poem; second, we can, by knowing how scansion aids reading aloud, approach a complete understanding of a poem, an understanding which is denied us if we do not recognize exactly what the poet is doing.

For example:

> For his teeth seem for laughing round an apple.

Unless we accent the word *his* we are likely to miss the contrast established between the hunger of the *fine zinc teeth* in the previous stanza and the hunger of the boy's teeth here.

Speech is rhythmical, and poetry attempts to reproduce human speech. Even though the predominant foot in English verse is the *iamb*, there are too many irregularities to enable us to pin down every sound and put a label on it. We even tend to write a kind of rhythm. (Scan the preceding nine words. They are iambic pentameter, just like the lines discussed earlier.)

Please go on to page 55.

[*from page 54*]

Does a poem have to rhyme? No, but most good English poetry does, although not necessarily at the end of each line. There has been what I call a brief flurry of non-rhyming poetry in this century, but good poets always try to heighten the effect of words above the level of prose. Without interesting use of sound, a poem is dull, regardless of its subject.

There are two types of rhyme: single (or masculine) rhyme, and double (or feminine) rhyme. (Triple and longer rhymes are usually reserved for humorous verse.) In masculine rhyme the similar sounds occur in single, final stressed beats; in feminine rhyme both the final and penultimate stresses sound alike. Which type of rhyme is exemplified by the last words of the two lines below?

For his teeth seem for laughing round an apple.
There lurk no claws behind his fingers supple;

Masculine. **page 45**

Feminine. **page 51**

They do not rhyme. **page 66**

[*from page 46*]

YOUR ANSWER: I don't know.

Your answer contains more truth than you may realize. If you have attempted to define literary terms before, you know the difficulties involved, and perhaps you have been a party to a few pointless arguments. I suggest, if you are not familiar with the terms *ode*, *sonnet*, and *elegy*, that you return to page 46 and read each of the answer pages. These will tell you what the poem is *not*, and why.

If you feel you know the terms well enough, perhaps you might read the suggested pages anyway and see what I think.

If neither of these options appeals to you, then accept the fact that the traditional lyric forms, with the exception of the sonnet, are seldom used today. Lyrics are lyrics, not much more, and there is no sense in attempting to classify where no classification applies. Most contemporary poetry is lyric; let it go at that. The right answer on page 46 is: it does not fit into any of these categories.

Now go on to page 53.

[*from page 53*]

YOUR ANSWER: I don't know.

Good for you. Here is the difference between free verse and blank verse. Free verse conforms to no set pattern of meter or rhyme.

I could
            for instance
write this entire section in free
                                                    verse,
and the only difference
between free verse and prose
would be in the way the whole thing
                                                            looked.

Blank verse, however, follows a regular five-beat meter, *without* end rhyme.

The best way that I know to demonstrate
What blank verse is, is just to show a line
Or two which corresponds to what I have
Defined above — de dum de dum de dum.

See the difference? When reading blank verse, you should not pause at the end of each line, nor should you overemphasize the beat of the lines. Perhaps the best blank verse occurs in the plays of Shakespeare and the poems of Milton. Although still occasionally used, blank verse in the modern period has for the most part given way to either free verse or strict rhyme schemes.

Return to page 53, reread the lines, and select another answer.

[*from page 47*]

YOUR ANSWER: The first is irregular; the second is iambic pentameter.

Sorry. You misread the first line:

For his teeth seem for laughing round an apple.

The first stress is on the word *his*, underlining the contrast between the boy's teeth and the "fine zinc teeth" of the previous stanza.

Traditional scansion often requires the reader to reduce a line to singsong sounds in order to scan it properly. Many poets dislike this singsong, so they go out of their way to make scansion difficult. But this process carried too far makes a choppy, irregular poem. Words have inherent rhythm, and good poets use the sound of words as well as their meaning to build a line.

Can you scan the first line to show the iambic pentameter? If so, go on to page 54. If not, turn to page 62.

[*from page 63*]

YOUR ANSWER: Wásh ing tő ni án.

Wrong. Let me represent this word another way, and perhaps you can see your error. Remember, the stress symbols represent those syllables which are emphasized. We can represent this by underlining.

Wash ing to ni an

Do you say "WASH ing TO ni AN"? Most persons say "WASH ing TO ni an," with more emphasis placed on the TO than on the WASH. Remember, in diagramming scansion, the heavy beats are represented by /, and the less emphasized beats by //. Some students of poetry put a ⌣ mark above unemphasized beats; but I prefer to leave unemphasized beats blank because, as we shall see later, it is the number of primary emphases in a line which determines the metrical length and gives the line its basic rhythm.

Return to page 63, review the stress symbols, and select another answer.

[*from page 71*]

YOUR ANSWER: It is written in iambic pentameter.

Right. Now you have an option. If you feel that you know the various feet well enough (*iamb*, *trochee*, *dactyl*, *spondee*, and *anapest*), then go on to page 54.

If you are uncertain about any of these, however, then I suggest you turn to page 68 for a further discussion.

Again — be honest.

[*from page 65*]

YOUR ANSWER: There is internal assonance.

You are not completely wrong, but you have selected an answer which shows that you have missed the intent of this discussion.

Certainly you can pick out a few examples of assonance if you wish to range far afield. The *a* sounds, for example, in the words *malice*, *madman*, and *famishing* in lines 3 and 4 certainly do exemplify assonance, but assonance is not repeated except sporadically and inconsistently.

There is an internal rhyme which runs *throughout* the poem and is consistently repeated in every single line. See if you can find it.

Return to page 65 and select another answer.

[*from page 47*]

YOUR ANSWER: I don't know.

Good, now we can get to work.

You are here because you are unfamiliar with some of the tools of poetry. Either you have forgotten, or this is your first experience with them. The important thing is to find out about them.

Let's begin.

Poetry is measurable, like anything else with dimensions. But instead of measuring size, shape, thickness, or distance, in poetry we measure sound patterns. We measure the emphases, the stresses of the human voice, the voice's *meter*.

As in other specialized fields, there is a system which applies to any series of written words. This system of measurement is called *scansion*.

Read the word "Mississippi" aloud. Do you hear the beats:

Mis sis sip pi?

If not, try again.

Are all the beats equal in intensity, or are some emphasized more than others? The answer to this should be obvious.

If you look up the word in the dictionary, you will find it written something like this:

Mis′ sis sip′ pi

meaning that two syllables (or beats) are stressed, and one syllable (the second) should receive more emphasis than the other one.

Please go on to page 63.

A similar system is used in the scansion of poetry to break each line into primary and secondary stresses, and to count the number of stresses in the line. Unaccented beats usually have no mark above them; secondary accents have two light lines above them (//), and primary accents are identified by a single heavy accent mark (/).

The word "Mississippi" would be represented thus:

// /
Mis sis sip pi

thereby identifying the three levels of emphasis: primary stress, secondary stress, and no stress at all.

Let's try it out. How would you scan the word "Washingtonian"?

/ // /
Wash ing to ni an. **page 59**

/ //
Wash ing to ni an. **page 67**

// /
Wash ing to ni an. **page 70**

[*from page 51*]

YOUR ANSWER: Consonance.

Right. Since the *ee* vowel sound of *heels* is dissimilar to the short *ur* sound of *curls*, assonance is ruled out. But the *l* and *s* sounds tie the words together by consonance. In fact, the entire poem consists of slant rhymes, some demonstrating assonance, others consonance.

Rhyme may also be used within a poem, producing what is called *internal* rhyme. Rudyard Kipling gives a familiar example of the internal rhyme:

> On the road to Mandalay, where the flying fishes play.

This is internal true rhyme. Instead of "true" rhyme, most contemporary poets prefer internal slant rhyme, reserving internal true rhyme for ballads and comic verse.

Cacophony (unpleasant or jarring sounds) and euphony (pleasant or smooth sounds) are often used internally, as can be seen in the following:

> Sharp with the sharpness . . . (euphonious consonance)
> There lurk no claws . . . (cacophonous consonance)
> Blue with all malice, like a madman's flash . . . (euphonious consonance)

This use of internal rhyme is common in contemporary poetry, and is found in Owen's poem. Note here that the internal rhyme is not restricted to one line, but runs throughout the entire poem.

Please go on to page 65.

[*from page 64*]

Arms and the Boy

Let the boy try along this bayonet-blade
How cold steel is, and keen with hunger of blood;
Blue with all malice, like a madman's flash;
And thinly drawn with famishing for flesh.

Lend him to stroke these blind, blunt bullet-heads
Which long to nuzzle in the hearts of lads,
Or give him cartridges of fine zinc teeth,
Sharp with the sharpness of grief and death.

For his teeth seem for laughing round an apple.
There lurk no claws behind his fingers supple;
And God will grow no talons at his heels,
Nor antlers through the thickness of his curls.

What can you see and hear which forms a consistent internal rhyme throughout the poem?

There is internal assonance. **page 61**

There is internal consonance. **page 72**

There is internal "true" rhyme. **page 75**

[*from page 55*]

For his teeth seem for laughing round an apple.
There lurk no claws behind his fingers supple;

YOUR ANSWER: They do not rhyme.

Oh yes they do. The final two syllables of each line are nearly identical.

Return to page 55 and try again.

[*from page 63*]

YOUR ANSWER: Wash íng to ni an.

Read the word again, as it is diagrammed above. There are no grounds for pronouncing it this way: WashINGtoNIan, with the accents on the ING and the I. We would scan the word "silly" in this manner:

síl ly, producing the sound SIL ly

not

sil lý, which sounds like sil LY.

Remember, the symbols / and // above a syllable represent emphasized beats, the / being the primary emphasis and the // the secondary, or lesser, emphasis. Some students of poetry put a ˘ mark above unemphasized beats. I prefer, however, to leave unemphasized beats blank because the number of primary accents determines the metrical length of the line and establishes the basic rhythm. We will study this in due course.

Return to page 63, review the example given, and select another answer.

[*from page 71*]

YOUR ANSWER: It is written in pentameter.

Right, and now let's get on to a discussion of the *types* of feet. Here are the four basic types of feet, and a fifth which has become accepted through repeated use:

Iamb — an unaccented beat followed by an accented one. This is the most common foot in English verse. Most of the feet in "Arms and the Boy" are iambic.

Which lóng | to núz|zle ín | . . . .

behínd | . . . .

Trochee — just the reverse. An accented beat followed by an unaccented one.

Héavy | hángs the | hámmer.

Dactyl — an accented beat followed by two unaccented ones.

Málachi | Múlligan

Chrístopher | Róbinson

Anapest — the reverse of the dactyl. Two unaccented beats followed by an accented one.

And the stár | of my fáte | hath declíned.

Spondee — two accented beats without an intervening unstressed beat. Spondees are rare in English verse. What one person might regard as a spondee another would consider an iamb or a trochee. For example:

The fórce | that thróugh | the gréen | fúse drívës | the flówer

Drívës my | gréen áge.

Fuse drives and *green age* may be considered spondees.

Please go on to page 69.

[*from page 68*]

Do not be misled into thinking that completely regular meter is desirable. Although few poems are written wholly in iambic feet or in trochaic feet, every good poem has a *normal meter*. The normal foot in "Arms and the Boy" is iambic. Although the poem consists mainly of iambic feet, there are trochaic substitutions, such as the first foot of the line:

> Lénd him | to stróke | these blínd, | blunt búl|let-heáds.

Bearing in mind that a poem containing various types of feet may still be normally iambic, return to page 47 and choose the correct answer.

[*from page 63*]

YOUR ANSWER: Wásh ing tó ni an.
(// over "Wash", / over "to")

Right. It is easy, isn't it? We say "WASHingTOnian," with more emphasis on the second accented syllable than on the first.

We had better establish a fact: *all* scansion, just like the interpretation of poems, is open to challenge. For example, the first of the two lines on page 53 can be scanned to show stresses in this manner:

/ over "teeth", / over "laugh", // over "round", / over "ap":

For his teeth seem for laugh ing round an ap ple.

Read aloud, the line would sound like this:

For his TEETH seem for LAUGH ing ROUND an AP ple.

In context with the rest of the poem, however, I prefer to scan it this way:

/ over "his", / over "seem", / over "laugh", / over "round", / over "ap":

For his teeth seem for laugh ing round an ap ple.

Read aloud, emphasizing the accents in a singsong manner, the lines sound like this:

For HIS teeth SEEM for LAUGH ing ROUND an AP ple.

I think that the word *his* and the word *seem* should be emphasized in reading, with the reader's voice rising toward the end of the line, stressing the word *apple* to contrast this food with that of the *fine zinc teeth* mentioned earlier.

Realize this: the scansion of a line of poetry is only a guide; it is *not* a precise formula for reading aloud because it does not determine the rate at which the line should be read. Whenever common sense or the meaning of a line makes a reader want to deviate in reading from the apparent demonstrable scansion of a line, then deviate he should.

Please go on to page 71.

[*from page 70*]

Let's proceed.

The basic element of a line of poetry is the *foot*, shown in scansion by a vertical line.

For hís | teeth séem | for láugh | ing róund | an ápple.

Although each foot *must* contain one primary stress, as seen above, there is no definite limit to the number of unaccented beats a foot may have. The number of feet determines the metrical length of the line.

In the above example there are five feet; therefore we call the line *pentameter*, meaning five-foot meter. The Greek prefix (*penta-* means "five") is used because of tradition; if you want to say "five-foot meter," do so.

Lines of other length are identified as follows:

One foot — <u>monometer</u>
Two feet — <u>dimeter</u>
Three feet — <u>trimeter</u>
Four feet — <u>tetrameter</u>
Six feet — <u>hexameter</u> (also called <u>alexandrines</u>)
Seven feet — <u>heptameter</u>

Few poets write in longer lines, and if you run across any, you can probably scan their lines in terms of shorter meters.

Here is another line from "Arms and the Boy."

And God will grow no talons at his heels, . . .

How would you scan this line?

It is written in iambic pentameter. **page 60**

It is written in pentameter. **page 68**

It is written in hexameter. **page 74**

[*from page 65*]

YOUR ANSWER: There is internal consonance.

Of course there is, and you will not find many other poems which use internal rhyme as well as this one does. The *n*, *m*, and *ng* sounds dominate the poem, giving a droning, continuous quality. In case you missed a few, here are the words which contribute to the internal consonance: *along*, *bayonet*, *keen*, *hunger*, *malice*, *madman*, *thinly*, *drawn*, *famishing*, *lend*, *blind*, *blunt*, *long*, *nuzzle*, *fine*, *zinc*, *sharpness*, *seem*, *laughing*, *round*, *behind*, *fingers*, *talons*, *antlers*, and *thickness*. Try sometime to create a poem along the same lines, consistently treating both subject and sound. This is a main concern of poets, and anyone who neglects sound for sense, or vice versa, does not create a complete poem.

There are a few more terms which you should be familiar with, not because I think they are vital to the understanding of any given poem, but because they crop up often in discussions of poetry, and you should have an idea of what each one means.

caesura — a break in a line requiring the reader to pause while reading. A *caesura* is usually set off by a comma, period, or other end mark. The line of Cunningham's epigram:

> And what is love? Misunderstanding, pain, contains one

caesura between *love* and *misunderstanding* and another after misunderstanding.

sibilance — repeated *s* sounds. "The silly snake slid slowly through the silver shrubbery." This is often used to produce a form of onomatopoeia.

onomatopoeia — the sounds of words used to represent their subject, as *tinkle*, *thud*, *clank*, *whiz*.

alliteration — a form of consonance in which intial consonant sounds are repeated successively. Owen's phrase "blind, blunt bullet-heads" shows alliteration of the *b* sounds. Alliterative *s* sounds produce *sibilance*.

Please go on to page 73.

[*from page 72*]

All right? Are we now, finally, finished with "Arms and the Boy"? We will never be through with it, because a work of art is permanent and because readers will always disagree. If the madness of war comes to be forgotten by future civilizations, readers of this poem will argue whether war actually *was* the voracious beast in Owen's poem.

As for the poem's title, perhaps you caught an echo of George Bernard Shaw's comedy *Arms and the Man.* But where did Shaw get the title? The phrase was first used by Vergil, in *The Aeneid.* The poem begins

"Arma virumque cano" (I sing of arms and the man).

The poem "Arms and the Boy" takes on new irony (the difference between what is and what seems to be) when you recognize the source of the title. "A young poet borrows; a mature poet steals," T. S. Eliot is quoted, and you must watch in contemporary poetry for allusions to earlier literature.

Now go on to page 76.

[*from page 71*]

YOUR ANSWER: It is written in hexameter.

You have miscounted. Are you certain that each of your six feet contains a primary stress?

Here is the way I would scan this line:

And Gód | will grów | no tál|ons át | his héels.

Count the feet, which are divided by the vertical lines: then, if you cannot remember the Greek prefixes, check on page 71 and select another answer.

[*from page 65*]

YOUR ANSWER: There is internal "true" rhyme.

I'm sorry. There is *no* "true" rhyme anywhere in this poem.

For a rhyme to be "true," words must sound as nearly identical as possible. *Cat . . . rat* is a "true" rhyme because the words sound nearly alike. Likewise, *whether . . . tether* is considered a "true" rhyme.

But what of one of the other examples given?

. . . other
. . . whether

Is this a "true" rhyme? Hardly. But the two words do sound somewhat alike, don't they? There are both assonance *and* consonance operating here, the assonance in the *e* sounds at the ends of the words, and the consonance evident in the *th* and *r*. *Blue*, *true*, *who*, *too*, and *do* all constitute "true" rhymes; *other*, *whether*, *either*, *gather* are feminine half or slant rhymes by assonance or consonance.

Return to page 65 and select another answer.

CHAPTER IV

Subject: What Is a Poem Really About?

In this chapter we will discuss the subject of the poem — what the poem is written about. To say that a poem is about life, death, truth, love, or mortal existence is vague; what we must determine is the poem's true subject, a subject which we first see exemplified by what I will call the *occasion* for the poem.

The occasion for the poem is that person, place, thing, or incident which is defined in and by the poem. We notice a person or a place being described, an incident narrated, an idea discussed, but we should not limit ourselves to a consideration only of this most obvious part of the poem. If we see no more than a description or a narration, aren't we ignoring the metaphoric nature of poetry?

Here is a table of the poems we have already read:

POEM	OCCASION	SUBJECT
"And what is love?"	The sipping of brandy.	Love.
"I saw a man pursuing"	A man chasing the horizon.	Man's determination.
"Night Clouds"	The sight of clouds at night.	Inevitability.
"Arms and the Boy"	A boy playing with the weapons of war.	War's predatory hunger.

As you can see from the above, the subject of a poem is far more abstract than its occasion. Poets rarely can present pure subject in a poem; almost without exception they choose a specific occasion, a person, place, thing, or incident, which represents the pure subject which concerns them.

Please go on to page 77.

[*from page 76*]

The question you should ask yourself when considering the subject of a poem is this: What interested the poet so much that he chose this occasion? When you are able to answer, you will have seen beneath the surface of the poem and discovered the poem's true subject, what the poet is really writing about.

Many contemporary poets use a specific person as the occasion for a poem. Read the following poem by Louis Simpson, trying first to discover the occasion for this poem.

A Woman Too Well Remembered

Having put on new fashions, she demands
New friends. She trades her beauty and her humor
In anybody's eyes. If diamonds
Were dark, they'd sparkle so. Her aura is
The glance of scandal and the speed of rumor.

One day, as I recall, when we conversed
In kisses, it amused her to transmit
"What hath God wrought!" — the message that was first
Sent under the Atlantic. Nonsense, yet
It pleases me sometimes to think of it.

Noli me tangere was not her sign.
Her pilgrim trembled with the softest awe.
She was the only daughter of a line
That sleeps in poetry and silences.
She might have sat upon the Sphinx's paw.

Then is she simply false, and falsely fair?
(The promise she would break she never made)
I cannot say, but truly can compare,
For when the stars move like a steady fire
And I think of her, other faces fade.

What is the occasion for this poem?

The poet's former lover. **page 80**

A woman of fashionable society. **page 83**

A memory. **page 86**

[*from page 85*]

YOUR ANSWER: Recurring memory.

Wrong. Memory is the *vehicle* by which the subject is presented to the poet, not the subject itself. The poem is more specific than memory. An attempt to treat memory in only twenty lines would probably produce nothing but unsupportable, incomplete generalizations.

The true subject of a poem is defined as "that which concerns the poet so deeply that he has chosen this incident, this example to write about." The subject of a poem does *not* contain the personal views of the author; rather, the subject is completely impersonal, and from a full understanding of the poem we can induce what the author is trying to show *about* his subject, to be defined later as *theme*.

Reread the poem, looking for a subject which justifies the poet in using this woman as the occasion for a poem.

Return to page 85 and select the correct answer.

[*from page 89*]

YOUR ANSWER: The retirement of a high-ranking officer.

No, I am afraid you are not considering the entire poem. Certainly, in the second part the officer is retired, but the occasion should be evident throughout, defined *by* and *in* the poem.

Reread the poem, looking this time for the incident or action (in this poem, the occasion is not a specific person, place, or thing) which is described in the first and second parts of the poem. When you can see this, then we can proceed.

Return to page 88, reread the poem, and select another answer from those on page 89.

[*from page 77*]

YOUR ANSWER: The poet's former lover.

I would say so. We can only imagine what made the poet think of this woman — perhaps he has seen her again, or heard someone talk about her — but she is obviously the occasion for this poem.

Notice the interesting regular rhyme scheme in each stanza. Here is the first stanza again:

Having put on new fashions, she demands	a
New friends. She trades her beauty and her humor	b
In anybody's eyes. If diamonds	a
Were dark, they'd sparkle so. Her aura is	a+
The glance of scandal and the speed of rumor.	b

The first and third lines rhyme, as do the second and fifth, while the fourth is connected to the first and third by consonance (here the *s* sound). The rhyme scheme of abaa+b (a+ standing for the slant rhyme) is continued regularly throughout the poem.

Structurally, the first stanza creates the picture of a woman we may have seen many times, the vivacious, sparkling coquette whom we perhaps dislike, but to whom men are invariably attracted. The poet is careful to use words which will initiate our dislike, such as: "new fashions," "demands new friends," "trades in anybody's eyes," "glance of scandal," "speed of rumor." Until the second stanza, we do not know the relationship of this woman to the poet.

I do not consider this poem particularly difficult to understand, because the poet makes few assumptions about the experience of the reader. Often the occasion of a poem may be obvious, while the subject is revealed only after the reader learns certain facts. Here, for example, Simpson assumes that everyone knows the meaning of the Latin *noli me tangere* ("touch me not"), and he even gives what he believes to be the source of the quotation, "What hath God wrought." Many modern poets do not cite their sources within the body of the poem.

Please go on to page 81.

[*from page 80*]

The first two stanzas concern only the particular woman. The third contains a general comparison.

Here is the third stanza again:

> *Noli me tangere* was not her sign.
> Her pilgrim trembled with the softest awe.
> She was the only daughter of a line
> That sleeps in poetry and silences.
> She might have sat upon the Sphinx's paw.

Which of the following is correct?

A Christian-pagan comparison is being made. **page 84**

She is being compared to Cleopatra. **page 87**

The Latin phrase and the Sphinx are dishonest referents; hence there is an invalid metaphor. **page 92**

There is no use of a symbol. **page 96**

[*from page 85*]

YOUR ANSWER: Unrequited love.

You are bringing your own experience into the poem, and have attached to it a common label that is concerned with a different subject.

Is there anything in the poem which implies that either the poet or the woman did *not* part amicably? that one or the other was jilted? Not at all. And there is no indication that their relationship was at all unhappy, or that the poet is whining over his loss of the woman.

Properly speaking, "unrequited love" is not the subject of *any* poem, for it implies a personal judgment. When we see the poet expressing his opinion, we approach the matter of *theme*, a subject we will study later.

So try to determine what particular subject has made the author write a poem using this particular woman as its occasion.

Return to page 85 and select another answer.

[*from page 77*]

YOUR ANSWER: A woman of fashionable society.

Not necessarily. Perhaps you got this impression from the references to fashions, diamonds, and scandal, but I think that you have insufficient evidence for saying that the woman is a member of fashionable society.

The "occasion for the poem" is the incident, person, place, or thing which is defined *in* and *by* the poem, not necessarily the incident, person, place, or thing which caused the poem to be written, because often the cause of the poem is never revealed to the reader. In "Night Clouds," for example, the occasion for the poem is the sight of clouds at night, but at no time do we have to speculate about *which* night the poet is describing.

The occasion for the poem must be defined *within* the poem, and also must be defined *by* the poem. In Crane's poem, "I saw a man pursuing the horizon," the occasion is stated in the first line, even though we understand that the sight of a man chasing the horizon occurs only in the author's imagination.

We might further define the occasion for the poem as that surface action which the reader sees taking place, whether in narrative or descriptive form.

We must, however, attempt to see the whole occasion, not just one of its parts. By saying that this poem concerns a woman of fashionable society, you gathered your impression from the first stanza and did not pay close enough attention to the whole poem.

Return to page 77 and select another answer.

[*from page 81*]

YOUR ANSWER: A Christian-pagan comparison is being made.

Right.

The reference to the Sphinx in this poem is obvious; *femmes fatales* have commonly been pictured lounging in Egyptian boudoirs, being fanned by huge slaves. But how does this relate to the pilgrim?

The pilgrim is the poet (and perhaps, from what he knows of this woman, pilgrim*s* might be better), trembling softly in the presence of a woman who does *not* have as a "sign" *noli me tangere*. These were Christ's words to his "pilgrim," Mary Magdalene, upon His resurrection, and the Christian "line" sleeps in Heaven, not in "poetry and silences." For this woman, the poet has become a pilgrim to love, and by these references the woman becomes a symbol of pagan love to which the poet has paid homage.

Now let's tie some elements of the poem together. Read it again.

A Woman Too Well Remembered

Having put on new fashions, she demands
New friends. She trades her beauty and her humor
In anybody's eyes. If diamonds
Were dark, they'd sparkle so. Her aura is
The glance of scandal and the speed of rumor.

One day, as I recall, when we conversed
In kisses, it amused her to transmit
"What hath God wrought!" — the message that was first
Sent under the Atlantic. Nonsense, yet
It pleases me sometimes to think of it.

Noli me tangere was not her sign.
Her pilgrim trembled with the softest awe.
She was the only daughter of a line
That sleeps in poetry and silences.
She might have sat upon the Sphinx's paw.

Then is she simply false, and falsely fair?
(The promise she would break she never made)
I cannot say, but truly can compare,
For when the stars move like a steady fire
And I think of her, other faces fade.

Please go on to page 85.

[*from page 84*]

What is it that concerns the poet so much that he has chosen this woman as the occasion for this poem?

Recurring memory. **page 78**

Unrequited love. **page 82**

Sexual love. **page 88**

[*from page 77*]

YOUR ANSWER: A memory.

No, I'm afraid not. To say that the occasion for this poem is a memory is far too vague. Actually, every poem could be said to be the product of a memory, for I know of no poem ever written which was completed *at the exact time* its occasion took place.

Certainly memory is present in the poem. But the occasion for the poem is that person, place, thing, or incident which is defined *by* and *in* the poem. Remembering may produce the occasion for the poem, but is not itself the occasion for the poem.

Return to page 77, read the poem again, and select another answer.

[*from page 81*]

YOUR ANSWER: She is being compared to Cleopatra.

Careful. You're jumping to conclusions from one word in one line. Just because the woman "might have sat upon the Sphinx's paw" does not mean that she is being compared to Cleopatra. Where is the river Nile? Where are the barges? And, for that matter, where is Mark Antony?

Perhaps you have not exhausted the phrase *noli me tangere*. Look the phrase up in your dictionary; then read the *New Testament*, *John* xx:17. See what connection you can make between this information and the use of the word *pilgrim*. Then see if a contrast to this idea is created by the woman's sitting "upon the Sphinx's paw."

Return to page 81, read the stanza again, and select another answer.

[*from page 85*]

YOUR ANSWER: Sexual love.

Right, and you can now see how we have progressed from the occasion for the poem, a particular woman, to the subject of the poem, sexual love. Why not just love in general? It is too inclusive, and the references to the conversing in kisses, plus the picture we are given of the woman, show that the relationship between the poet and the woman was mainly physical.

When we consider subject, we are not yet concerned with the author's attitude toward his subject; nor do we discuss what the author uses his subject for. All we wish to do at this point is determine what the author is writing about. In Cunningham's epigram about love, the subject was obvious; in "A Woman Too Well Remembered," we had to do a little digging.

Many times, in our specialized age, poets have used the language of particular trades in their poems, sometimes consciously, often unconsciously. Here is a poem by Peter Kane Dufault, at one time a combat airman in North Africa and Italy.

General Salute

Airplanes would lift for him. —
Five hundred heavies of the AAF, once
while he squinted from a promontory
gaggled between the sun
and shattered Adriatic. Their salute
into the infinite for him
arced upward half a day and dropped
all afternoon. . . . Old Man . . .
Now when he lays his trowel down
in a rose garden on the Rappahannock,
visoring hand returns, returns, —
to a scatter of starlings,
or a detouring plane, —
the all-culminating violence,
dominion,
vertigo.

Please go on to page 89.

[*from page 88*]

The comparison between what was *once* and what *now* is introduces the occasion for the poem, that person, place, thing, or incident which is defined in and by the poem. But before we go any further, there is some aviation and military jargon which you must understand. *Heavies* refers to the heavy bombers of the AAF, Army Air Forces. The word *gaggle* is a specific term meaning the execution of aerial maneuvers in combat. *Old Man* is the nickname often given commanders of military organizations, and the last word of the poem, *vertigo*, has a particularly unpleasant connotation for pilots, describing as it does a dizziness causing loss of orientation.

Now reread the poem on page 88 and determine the occasion for the poem.

The retirement of a high-ranking officer. **page 79**

A salute toward the sky. **page 94**

War and peace. **page 97**

[*from page 94*]

YOUR ANSWER: Aírplanes would lift fór him. —

This is the way I read it, but I will not argue if you do not like the secondary stress on the word *lift*, nor would I challenge any other emphasis, as long as the word *for* stands out. Why this insistence on one word? Because the opening line, set off as it is by itself (note the use of the period *and* the dash), introduces the first hint of the subject. "Airplanes would lift *for* him," the poem says, establishing an important contrast between what was and what is now. Now the retired officer works in his garden with a trowel, and airplanes fly overhead without a word from him.

The use of words with two or more meanings has been a common practice of poets for centuries. Modern poets still use puns to give breadth to their work. Look at the title, "General Salute." We can read it two ways: first as a salute *by* a general, then as a salute *in* general. And the word *lift* can mean the act of raising and carrying an object, or the lifting of an airplane off the ground to start its flight. What about *Old Man*? The military connotation has already been noted, but the *Old Man* has become an old man, literally, and this one word helps us to see both the past and the present.

When we notice a double meaning we should ask ourselves, "Are all the possible meanings of this word consistent with the rest of the poem?" If our answer is yes, we can applaud the pun and see once more how one word or phrase can create a complex of meaning.

Please go on to page 91.

[*from page 90*]

The *occasion* for this poem is a salute toward the sky. When we consider why a salute is tendered in the first place, we can discover the *subject* of the poem.

Read the poem again, looking for the subject.

General Salute

Airplanes would lift for him. —
Five hundred heavies of the AAF, once
while he squinted from a promontory
gaggled between the sun
and shattered Adriatic. Their salute
into the infinite for him
arced upward half a day and dropped
all afternoon. . . . Old Man . . .
Now when he lays his trowel down
in a rose garden on the Rappahannock,
visoring hand returns, returns, —
to a scatter of starlings,
or detouring plane, —
the all-culminating violence,
dominion,
vertigo.

The first part describes the salute of the heavy bombers to the general; the second is concerned with the return of the "visoring hand." What is the major difference between what we see on the promontory and in the "rose garden on the Rappahannock"?

The general does not salute in both scenes. **page 95**

The first scene is orderly; the second is disorderly. **page 98**

There is no difference. **page 102**

[*from page 81*]

YOUR ANSWER: The Latin phrase and the Sphinx are dishonest referents; hence there is an invalid metaphor.

Good for you, you are taking a stand. Unfortunately, this time you are wrong. You have probably not exhausted the symbolic possibilities of the stanza.

If you recognized the biblical reference in the first line, good; if not, look up *John* xx:17. This will help to explain why the poet is described as a "pilgrim" in the second line, and add to your understanding of who "sleeps in poetry and silences." Certainly not the descendants of the speaker of the first *noli me tangere*; they sleep in Heaven. Which "line" cannot sleep in heaven (here the word *sleep* should be taken in its final sense)? And how does the Sphinx have anything to do with this particular "line"?

I think this is an honest symbol, used to make more nearly universal a woman who is first shown only as a former lover of the poet.

Return to page 81 and select the correct answer.

[*from page 99*]

YOUR ANSWER: Frustration.

I'm afraid not. Who is frustrated? The general? From the context of the poem, I rather doubt it. If you subscribe to the common but erroneous belief that generals are dissatisfied without a war to fight, you would have grounds for seeing frustration in the poem. But there are too many if's, and to pursue this line of interpretation would be dishonest.

There is no evidence that the general is not happy in his rose garden, or that he feels anything at all when he instinctively raises his hand to shade his eyes to look at birds or airplanes. Something about this semblance of a salute bears directly on the poem's subject. Why, for instance, does Dufault say that the general's "visoring hand returns, returns, — " using the dash to slow down the reading and emphasize what it is that the general *now* salutes? What in the general's experience makes him search the sky again and again, even long after fighting is over? We are the sum of all our experiences, but some affect us more than others.

Return to page 99 and select another answer.

[*from page 89*]

YOUR ANSWER: A salute toward the sky.

Right. The specific incident is the sight of a military officer first in the act of saluting "five hundred heavies," then saluting a "scatter of starlings."

Dufault writes economically and tightly. *Scatter*, for instance, is not fully understood until we see its relationship to *vertigo*, a scattering of the senses, and we see a further development through assonance when we look back on the "shattered" Adriatic. The misreading or misunderstanding of one word or phrase in this poem is likely to make the entire structure meaningless.

Look at the metrics. How would you scan the first line?

Airplanes would lift for him. —

/ // /
Airplanes would lift for him. **page 90**

// /
Airplanes would lift for him. **page 100**

// /
Airplanes would lift for him. **page 103**

[*from page 91*]

YOUR ANSWER: The general does not salute in both scenes.

Yes, he does. On page 94 I referred to the salute toward the sky as common to both scenes, and I called it the occasion for the poem. So how could the general *not* salute in both scenes?

An answer might be that the poet doesn't *show* him saluting in the first scene, to which I would reply, "Yes, he does. He does not, however, *tell* us as he does in the second scene."

I would like to conduct an experiment to demonstrate how a poet can show something definite without appearing to say anything about it.

Here is line 3:

while he squinted from a promontory

Why is he squinting? If you stand outdoors and attempt to focus on an object which is almost in a direct line between you and the sun, you will squint. *Then* what will you do? What is that hand doing at your forehead? Trying to shade your eyes? And doesn't this gesture resemble a salute?

Return to page 91, reread the poem, and select another answer.

[*from page 81*]

YOUR ANSWER: There is no use of a symbol.

Well, there is.

Perhaps it might help to remember the definition of the literary symbol: something which is itself and at the same time is something else as well. The something here is the woman, the former lover of the poet. But she is also called "the only daughter of a line/ That sleeps in poetry and silences." Is she really a relative of an ancient tribe or clan, or is she supposed to represent what *could* possibly be?

We are not able to see what is being symbolized, but we must see the symbol itself, in this case the woman. By means of our intellect we can make the comparison between what the woman *is* and what she *represents*; then we can imagine the woman to be that which she represents, in this case a member of a pagan race. If we say, "That woman is a pagan," we do not mean that she falls down and worships stone idols, but we do mean that she has certain pagan characteristics; in other words, she is a *symbol* of paganism.

If you still do not see the use of the woman as a symbol, place a marker here and return to page 25, and reread the discussion of the symbol. Try to see first what the symbol is, then how it is used. When you feel you understand, return to page 81 and select another answer.

[*from page 89*]

YOUR ANSWER: War and peace.

Wrong. This answer is too vague.

I think you fail to understand the definition of the "occasion for the poem." A poet may decide upon a subject to write and then search for a representative example. The example he chooses must represent his subject, but it must also be suitable for honest, consistent, and complete treatment within the limits of the poem.

Or the poet may work another way, seeing or imagining a specific person, place, thing, or incident which has in it qualities of a much more abstract *subject*. The requirements of honesty, consistency, and completeness naturally must still be in force.

For instance, let's assume that Wilfred Owen felt appalled by the impression of predatory hunger that war gave him. How could he *show* war's predatory hunger? Predatory animals feed on smaller animals; they prey on the young, the offspring which do not know enough to hide. War also devours the young. Perhaps this was how Owen arrived at the occasion for the poem "Arms and the Boy," an occasion which we have seen stated as the sight of a young man playing with weapons of war.

"General Salute" has as its occasion a similarly minor incident which the author has connected with his much larger, more inclusive *subject*.

Return to page 88, reread the poem, and select another answer from those on page 89.

[*from page 91*]

YOUR ANSWER: The first scene is orderly; the second is disorderly.

Right. To understand this relationship is to begin to see what the poet means. The first scene shows the general standing on a promontory (as far out as he can go) watching *his* airplanes salute the infinite "between the sun and shattered Adriatic." He watches them go out for their mission in the morning, then sees them return in the afternoon. The word *dropped* may be a pun, denoting both a return to the airfield as well as the actual dropping of their bombs.

The second scene, however, is quite different. Now the general stands in a peaceful rose garden, his hand in the attitude of a salute (as it was before when he "squinted" from the promontory), this time not to a formation of airplanes but to a *scatter* of birds or an airplane which is *off* its planned course. These flying objects are no longer under his control. His days of command in war and death are past; his occupation now is one of peace and creation, symbolized by the rose garden in which he is working.

So, the occasion for the poem — a salute toward the sky — is seen performed twice: first under orderly circumstances, second by habit in a haphazard situation. When you consider the reasons for a salute, and notice the reference to the airplanes lifting *for* the "Old Man," you should be able to arrive at the subject of the poem.

Please go on to page 99.

[*from page 98*]

Here is the poem once more:

General Salute

Airplanes would lift for him. —
Five hundred heavies of the AAF, once
while he squinted from a promontory
gaggled between the sun
and shattered Adriatic. Their salute
into the infinite for him
arced upward half a day and dropped
all afternoon. . . . Old Man . . .
Now when he lays his trowel down
in a rose garden on the Rappahannock,
visoring hand returns, returns, —
to a scatter of starlings,
or detouring plane, —
the all-culminating violence,
dominion,
vertigo.

What is the subject of the poem?

Frustration. **page 93**

War. **page 107**

Control. **page 110**

[*from page 94*]

YOUR ANSWER: Aírplanes would líft for him.

Reread this line the way you wish to emphasize it. What else do airplanes do? Drag? Push? Why does the poet want to emphasize the *lifting* of an aircraft, when the thought is not original and contributes nothing to the poem?

Dufault places great importance on single words, and to read the first line as you wished results in little more meaning than "Airplanes fly in the sky." Try reading it by placing the primary emphasis on the one word which introduces the major consideration of the poem and provides an important clue to the subject.

Return to page 88, reread the poem, and select another answer from those on page 94.

[*from page 111*]

YOUR ANSWER: Suffering.

No, it isn't. The painting mentioned in the poem has suffering as its subject, and Auden comments that the Old Masters were never wrong about suffering. But suffering is accepted here and is shown as only one part of life, like truth, hope, happiness, or death, about which the Old Masters could also be said to be right.

Read the poem again, looking for its occasion on the concrete level.

Musée des Beaux Arts

About suffering they were never wrong,
The Old Masters: how well they understood
Its human position; how it takes place
While someone else is eating or opening a window or just
walking dully along;
How, when the aged are reverently, passionately waiting
For the miraculous birth, there always must be
Children who did not specially want it to happen, skating
On a pond at the edge of the wood:
They never forgot
That even the dreadful martyrdom must run its course
Anyhow in a corner, some untidy spot
Where the dogs go on with their doggy life and the torturer's horse
Scratches its innocent behind on a tree.

In Brueghel's *Icarus*, for instance: how everything turns away
Quite leisurely from the disaster; the ploughman may
Have heard the splash, the forsaken cry,
But for him it was not an important failure; the sun shone
As it had to on the white legs disappearing into the green
Water; and the expensive delicate ship that must have seen
Something amazing, a boy falling out of the sky,
Had somewhere to get to and sailed calmly on.

What is the occasion for the poem?

The sight of people suffering. **page 106**

A work of art. **page 108**

The sight of people being unconcerned about others. **page 112**

[*from page 91*]

YOUR ANSWER: There is no difference.

Good enough. Let me point out the differences, and then you can draw your own conclusions. Here is the poem again, with certain words underlined:

General Salute

Airplanes would lift for him. —
Five hundred heavies of the AAF, once
while he squinted from a promontory
gaggled between the sun
and shattered Adriatic. Their salute
into the infinite for him
arced upward half a day and dropped
all afternoon. . . . Old Man . . .
Now when he lays his trowel down
in a rose garden on the Rappahannock,
visoring hand returns, returns, —
to a scatter of starlings,
or detouring plane, —
the all-culminating violence,
dominion,
vertigo.

The poet shows the conflict between symbols of flight and time which at first may seem insignificantly different but on close inspection prove very dissimilar. Perhaps you have seen formations of aircraft taking off and landing, forming V's, diamond shapes, or straight lines in the sky. Five hundred is a lot of aircraft, and their departure in the morning and their return in the afternoon implies a consistent picture of orderly motion.

But what about the "scatter of starlings" and the "detouring plane"? How do these aerial sights differ from the well-planned, organized take-offs and landings of bombers? Visualize the difference; then return to page 91 and select the correct answer.

[*from page 94*]

YOUR ANSWER: Aírplanes would lift for him.

I do not read it this way at all, primarily because of the confusion created by various interpretations of the word *would.* Does the phrase mean "used to lift," or is the conditional used with an implified "if" to follow?

Read this line in context with the rest of the poem on page 88. By giving one word primary emphasis, you can see the subject of the poem introduced. Try various combinations, and decide which one best introduces this poem.

Return to page 94 and select another answer.

[*from page 111*]

YOUR ANSWER: Art's relationship to life.

Precisely. You have discovered what concerned the poet so deeply that he chose a work of art by one of the Old Masters as the occasion for his poem.

This poem contains an approach to its subject different from those used in poems discussed earlier. The subjects — love and dominion — of the other poems are recognized and commented on by the poets. This is not the case here, for Auden shows art's importance by his initial comment that "the Old Masters were never wrong about suffering," then investigates how the Old Masters *show* that they were never wrong.

In the painting *The Fall of Icarus* the "ploughman" and the "delicate ship" did not just *happen* to be there; they were placed in the painting by the artist for a specific purpose — with the result that to Auden the true nature of suffering is shown.

The subject of this poem, art's relationship to life, is demonstrated for us by Auden's comments on the Old Masters. Go on to page 105, reread the poem, and attempt to determine what parts of this relationship Auden is concerned with.

[*from page 104*]

Musée des Beaux Arts

About suffering they were never wrong,
The Old Masters: how well they understood
Its human position; how it takes place
While someone else is eating or opening a window or just
    walking dully along;
How, when the aged are reverently, passionately waiting
For the miraculous birth, there always must be
Children who did not specially want it to happen, skating
On a pond at the edge of the wood:
They never forgot
That even the dreadful martyrdom must run its course
Anyhow in a corner, some untidy spot
Where the dogs go on with their doggy life and the torturer's horse
Scratches its innocent behind on a tree.

In Brueghel's *Icarus*, for instance: how everything turns away
Quite leisurely from the disaster; the ploughman may
Have heard the splash, the forsaken cry,
But for him it was not an important failure; the sun shone
As it had to on the white legs disappearing into the green
Water; and the expensive delicate ship that must have seen
Something amazing, a boy falling out of the sky,
Had somewhere to get to and sailed calmly on.

Assuming that art has a relationship to life, what, according to Auden, must be recognized first in order to understand this relationship?

That the Old Masters are the best. **page 113**

That art is important to everyday existence. **page 116**

That art differs from life because art is created by man. **page 120**

[*from page 101 or 122*]

YOUR ANSWER: The sight of people suffering.

I'm sorry, you are wrong. Please realize that although suffering plays an important part in the poem, it is neither the subject nor the occasion for the poem.

Let me ask this. According to our definition, the occasion for the poem is that person, place, thing, or incident which is defined *by* and *in* the poem. Is suffering present in "Musée des Beaux Arts"? Is there any discussion of what suffering is? What it does? If suffering were so important to Auden here, don't you think he might have been more interested in the torturer than in the "innocent behind" of the torturer's horse?

Turn to page 101 and concentrate on the second stanza. How does Auden know that the Old Masters were never wrong about suffering? Consider the first stanza as a commentary on what Auden sees in the painting *The Fall of Icarus*.

Now return again to page 101, reread the poem, and select another answer.

[*from page 99*]

YOUR ANSWER: War.

I'm sorry, but war is no more the subject of this poem than it is the subject of the poem "Arms and the Boy."

Here is an exercise for you. Dufault, unlike many poets we shall see, sums up his subject with one specific word that underlines everything he points to in the poem. Look at the one word in the first line that must be accented:

Airplanes would lift <u>for</u> him. —

This line, when understood, introduces the subject, explaining why it is that the "visoring hand returns, returns," again and again.

Return to page 99, reread the poem, and select another answer.

[*from page 101 or 122*]

YOUR ANSWER: A work of art.

Right. The reason I consider the occasion for this poem to be a work of art is as follows: Brueghel's painting *The Fall of Icarus* is described and defined in and by the poem. It is presented not for its own sake, but as representative of all the works of art created by the Old Masters. "How well they [the Old Masters] understood" the nature of suffering, Auden says in the beginning. He gives a brief example of the kind of suffering he means. "They never forgot . . ." Auden continues, and he shows by example what the Old Masters always remembered.

To discover the subject of this poem, you must determine what concerned Auden so deeply that he used a work of art as the occasion for his poem.

You have recognized the emphasis on suffering and human unconcern. Both parts of the human condition are subjects of the Old Masters' art. Reread the poem on page 109, and notice how suffering and human unconcern function within it.

[*from page 108*]

Musée des Beaux Arts

About suffering they were never wrong,
The Old Masters: how well they understood
Its human position; how it takes place
While someone else is eating or opening a window or just
walking dully along;
How, when the aged are reverently, passionately waiting
For the miraculous birth, there always must be
Children who did not specially want it to happen, skating
On a pond at the edge of the wood:
They never forgot
That even the dreadful martyrdom must run its course
Anyhow in a corner, some untidy spot
Where the dogs go on with their doggy life and the torturer's horse
Scratches its innocent behind on a tree.

In Brueghel's *Icarus*, for instance: how everything turns away
Quite leisurely from the disaster; the ploughman may
Have heard the splash, the forsaken cry,
But for him it was not an important failure; the sun shone
As it had to on the white legs disappearing into the green
Water; and the expensive delicate ship that must have seen
Something amazing, a boy falling out of the sky,
Had somewhere to get to and sailed calmly on.

Specifically, how do the people and animals react to the suffering present in both stanzas of the poem?

They realize there is nothing they can do about it. **page 114**

They do not recognize it as suffering. **page 118**

They accept it as a necessity of life. **page 123**

[*from page 99*]

YOUR ANSWER: Control.

Correct. Control (*dominion*, as Dufault calls it in the poem) is the subject, symbolized by the salutes of the general and the airplanes. Dominion is perpetual, the poet shows, whether it is seen to be violent in wartime or habitual in a peaceful rose garden.

We have not concerned ourselves with what the poet says about his subject; that will be treated in detail in a following chapter, but you should notice here the difference in approach between this poem and "A Woman Too Well Remembered." Simpson made a direct comment at the end of his poem, while here, Dufault is much more obtuse. The final lines:

> The all-culminating violence,
> dominion,
> vertigo.

are not so concrete as the closing lines of "A Woman Too Well Remembered." Do you think Dufault is passing judgment here, or is he expressing his inability to understand the dominion which can produce the "all-culminating violence" of war? Do you see any connection between the first and last lines? Try reading them as one framing sentence: "Airplanes would lift for him . . . the all-culminating violence." Is this one complete thought, and the rest of the poem a justification of the officer's attitude? The poet leaves the reader to ponder the question in any way he likes.

So far in this chapter we have seen two poems which deal directly with what we might call the human condition, each using an occasion which is easily recognizable. The next poem is more complex, because here what may appear to be the subject actually is not. One of the major concerns of artists is their art itself. They are rarely satisfied just to comment on life; instead, their approach is to try to mold, design, and create some artifact (the work of art, a painting, poem, or piece of prose) which actually improves on life. Because many artists feel that life itself is haphazard and misleading, they attempt to make an artifact which is real and honest, without the frills and trivialities of everyday existence.

Please go on to page 111.

[*from page 110*]

Let us investigate this purpose by reference to the following poem by W. H. Auden.

Musée des Beaux Arts

About suffering they were never wrong,
The Old Masters: how well they understood
Its human position; how it takes place
While someone else is eating or opening a window or just
walking dully along;
How, when the aged are reverently, passionately waiting
For the miraculous birth, there always must be
Children who did not specially want it to happen, skating
On a pond at the edge of the wood:
They never forgot
That even the dreadful martyrdom must run its course
Anyhow in a corner, some untidy spot
Where the dogs go on with their doggy life and the torturer's horse
Scratches its innocent behind on a tree.

In Brueghel's *Icarus*,* for instance: how everything turns away
Quite leisurely from the disaster; the ploughman may
Have heard the splash, the forsaken cry,
But for him it was not an important failure; the sun shone
As it had to on the white legs disappearing into the green
Water; and the expensive delicate ship that must have seen
Something amazing, a boy falling out of the sky,
Had somewhere to get to and sailed calmly on.

Let's try a direct jump. What is the subject of this poem?

Suffering. **page 101**

Art's relationship to life. **page 104**

Human unconcern. **page 122**

---

* *The Fall of Icarus,* a painting by Pieter Brueghel (1525?-69) which depicts the mythical death of Icarus, the son of Dedalus, after he flew too close to the sun and his wax wings melted.

[*from page 101 or 122*]

YOUR ANSWER: The sight of people being unconcerned about others.

I'm sorry, but your concern with human *un*concern has misled you. Human unconcern is present in the poem, but it is neither the subject of nor the occasion for the poem.

A bit of review is in order. The occasion for the poem is the person, place, thing, or incident which is defined *by* and *in* the poem. Is this the case with human unconcern? Is there any consideration of what human unconcern *is*, or why it exists? Not at all. Auden does not care here *why* the children do not "specially" care about the old people's patient wait for death. He does not berate the torturer's horse for being unconcerned, nor does he attempt to explain why the "ploughman" and the "delicate ship" pay no attention to the suffering of Icarus. Auden accepts this indifference as a part of life.

Return to page 101 or 122 and concentrate on the second stanza. The second stanza describes a painting, one of many hanging in the art gallery. How does the author *know* that the Old Masters were never wrong about suffering? Finally, determine what person, place, thing, or incident is defined in and by the poem *on the literal level.*

Now return again to page 101 or 122, reread the entire poem, and select another answer.

[*from page 105 or 127*]

YOUR ANSWER: That the Old Masters are the best.

Wrong. There is no comparison here between the Old Masters and any other group of artists. The Old Masters are used as examples of what Auden considers good artists. Notice the use of the present tense in the first stanza: how suffering "takes place while someone else *is* eating or opening a window or just walking." Had Auden been concerned only with what the Old Masters *were* able to do, why would he have used the present tense?

Remember, we have established that Auden is writing about art's relationship to life, but something else is involved. You can see a comparison between what really *is* (suffering) and what *appears to be* (the nonexistence of suffering suggested by the lack of attention paid to it). Ordinary life does not equip people to see and understand suffering, but art is different from life. Think about this difference. How does a painting of a scene differ from the scene itself?

Turn to page 127, reread the poem, and choose another answer.

[*from page 109 or 123*]

YOUR ANSWER: They realize there is nothing they can do about it.

Who does? The children? The "doggy" dogs? The aged who have transmuted what Auden thinks is suffering into a reverent wait for the "miraculous birth"? Not at all.

In order to realize that you can do nothing about a particular human condition, you must first *see* it and then make up your mind. You cannot, for example, know that an accident victim is beyond all help unless you are at the scene of the accident. You cannot feel a sense of futility toward a person with an incurable disease unless you are certain that he *has* this particular disease.

The necessity for recognition is Auden's comment on the reaction of people toward suffering in general. Certainly the person (not present in the poem) who is being tortured realizes what suffering is, and certainly Icarus, his wings melted by the sun, knows suffering when he plunges toward the ocean. But what about the rest of humanity who are opening windows or "just walking dully along"? Even if they *see* forms of suffering, do they recognize it as such and feel anything?

Return to page 109, reread the poem, and select another answer.

[*from page 119*]

YOUR ANSWER: By observing more closely what goes on around us.

This solution might work for some persons, but it is not the answer Auden suggests. Notice his use of the aged people. Shouldn't they know about suffering? After all, they are about to die. Instead of recognizing their slow departure from life as a form of suffering, they substitute a passionate, reverent hope for a "miraculous birth." The men of the "delicate" ship *must* have seen, Auden says, but because they had "somewhere to get to" they did not stop to help.

All of the examples given in the poem suggest that people will always ignore suffering, either because they do not want to see it or else are unable to see it.

But Auden does have a solution, one that concerns something men can do to recognize suffering.

Return to page 119, reread the poem, and select another answer.

[*from page 105 or 127*]

YOUR ANSWER: That art is important to everyday existence.

Your answer is true, but not relevant to this question. Isn't the importance of art assumed from the beginning of the poem? Anyone who is "never wrong" about suffering certainly does have something important to give humanity, but would this by itself account for the relationship of art to life? And if we *do* understand that art is important to life, how does this help us to see the relationship?

Let's investigate further. Assuming that art does have a relationship to life, why does it? How is a painting different from a photograph? A photograph could depict aged people, the opening of windows, people walking dully along, dogs and tethered horses, but it might not show that suffering was in some way common to all of them. The Old Masters, however, could delineate this suffering, and it is how they managed to succeed that Auden is investigating. He writes about his subject, the relationship of art to life, by showing what this relationship is and *how* it is accomplished. In order to do so, he must prove that art can emphasize what life consists of while not being itself at all *like* life.

Turn to page 127, reread the poem, and select another answer.

[*from page 121*]

YOUR ANSWER: The artist can show life exactly as it is.

No, he can't. Remember my statement that no art is truly "realistic"? If you forgot this, return now to page 120, read the second paragraph (which isn't so much of a digression after all) and subsequent material, then choose another answer. If, however, you disagree with my statement that no art is "realistic," read on, and if you still wish to argue, write to me in care of the publishers. I'm always willing to learn.

Art is not "realistic." Let's define terms. For the sake of argument, let us accept that what is real is that which we can see, feel, hear, taste, or touch.

All right, now for an example. You see a beautiful woman. She has been created by life processes which are still largely unknown. We know how life is created, but we can't pin down details. Could you, by any stretch of the imagination, create such a woman yourself? Can any person? This is what I mean by art's *not* being "realistic." The writer James Joyce calls all art "fake" as opposed to what is "real." This is a valid comment, because anything made by man is an imperfect copy of that which is made by nature or God.

Do you now agree that art cannot be "realistic"? If not, please accept the terms I use as stepping stones to greater understanding, return to page 121, and choose another answer.

[*from page 109*]

YOUR ANSWER: They do not recognize it as suffering.

Exactly. When does suffering take place?

> While someone else is eating or opening a window or just
> walking dully along;

These are everyday occurrences which emphasize the presence of suffering at all times. The aged (in violent contrast to the youth, Icarus) wait stoically, not realizing they are suffering, hoping for the "miraculous birth" into the life after death. The children skating *near* the woods do not know enough about suffering to care; they don't "specially" want it to happen. The "doggy" dogs and the torturer's horse do not recognize suffering any more than do the people on the "expensive delicate ship" which has somewhere to go. This phrase is ironic when we think of how expensive and delicate human life really is.

Everyone turns away from suffering, says Auden; yet suffering exists. There ought to be a way for those of us not experiencing pain, torture, or death to recognize and understand what suffering is.

Please go on to page 119, reread the poem, and see if you can find Auden's solution.

[*from page 118*]

Musée des Beaux Arts

About suffering they were never wrong,
The Old Masters: how well they understood
Its human position; how it takes place
While someone else is eating or opening a window or just
    walking dully along;
How, when the aged are reverently, passionately waiting
For the miraculous birth, there always must be
Children who did not specially want it to happen, skating
On a pond at the edge of the wood:
They never forgot
That even the dreadful martyrdom must run its course
Anyhow in a corner, some untidy spot
Where the dogs go on with their doggy life and the torturer's horse
Scratches its innocent behind on a tree.

In Brueghel's *Icarus*, for instance: how everything turns away
Quite leisurely from the disaster; the ploughman may
Have heard the splash, the forsaken cry,
But for him it was not an important failure; the sun shone
As it had to on the white legs disappearing into the green
Water; and the expensive delicate ship that must have seen
Something amazing, a boy falling out of the sky,
Had somewhere to get to and sailed calmly on.

How, according to Auden, can suffering be communicated to those not at the moment experiencing it?

By observing more closely what goes on around us. **page 115**

By having really experienced suffering once. **page 124**

By observing a work of art which deals with suffering. **page 126**

[*from page 105 or 127*]

YOUR ANSWER: That art differs from life because it is created by man.

Correct. A work of art, as opposed to a work of nature or God, is the only creation that man is able to fashion himself by his own ingenuity. Technically, anything *made* by man is a work of art — a house, an automobile, a fence, a novel, poem, or play. Man in the role of creator is thereby an *artisan*, a maker, and in building a house, for instance, he does not copy a shelter made by nature (a cave, a clump of trees, a rocky overhang) but uses his abilities to improve on nature.

This is precisely what an artist does with a painting, poem, novel, or play. Nothing written is truly "realistic." If it were, each time a new day dawned in a book, every character would be seen to get up, yawn, stretch, go to the bathroom, brush his teeth, eat breakfast, and so on. But authors usually omit these details from their books. Why? Because these events are not important to the author's purpose in writing the book.

Simple, isn't it? Yet understanding what is "real" is vital to an understanding of the function of art.

Does this simple approach tread on your understanding and use of the terms "naturalism," "realism," "surrealism," and the like? Does it mean that the various schools of poetry and fiction do not exist, because there is no such thing as "realistic writing"? Not at all. Literary people are label-pinners and school creators by habit; they can't help themselves, and all that is meant by a particular name applied to a style of writing is that the artists who belong to a particular school differ from artists of another school in their choice of *what* they select from life to use in their art. You can take practically any incident from life and reproduce it naturalistically, realistically, imagistically, and so on.* But let's leave this discussion of schools and return to the poem.

Please go on to page 121.

---

* For extended definitions of these terms, consult *A Handbook to Literature* as listed in the Appendix.

[*from page 120*]

The artist believes that he improves on life, succeeding because art makes people see what life cannot show them. Read the poem again.

Musée des Beaux Arts

About suffering they were never wrong,
The Old Masters: how well they understood
Its human position; how it takes place
While someone else is eating or opening a window or just
walking dully along;
How, when the aged are reverently, passionately waiting
For the miraculous birth, there always must be
Children who did not specially want it to happen, skating
On a pond at the edge of the wood:
They never forgot
That even the dreadful martyrdom must run its course
Anyhow in a corner, some untidy spot
Where the dogs go on with their doggy life and the torturer's horse
Scratches its innocent behind on a tree.

In Brueghel's *Icarus*, for instance: how everything turns away
Quite leisurely from the disaster; the ploughman may
Have heard the splash, the forsaken cry,
But for him it was not an important failure; the sun shone
As it had to on the white legs disappearing into the green
Water; and the expensive delicate ship that must have seen
Something amazing, a boy falling out of the sky,
Had somewhere to get to and sailed calmly on.

What can the artist do (according to Auden) to show the observers of his art what life cannot show them?

The artist can show life exactly as it is. **page 117**

The artist is able to capture emotion. **page 125**

The artist can select and discard. **page 128**

[*from page 111*]

YOUR ANSWER: Human unconcern.

Not quite. Although human unconcern is shown in the poem, it is not the subject. Human unconcern is taken for granted, just as war is accepted in Dufault's "General Salute." We must accept unconcern and live with it.

Let us attempt to establish the occasion for the poem.

Musée des Beaux Arts

About suffering they were never wrong,
The Old Masters: how well they understood
Its human position; how it takes place
While someone else is eating or opening a window or just
    walking dully along;
How, when the aged are reverently, passionately waiting
For the miraculous birth, there always must be
Children who did not specially want it to happen, skating
On a pond at the edge of the wood:
They never forgot
That even the dreadful martyrdom must run its course
Anyhow in a corner, some untidy spot
Where the dogs go on with their doggy life and the torturer's horse
Scratches its innocent behind on a tree.

In Brueghel's *Icarus*, for instance: how everything turns away
Quite leisurely from the disaster; the ploughman may
Have heard the splash, the forsaken cry,
But for him it was not an important failure; the sun shone
As it had to on the white legs disappearing into the green
Water; and the expensive delicate ship that must have seen
Something amazing, a boy falling out of the sky,
Had somewhere to get to and sailed calmly on.

What is the occasion for the poem?

The sight of people suffering. **page 106**

A work of art. **page 108**

The sight of people being unconcerned about others. **page 112**

[*from page 109*]

YOUR ANSWER: They accept it as a necessity of life.

I'm sorry, you are wrong. You have chosen this answer for the same reason someone else selected the answer "They realize there is nothing they can do about it." In both cases, suffering must be seen and understood to form a judgment about it, and Auden does not believe that people are able to recognize true suffering.

Go on to page 114 and continue reading.

[*from page 119*]

YOUR ANSWER: By having really experienced suffering once.

Not in this poem. Experience may be the best teacher in some fields, but not, according to Auden, with regard to suffering. Can you assume that the aged people or the "ploughman" have suffered in some manner during their lifetimes? Certainly, and Auden hardly assumes that a person only suffers once and is then immune. The unseen torturer is a particularly good image, because we react to the word's connotations of dire, drawn-out pain. But will the person being tortured, once set free, react any differently to the suffering of *others* while *he* is "opening a window or just walking dully along"? If your answer is yes, then you have a much rosier outlook on humanity than Auden does, and I would not even begin to argue with you.

We are concerned here with what the *poem* says, not with your personal (and commendable) opinion. Once we understand a poem in its entirety, *then* we may agree or disagree. In asserting your disagreement, you are likely to miss the whole point of the poem, a poem that uses suffering only as an example. You could insert truth, happiness, fear, or any abstraction not easily defined by the senses and the poem would mean the same as it does when suffering is discussed.

So please accept the use of suffering as an example that serves to carry the mind on to larger and more important considerations.

Return to page 119 and select the correct answer.

[*from page 121*]

YOUR ANSWER: The artist can capture emotion.

No. It's funny, isn't it, how often the well-known phrases trap us. First, art cannot capture emotion, and second, even if it could, this is not what Auden is talking about.

Try to see the meaning of words as they are used. Perhaps you (like me) have often said of a poem, play, or novel, "That work really captures the emotion." But what have you said? Whose emotion has been "captured"? Yours or mine? The character's emotion? The author's emotion? And once captured, what is done with the emotion? Is it kept in a cage? A glass jar? Think of the many possible meanings of this dishonest, inconsistent, and incomplete metaphor ("capture the emotion") and you will perhaps understand why fighting often results when the use of words fails to solve a problem.

Art can *create* emotion, can't it? Haven't you at one time or another felt happiness, sadness, or anger when observing some form of art? A play, perhaps, or a movie? And life can create emotion, too, by means of the many incidents which affect us in varying ways. This is obvious.

How, then, do art and life differ? We said earlier that art is created by man. All right. Regardless of how life is created and arranged, the *plan*, the *structure*, the *reason* for every incident is *not* known to man. With a good work of art, however, a human being must know what the plan consists of and why it exists. See the difference? An artist thinks that he can comprehend emotion where less perceptive persons cannot; then, by means of his art, he attempts to re-create that emotion in the person who reads, sees, or hears his art.

How the artist succeeds is what concerns us here, and what Auden shows in his poem as the relationship of art to life.

Return to page 121, reread the poem, and select another answer.

[*from page 119*]

YOUR ANSWER: By observing a work of art which deals with suffering.

Right. Auden considers a work of art capable of showing what true suffering is, and art can transmit what the artist feels to the person who observes the work of art. But how does a work of art succeed for people who cannot even recognize suffering when they see it in life? This is the question Auden seeks to answer, and in order to do so he has chosen as his subject the relationship between art and life.

This is his subject; everything else in the poem is a commentary on the relationship of a work of art to life. The occasion for the poem, a work of art, is the example Auden chooses to show the relationship; suffering and human unconcern are but two of the many elements of life which art can show its audience.

Once we discover the poem's subject, we find that further investigation is needed. In the previous poems, once we arrived at the subject, we found the author commenting upon his subject, expressing an opinion about it. Here, however, further definition is needed. Auden not only admits the relationship but also shows why and how this relationship exists, and in doing so answers the question "What value does art have for us?"

Therefore, this poem is not a comment upon a subject but an investigation of one. To justify his subject, Auden demonstrates something about art which is never mentioned in the poem, but which must be understood by the artist in order to present suffering, pain, fear, hope, truth, or any other subject he desires.

Please go on to page 127.

[*from page 126*]

Musée des Beaux Arts

About suffering they were never wrong,
The Old Masters: how well they understood
Its human position; how it takes place
While someone else is eating or opening a window or just
walking dully along;
How, when the aged are reverently, passionately waiting
For the miraculous birth, there always must be
Children who did not specially want it to happen, skating
On a pond at the edge of the wood:
They never forgot
That even the dreadful martyrdom must run its course
Anyhow in a corner, some untidy spot
Where the dogs go on with their doggy life and the torturer's horse
Scratches its innocent behind on a tree.

In Brueghel's *Icarus*, for instance: how everything turns away
Quite leisurely from the disaster; the ploughman may
Have heard the splash, the forsaken cry,
But for him it was not an important failure; the sun shone
As it had to on the white legs disappearing into the green
Water; and the expensive delicate ship that must have seen
Something amazing, a boy falling out of the sky,
Had somewhere to get to and sailed calmly on.

Specifically, let us assume that art has a relationship to life. What (according to Auden) must be recognized first in order to understand this relationship?

That the Old Masters are the best. **page 113**

That art is important to everyday existence. **page 116**

That art differs from life because it is created by man. **page 120**

[*from page 121*]

YOUR ANSWER: The artist can select and discard.

You are correct. Certainly art is capable of creating emotion in the observer, and perhaps it can present life, if not as it is, then as it might be. But Auden's concern here is the *way* art can succeed: an artist can select, discard, arrange, forge, and fuse in his creation *only* those items necessary to show what the artist wants to show. His intention is often to create in the observer the particular emotion that he, as artist, senses. In this poem, suffering is shown by selection of detail.

This is a rich poem, and there is one more aspect I would like to consider. The poem not only exemplifies a vital, contemporary concern with the what's, why's, and how's of art but also demonstrates a structural technique which you will probably encounter again. Auden says that art can provide answers we cannot get from ordinary life. But his poem is a work of art, is it not? Can we then take Auden's work of art and assume it is "never wrong" about his subject of art and life?

Let's see. Look at the poem again. See if you can determine what relationship the two parts have to each other, and why Auden chooses to divide his poem into two parts.

Please go on to page 129.

[*from page 128*]

Musée des Beaux Arts

About suffering they were never wrong,
The Old Masters: how well they understood
Its human position; how it takes place
While someone else is eating or opening a window or just
walking dully along;
How, when the aged are reverently, passionately waiting
For the miraculous birth, there always must be
Children who did not specially want it to happen, skating
On a pond at the edge of the wood:
They never forgot
That even the dreadful martyrdom must run its course
Anyhow in a corner, some untidy spot
Where the dogs go on with their doggy life and the torturer's horse
Scratches its innocent behind on a tree.

In Brueghel's *Icarus*, for instance: how everything turns away
Quite leisurely from the disaster; the ploughman may
Have heard the splash, the forsaken cry,
But for him it was not an important failure; the sun shone
As it had to on the white legs disappearing into the green
Water; and the expensive delicate ship that must have seen
Something amazing, a boy falling out of the sky,
Had somewhere to get to and sailed calmly on.

Let us forget for the moment what the stanzas *say* and concentrate on what they *are*. Do you remember the definitions of image and symbol? If not, mark this place and turn to pages 20 and 25 for review, then return here.

As a group of words on the page, each stanza is a composite symbol. Stanza 1 is a symbol of ordinary life, dogs going on with their doggy life, people walking dully along, and so on. Stanza 2 is a symbol of art; a painting is being described, but unlike the elements of the first stanza (life), everything we see in the second stanza is there for a specific purpose, designed to show the central idea of the work of art, human suffering. By arranging his material in this way, the painter produced a scene which immediately strikes us with its message: no one cares when others suffer.

Please go on to page 130.

[*from page 129*]

By choosing Icarus as his central figure, Brueghel intensifies the pathos, for the suffering and death are those of a young man who has every reason to live. Yet no one in the painting cares.

Life, as shown by Auden in the first stanza, contains many different and opposing impressions which are sometimes seen but rarely understood. These impressions can only be brought into focus by the artist's ability to create his art by the proper selection of detail, and this process is *shown* by the second stanza, the symbol of art itself.

By first showing life, then art, Auden not only discusses the creative process but also demonstrates it before our eyes. Using suffering as an example, he presents the ordinary view first, then the artist's view — that is, the work of art itself. And in so doing, Auden creates his own work of art, his poem.

So we end with a work of art which explains its own creation, and an extremely complex poem which justifies itself.

Please go on to page 131.

[*from page 130*]

We have seen thus far how a person (a woman), an action (a salute), and a work of art (a painting) have led us into subjects of sexual love, dominion, and the relationship of art to life. In each case we have used the process of abstraction to arrive at the subject, starting with the occasion for the poem at the literal level, then proceeding to the pure idea behind it.

Let us look at another poem now, this one by Robert Frost. At first appearing deceptively simple, this poem is seen to be complex when studied carefully.

The Oven Bird

There is a singer everyone has heard,
Loud, a mid-summer and a mid-wood bird,
Who makes the solid tree trunks sound again.
He says that leaves are old and that for flowers
Mid-summer is to spring as one to ten.
He says the early petal-fall is past
When pear and cherry bloom went down in showers
On sunny days a moment overcast;
And comes that other fall we name the fall.
He says the highway dust is over all.
The bird would cease and be as other birds
But that he knows in singing not to sing.
The question that he frames in all but words
Is what to make of a diminished thing.

First — what type of poem is it?

It is a Shakespearean sonnet. **page 134**

It is a sonnet. **page 137**

It falls into no specific category, other than lyric. **page 140**

[*from page 140*]

YOUR ANSWER: It is written in iambic pentameter.

Right.

Next question. What is the specific name for a fourteen-line poem written in iambic pentameter? If you do not know, return to page 49, read the discussion, and return here.

When you know what a fourteen-line poem written in iambic pentameter is, return to page 131 and select the correct answer.

[*from page 137*]

YOUR ANSWER: There are two couplets, a quatrain, and a sestet.

Right. The rhyme scheme of this poem is not obvious on first reading; all we know is that there are interlinking, similar sounds, but, looking closer, we see that the poem contains first a couplet (rhyme scheme is *aa*), then a sestet (*bcbdcd*), another couplet (*ee*), and finally a quatrain (*fgfg*).

Robert Frost is not considered a "scholarly" poet. He does not, for instance, use references to historic or literary incidents which must be understood before even the occasion, much less the subject, can be discerned. He writes mainly of commonplace rural scenes familiar to most Americans.

Here he describes the singing of a bird, a sound which he says at first that "everyone has heard." But have you? Do you know what an ovenbird's song is like? If so, then you can immediately sense what Frost is describing. If not, you are at a slight disadvantage, able to perceive only generally that a bird's song is mentioned.

By the way, what is an ovenbird? (Most dictionaries spell *ovenbird* as one word.)

It belongs to the crow family. **page 136**

It belongs to the wood-warbler family. **page 138**

It belongs to the weaverbird family. **page 141**

[*from page 131*]

YOUR ANSWER: It is a Shakespearean sonnet.

Consider this a reprimand: you could not have arrived here unless you decided to guess, and as is not unusual when you guess, your answer is wrong.

A Shakespearean sonnet does have fourteen lines; it is in iambic pentameter; but it is written in three quatrains (four line divisions) and one couplet. A Shakespearean sonnet looks like this:

XXXXXXXXXXXXXXXXXXXXX A
XXXXXXXXXXXXXXXXXXXXX B
XXXXXXXXXXXXXXXXXXXXX A
XXXXXXXXXXXXXXXXXXXXX B

XXXXXXXXXXXXXXXXXXXXX C
XXXXXXXXXXXXXXXXXXXXX D
XXXXXXXXXXXXXXXXXXXXX C
XXXXXXXXXXXXXXXXXXXXX D

XXXXXXXXXXXXXXXXXXXXX E
XXXXXXXXXXXXXXXXXXXXX F
XXXXXXXXXXXXXXXXXXXXX E
XXXXXXXXXXXXXXXXXXXXX F

XXXXXXXXXXXXXXXXXXXXX G
XXXXXXXXXXXXXXXXXXXXX G

The individual stanzas may be closed up to look like Frost's poem, but the three quatrains and the couplet must appear in this order for a sonnet to be called Shakespearean. Also, though the rhyme scheme may vary, the basic structure must be as shown above.

Return to page 131 and try again.

[*from page 140*]

YOUR ANSWER: It is written in iambic hexameter.

You are wrong. Perhaps you have forgotten the nomenclature of metrics. Here is some of it again:

monometer — one-foot lines
dimeter — two-foot lines
trimeter — three-foot lines
tetrameter — four-foot lines
pentameter — five-foot lines
hexameter — six-foot lines

Return to page 140, reread the poem, and select another answer.

[*from page 133*]

YOUR ANSWER: It belongs to the crow family.

It most certainly does not. You didn't guess, did you? Will you please get a dictionary and look up *ovenbird*.

When you have determined what an ovenbird is, return to page 133 and choose the correct answer.

[*from page 131*]

YOUR ANSWER: It is a sonnet.

Right. This poem typifies the contemporary use of the sonnet form. It has, of course, fourteen lines and is written in iambic pentameter. But here all similarity to the two traditional sonnet forms ends, because this poem has its own, unique rhyme scheme, one which is regular and consistent. Throughout most of his poetry, Frost creates his own individual rhyme patterns, and some of his intricate constructions do not appear to be regular until the poem is inspected closely.

Here is the poem again. Determine the pattern of rhyme Frost uses.

The Oven Bird

There is a singer everyone has heard,
Loud, a mid-summer and a mid-wood bird,
Who makes the solid tree trunks sound again.
He says that leaves are old and that for flowers
Mid-summer is to spring as one to ten.
He says the early petal-fall is past
When pear and cherry bloom went down in showers
On sunny days a moment overcast;
And comes that other fall we name the fall.
He says the highway dust is over all.
The bird would cease and be as other birds
But that he knows in singing not to sing.
The question that he frames in all but words
Is what to make of a diminished thing.

Which of the following describes the rhyme scheme of this poem?

There are two couplets, a quatrain, and a sestet. **page 133**

There are a couplet and three quatrains. **page 144**

There are rhymes, but they do not fit into any regular pattern. **page 148**

[*from page 133*]

YOUR ANSWER: It belongs to the wood-warbler family.

Correct. I hope you have found this out by reference to a good dictionary or an encyclopedia.

This was an easy reference, one that could almost be understood from the — Just a minute. Did you guess?

Let's see.

Where does the ovenbird build its nest?

In a tree. **page 142**

In attics, garages, and similarly sheltered areas. **page 145**

On the ground. **page 154**

[*from page 154*]

YOUR ANSWER: A bird singing.

Right. Isn't it strange how often we overlook the obvious? The singing of a particular bird is the occasion for this poem, and when we investigate the reason for the singing we are on the way toward discovering what the poet is writing about.

As I mentioned, however, the deceptive simplicity of this poem is distracting. Everything is quite clear until the last four lines; then, in the crux of the poem, Frost appears to be playing with words and becoming obscure. Read the poem again, concentrating on the last four lines.

The Oven Bird

There is a singer everyone has heard,
Loud, a mid-summer and a mid-wood bird,
Who makes the solid tree trunks sound again.
He says that leaves are old and that for flowers
Mid-summer is to spring as one to ten.
He says the early petal-fall is past
When pear and cherry bloom went down in showers
On sunny days a moment overcast;
And comes that other fall we name the fall.
He says the highway dust is over all.
The bird would cease and be as other birds
But that he knows in singing not to sing.
The question that he frames in all but words
Is what to make of a diminished thing.

Now, what is the subject of this poem?

Reality and the imagination. **page 146**

Nature. **page 149**

I don't know yet. **page 152**

[*from page 131*]

YOUR ANSWER: It falls into no specific category, other than lyric.

Wrong. This poem is one of the most tightly structured poems we will discuss and there is a name for it, one discussed earlier.

Here is the poem again. Count the lines and then scan the poem, placing the accent marks and identifying the individual feet.

The Oven Bird

There is a singer everyone has heard,
Loud, a mid-summer and a mid-wood bird,
Who makes the solid tree trunks sound again.
He says that leaves are old and that for flowers
Mid-summer is to spring as one to ten.
He says the early petal-fall is past
When pear and cherry bloom went down in showers
On sunny days a moment overcast;
And comes that other fall we name the fall.
He says the highway dust is over all.
The bird would cease and be as other birds
But that he knows in singing not to sing.
The question that he frames in all but words
Is what to make of a diminished thing.

Now, how would you describe the scansion of this poem?

It is written in iambic pentameter. **page 132**

It is written in iambic hexameter. **page 135**

It is written in trochaic hexameter. **page 151**

[*from page 133*]

YOUR ANSWER: It belongs to the weaverbird family.

I see you have heard of the weaverbirds, alias finches. But an ovenbird is not a member of this family, not even a distant cousin.

If you are at this moment marooned on a desert island or alone on the top of a mountain, then you may guess. In any other situation, however, please use a dictionary or an encyclopedia.

After looking up *ovenbird*, return to page 133 and choose the correct answer.

[*from page 138*]

YOUR ANSWER: In a tree.

I see.

Your answer is wrong. As it usually does, guessing leads you up a blind alley.

Now what?

Why not look up *ovenbird* in a dictionary under the O section?

When you have done this, return to page 138 and choose the correct answer.

[*from page 157*]

YOUR ANSWER: Time.

Wrong, I'm afraid. Time is a subject which is often considered by poets, but Frost is not discussing it here. True, time does play a part in the poem, for without it the seasons could not change and we would have nothing to remember. But if Frost were concerned with time here, don't you think he might attempt to investigate *why* the seasons change? Perhaps he would discuss *how* this cyclical change is an expression of time, or else comment upon spring with its fruitfulness as a symbol of youth, and fall with its decay as a symbol of age.

But he does not do so. Time appears here only as that essence without which nothing could happen.

On second thought, let's use your answer as a springboard. The subject of this poem concerns two items; first, something which does happen *in* time, seasonal change, growth and decay; second, something which is *not* related to time but occurs only in the mind. How long is a thought? Who can know? A memory? No one can tell.

So reread the poem and see how spring, which *did* occur, is shown contrasted with summer and fall, which are in existence when the bird sings. Spring and its fruitfulness are seen in later seasons as a "diminished thing," but for a human being it is possible to "see" spring in all its beauty. How? To answer this question is to recognize the subject of this poem.

Return to page 157, reread the poem, and select another answer.

[*from page 137*]

YOUR ANSWER: There are a couplet and three quatrains.

No. Couplets there are, but not three quatrains. Here is the poem again, this time broken into parts.

The Oven Bird

There is a singer everyone has heard,
Loud, a mid-summer and a mid-wood bird,

Who makes the solid tree trunks sound again.
He says that leaves are old and that for flowers
Mid-summer is to spring as one to ten.
He says the early petal-fall is past
When pear and cherry bloom went down in showers
On sunny days a moment overcast;

And comes that other fall we name the fall.
He says the highway dust is over all.

The bird would cease and be as other birds
But that he knows in singing not to sing.
The question that he frames in all but words
Is what to make of a diminished thing.

What do you see now? Remember, a quatrain consists of a group of four lines with a particular rhyme scheme; a sestet is a group of six lines with any regular rhyme; an octave is a group of eight lines with its own rhyme scheme; and a couplet is nothing more than two successive lines which rhyme.

How many of each do you see?

Return to page 137 and choose another answer.

[*from page 138*]

YOUR ANSWER: In attics, garages, and similarly sheltered areas.

They do? If you have seen ovenbirds nesting in these places, I suggest you consult the nearest ornithologist or bird watcher. Or perhaps you should

USE YOUR DICTIONARY

Please?

Guessing will sooner or later lead you up a blind alley, as it has here.

After you have looked in the dictionary under O, return to page 138 and choose another answer.

[*from page 139, 157 or 164*]

YOUR ANSWER: Reality and the imagination.

Precisely. You have identified a subject which is treated again and again in contemporary poetry. Frost considers this subject in many of his poems.

Many times (and I do not offer this in praise of contemporary poetry) in order to understand one poem by a particular author, you need to be familiar with his other works, both poetry and prose. This requirement is something new in the history of the world's literature.

Before the middle of the eighteenth century, the well-ordered world allowed man no misunderstanding of himself, science, God, or the universe. People *knew* how large the universe was; they knew there were only four elements, earth, water, air, and fire. To understand the literature of several centuries back, all that is needed is a knowledge of the history and ideas of the period. If you have this knowledge, the author and his writing are not difficult to understand.

Science, however, did away with all this regularity. Galileo started the disruption; Newton aided it; and Darwin completed the successful challenging of ideas which had existed as truths for centuries. Rather than look back on what had always been true, people were forced to make their own laws and look ahead, where often they saw nothing but chaos.

As a result, literature became diverse, and to understand what a modern writer is talking about, the reader must investigate him personally, his "circle," his "movement," his ideology. You must read as much of what he has written as possible, not as you would with an earlier author to see *how* he is saying something, but in order even to begin to understand what the later writer is trying to say. The new theories, beliefs, and systems of many contemporary writers become interesting when one realizes that this inquiry into the unknown, this dissatisfaction with and distrust of conventional beliefs is comparatively new. After all, what are two or three hundred years in the total sum?

Please go on to page 147.

[*from page 146*]

Frost, like most moderns, has a particular attitude toward reality, shown in this and many of his other poems. Everyone knows, he says, that leaves fall, flowers wither, and dust covers. This is reality, and during late summer and fall, spring and all its blossoms are only figments of the imagination.

The ovenbird knows too, but not because of his intellect. He is a product of nature and *must* sing during summer and fall, even though he does not know why.

Here is the final quatrain again. Read it and determine if Frost appears to be making any recommendations.

The bird would cease and be like other birds
But that he knows in singing not to sing.
The question that he frames in all but words
Is what to make of a diminished thing.

How should we react, according to Frost, to nature and her ways?

We should appreciate spring while we have it, because the other seasons are dull and dreary. **page 150**

We should attempt to make our living conditions as much like spring as possible. **page 155**

Because of our knowledge of nature's ways, we should accept and live with what she gives us. **page 158**

[*from page 137*]

YOUR ANSWER: There are rhymes, but they do not fit into any regular pattern.

You have not looked at the poem closely enough. Many times poets create patterns which at first seem highly irregular but are actually well planned and orderly.

Such is the case here. The poem is reproduced below, this time broken into parts.

The Oven Bird

There is a singer everyone has heard,
Loud, a mid-summer and a mid-wood bird,

Who makes the solid tree trunks sound again.
He says that leaves are old and that for flowers
Mid-summer is to spring as one to ten.
He says the early petal-fall is past
When pear and cherry bloom went down in showers
On sunny days a moment overcast;

And comes that other fall we name the fall.
He says the highway dust is over all.

The bird would cease and be as other birds
But that he knows in singing not to sing.
The question that he frames in all but words
Is what to make of a diminished thing.

The two-line sections are easily recognizable as couplets because of the true rhyme at the end of each line, but what of the other sections? Place a letter at the end of each rhyme, and see if you can find the pattern which is consistent in the two longer sections (each section has its own rhyme scheme).

When you have determined what the pattern is, return to page 137 and select another answer.

[*from page 139*]

YOUR ANSWER: Nature.

Not really. Don't be misled by the contemporary poet's use of nature in his poems. Seldom is nature used as a subject, as it often was in past centuries. Earlier writers saw nature as an expression of the regularity of existence (man, the world, the universe were also regular and understandable); when science began destroying the traditional beliefs, many poets came to view nature as the *only* remaining example of constancy and truth. Neither of these attitudes is prevalent today, and nature appears in poetry mainly as a source of metaphor.

Often, when attempting to discover what the poet is writing about, a reader has difficulty discovering the occasion for the poem. Nothing really has to happen in a poem, and in "The Oven Bird" we have agreed that the occasion is only the song of a bird. The linking in our minds of nature and birds does not mean that a poem with birds in it has to be about nature.

Try to see what concerns Frost about the singing of this bird. Why is the bird unable to "be as other birds"? What is the "question that he frames in all but words"? Answer these questions, apply the solutions to humanity, and you will have the subject of the poem within your grasp.

Return to page 139, reread the poem, and select another answer.

[*from page 147*]

YOUR ANSWER: We should appreciate spring while we have it, because the other seasons are dull and dreary.

"Gather ye rosebuds while ye may," Robert Herrick said in the seventeenth century. This appears to be your view, and it is not at all what Frost recommends. If this were so, wouldn't the bird bemoan the passing of spring? Would he not sing praises of everything springlike?

But he does not, and neither does Frost. "What to make of a diminished thing" is the consideration here. To use our imagination *during* spring to think ahead to a period of dullness and dreariness is as bad as looking back and wishing for something past.

Why does the bird know "in singing not to sing"? Why does anyone sing? Isn't it usually to express joy over something? The bird is not necessarily ecstatic over the passing of spring, but he certainly is not rueful. He accepts it, and sings anyway, not because he particularly wants to, but because he has to. He may not know *why* he sings, but we, human beings with the ability to think and imagine, do know why, and we also know the dangers of living too long in our imagination.

This is Frost's point: we must accept what is real and determine for ourselves "what to make of a diminished thing," the "good old days," for instance, or our long lost youth.

Now return to page 147 and choose another answer.

[*from page 140*]

YOUR ANSWER: It is written in trochaic hexameter.

Wrong. Selecting this answer at this stage of the game shows that either you did not answer quite truthfully in Chapter Three, or else you did not see fit to follow suggestions I made at the time.

In any event, you need some review, so mark this page in your book, turn now to page 62 and read the material on scansion, then return here.

All right?

Now go back to page 140 and select the correct answer.

[*from page 139*]

YOUR ANSWER: I don't know yet.

Your honesty is gratifying. Don't be upset if you could not immediately grasp an extremely abstract idea.

I can provide no formula to enable you to decipher any modern poem, but I can help you to begin your investigation; then, once you have read a few poems, your appreciation of other poems will increase and you will find poems easier to understand.

According to modern architects, isn't simplicity the ultimate in design? Isn't the phrase *clean lines* a cliché applied to almost every new building? This phrase could be applied to poetry as well.

Clean lines as such, however, often give little indication of what the object, building, or machinery is supposed to do. Can you, by observing the outside of a rectangular, glass-walled structure, determine what goes on inside? Rarely. You can read the sign out front? Perhaps, but U. S. Industries' Educational Science Division had a hand in the making of this book, and if you stand outside their office and read the sign, what does it tell you about lyric poetry? Absolutely nothing.

Usually, however, you can tell a factory from a church, a house from an office building: thus you have a starting point. In modern poetry the starting point is the recognition of metaphor.

So — Rule 1 — always realize that you are reading metaphor whenever you tackle a poem. What the poet *shows* in his poem usually stands for something else.

Rule 2 — determine the occasion for the poem, keeping in mind that nothing has to happen, nothing has to change, no one has to die or win a battle. But nearly all contemporary poetry (I must exclude here the pleasing nonsense verses we read as fillers in magazines) contains conflict, usually between one idea and another. The conflict can be between what *is* and what *was*, what *was* and what *should have been*, what *is* and what *will be*, what *is* and what *should be*, and so on. It is the poet's recognition that such conflict exists that stirs him to create the poem, perhaps because he sees beauty where there is thought to be none, deceit taking the guise of truth, inconstancy the guise of consistency, and many other paradoxes.

Please go on to page 153.

[*from page 152*]

So — Rule 3 — try to identify the elements in conflict, realizing that the occasion for the poem may represent only one side, perhaps not the one which the poet thinks is right.

Finally — Rule 4 — attempt to comprehend the *controlling* metaphor, a composite of simile, image, and symbol, a comparison which is suggested by the occasion for the poem. Remember "General Salute"? The salute toward the sky was but one of many examples of dominion, yet by its use in the poem it became a symbol of dominion. And in Auden's poem, the ability of the artist to select and discard symbolized the representation of what life really contains. Most poems have a controlling metaphor to which all other metaphors contribute.

Keeping in mind, then, that the occasion for this poem, "The Oven Bird," is a bird singing, reread the poem and determine what elements are in conflict.

The Oven Bird

There is a singer everyone has heard,
Loud, a mid-summer and a mid-wood bird,
Who makes the solid tree trunks sound again.
He says that leaves are old and that for flowers
Mid-summer is to spring as one to ten.
He says the early petal-fall is past
When pear and cherry bloom went down in showers
On sunny days a moment overcast;
And comes that other fall we name the fall.
He says the highway dust is over all.
The bird would cease and be as other birds
But that he knows in singing not to sing.
The question that he frames in all but words
Is what to make of a diminished thing.

What two qualities of nature are shown in opposition?

Fruitfulness and decay. **page 156**

Heat and coldness. **page 160**

Animal life and vegetable life. **page 165**

[*from page 138*]

YOUR ANSWER: On the ground.

Right, and it is called the ovenbird because of the peculiar domed shape of its nest.

If you were familiar with the ovenbird all along, well and good, but think of the readers of this poem who have never seen or heard one. Those who are familiar with this bird have an intellectual advantage much like that of a Greek scholar confronted with one of the more complex offerings of William Butler Yeats or T. S. Eliot, not to mention the work of Ezra Pound and James Joyce. With few exceptions, however, all the background material for contemporary poetry is at our finger tips, if we make frequent and thorough use of dictionary, Bible, and encyclopedia.

Please read the Frost poem again.

The Oven Bird

There is a singer everyone has heard,
Loud, a mid-summer and a mid-wood bird,
Who makes the solid tree trunks sound again.
He says that leaves are old and that for flowers
Mid-summer is to spring as one to ten.
He says the early petal-fall is past
When pear and cherry bloom went down in showers
On sunny days a moment overcast;
And comes that other fall we name the fall.
He says the highway dust is over all.
The bird would cease and be as other birds
But that he knows in singing not to sing.
The question that he frames in all but words
Is what to make of a diminished thing.

What is the occasion for this poem?

A bird singing. **page 139**

Spring and summer. **page 159**

Falling leaves. **page 162**

[*from page 147*]

YOUR ANSWER: We should attempt to make our living conditions as much like spring as possible.

Please. I feel that you are precisely the person Frost had in mind when he wrote this poem in 1916. You see, your ideas have been held by people for a long time, and there will doubtless be many others who agree with you in years to come.

But is there not a limit to one's imagination? Can you, while dreaming of spring and balmy breezes, walk out into a blizzard and stay warm? Mind has some power over matter, but not this much. We must, Frost is saying, accept the highway dust and the falling leaves; we do not have to *like* them, but dreaming of spring will hardly make summer and fall any better.

Nature, to Frost, has created nothing ideal. Everything changes, and man should recognize this, being simultaneously a part of nature and also, because of his ability to think, more advanced than nature. Ideals are created by the mind, and they are fine to wish for and strive for, as long as we realize they are unattainable. We should answer the question "what to make of a diminished thing" for ourselves, individually, always recognizing that "things" will become diminished no matter what we can do or say.

I am not asking you to agree. But please recognize that Frost does *not* ask us to create anything unattainable in our imaginations.

Return to page 147 and select another answer.

[*from page 153*]

YOUR ANSWER: Fruitfulness and decay.

Right, shown by the old leaves, the smaller number of flowers, the "petal-fall" which is past, and the autumn highway dust, all of which provide a contrast to the lushness of spring. Spring is over, and has been replaced by the seasons of growth and decay, summer and fall.

Notice the repetition of the phrase "he says," referring to the bird. The bird's comment hardly tells us anything we do not already know; no hidden truths are revealed, nothing pointed out that we might have missed. Everything he sings about is an obvious, well-known fact.

But then what? We have a bird singing about nature's cyclical changes, specifically the change from fruitfulness to decay. This change is real; we know that it happens each year and that there is nothing we can do about it.

But haven't you often wished that you could do something about falling blossoms, the withering leaves and grass, the dusty highway? Trying to keep cool on a scorching August day, haven't you thought of an earlier day, perhaps in May or June, when you woke up to warm sunshine and a green lawn? Has this thought made the heavy, humid August day any more bearable? Perhaps for a moment, but like the effects of a cool drink, the memory soon leaves you where you started, sweltering. These are the results of wishful thinking.

Does the bird do this? Does he lament the fact that spring is gone? Not at all. He merely says it has, framing "in all but words . . . what to make of a diminished thing." He does not trill joyously, ushering in the season; neither does he warble plaintively, bemoaning the passing of beauty. Isn't the bird's acceptance of the change of seasons quite different from the way people react?

Please go on to page 157.

[*from page 156*]

We have now started discussing the controlling metaphor, shown here by the two symbols spring (fruitfulness) and summer/fall (decay) as well as the singing of the bird, which symbolizes to Frost what the attitude toward cyclical change *should* be.

To tie everything together, let us now ask: Where, in the poem, does spring exist? Do we see it in full bloom? Not at all. The bird, commenting on what he knows is real, says that "leaves *are* old," that "the early petal-fall *is* past," that "the highway dust *is* over all." Spring itself is merely a memory in this poem. What is real here is the decay of summer and fall.

Finally, where can we see spring long after it is gone? A simple answer: in the mind. We can only think about it, while that which we are experiencing is quite another thing. By accepting the contrast between what we experience and what we think about, we approach the subject of the poem.

Read it once more.

The Oven Bird

There is a singer everyone has heard,
Loud, a mid-summer and a mid-wood bird,
Who makes the solid tree trunks sound again.
He says that leaves are old and that for flowers
Mid-summer is to spring as one to ten.
He says the early petal-fall is past
When pear and cherry bloom went down in showers
On sunny days a moment overcast;
And comes that other fall we name the fall.
He says the highway dust is over all.
The bird would cease and be as other birds
But that he knows in singing not to sing.
The question that he frames in all but words
Is what to make of a diminished thing.

What is the subject of this poem?

Time. **page 143**

Reality and the imagination. **page 146**

I still don't know. **page 164**

[*from page 147*]

YOUR ANSWER: Because of our knowledge of nature's ways, we should accept and live with what she gives us.

Precisely. This is a common idea. It doesn't make August any cooler, but perhaps August becomes more bearable. Humans differ from animals, but man is also a product of nature; therefore he should not live for and in his imagination, because so doing will end only in unhappiness and frustration. To hope for a perpetual spring is vain, as impossible as the desire for the ideal woman or the fountain of youth. Whether the "diminished thing" is a product of the past, present, or future, we still must know what to make of it. For the ovenbird, and for man, spring is fine while it lasts, and it will come again next year.

The last poem we will consider in this chapter is one by E. E. Cummings. Read this poem aloud *first*, then read it silently to yourself.

PORTRAIT

Buffalo Bill's
defunct
who used to
ride a watersmooth-silver
stallion
and break onetwothreefourfive pigeonsjustlikethat
Jesus

he was a handsome man
and what i want to know is
how do you like your blueeyed boy
Mister Death

There is nothing difficult about this poem, but it is different from other poems, and it is as powerful as anything you will read.

What is the subject of the poem?

Death. **page 161**

Sorrow. **page 163**

Buffalo Bill. **page 166**

[*from page 154*]

YOUR ANSWER: Spring and summer.

Wrong. You have missed the obvious and jumped directly to an unsupportable conclusion.

Certainly spring and summer are mentioned in the poem, seen in the comment by the bird, "Midsummer is to spring as one to ten," but isn't fall also mentioned? Look:

> And comes that other fall we name the fall.
> He says the highway dust is over all.

How would fall fit into a poem for which the occasion was spring and summer?

This time, when you choose another answer, select the obvious. The occasion for this poem—the concrete, literal level—has already been discussed at length.

Return to page 154, reread the poem, and try again.

[*from page 153*]

YOUR ANSWER: Heat and coldness.

I'm afraid not. There may be an implied contrast between the pleasant warmth of spring and the stifling heat of summer, but it borders on the dishonest as far as this poem is concerned.

The seasons that are mentioned here are spring, summer, and fall, each used to symbolize something. They are the first type of symbol we discussed in Chapter Two, that symbol which has an accepted meaning because of frequent and consistent use in literature.

For years, spring has symbolized rebirth, growth, and beauty, while summer and fall have symbolized the cyclical end of all the bounty of spring. Leaves wither, flowers die, trees shed their leaves, and so on.

Frost is not deviating from this accepted use here; indeed, he rarely uses natural symbols differently from their normal function.

Return to page 153, reread the poem, and select another answer.

[*from page 158*]

YOUR ANSWER: Death.

Correct. The subject seems obvious to me. Don't be misled by literary people who say that the only good poetry is "difficult" poetry. This is untrue. Much "difficult" poetry is bad, and other poems are complex because of the complexity of subject matter.

What about love? It is a familiar concept, but can you define it? Can you write about it? How would you communicate your feeling to someone else, other than by saying "I love you"? What would happen if the person you were addressing said "Why?" What would you say that would not be trite and feeble? You might continue, "I love you more than anything in the world," to which your loved one might reply, "More than what?" See the problem? The poet must foresee all these questions and many more, and by attempting to be honest, consistent, and complete, he is often led into justifications that are very specific, personal, but to a reader often obscure.

E. E. Cummings prefers not to justify, however, but his presentation often causes equal confusion. He writes in what I will call a graphic style, designed to produce the same *sound* no matter who reads his poem.

Death, the subject, is discussed in an apparently offhand manner. Buffalo Bill, the hero, is dead, and the poet asks calmly, "How do you like your blueeyed boy Mister Death" Everyone dies, Cummings is saying, and his mild concern with the problem seems at the opposite pole from that of, for example, Wilfred Owen in "Arms and the Boy."

But is it really so mild? There is something not evident in this poem, something which makes it far more than a mere statement of fact.

Go on to page 167, and we will investigate further.

[*from page 154*]

YOUR ANSWER: Falling leaves.

Not quite. If you accept falling leaves as the occasion for the poem, what would you make of the dust, the bird, the flowers, the petal-fall, and the singing? What do *these* have to do with falling leaves?

Remember, the occasion for the poem should be seen most obviously on the literal, concrete level as that person, place, thing, or incident which is being defined *by* and *in* the poem. Usually the occasion is what you first see; then, by abstracting further, you arrive at the subject.

Return to page 154, reread the poem, and select the most obvious and simple answer.

[*from page 158*]

YOUR ANSWER: Sorrow.

Not at all. Cummings is far from being sorry about the death of Buffalo Bill, and even if he were, sorrow would hardly be the subject of the poem.

Sorrow and most other emotions are rarely the subjects of poetry; rather they are expressions of the poet's attitude toward his subject, to be defined as *tone* in the next section. Perhaps sorrow is what the poet feels and what he wants the reader to feel, but he cannot create this by writing about it. He must write about something else toward which you can feel sorry; then he achieves his purpose.

The subject of this poem is obvious; it is even referred to in the poem itself. Return to page 158, reread the poem, and determine what concerns the poet here so deeply that he has decided to write a poem about it.

[*from page 157*]

YOUR ANSWER: I still don't know.

Don't feel bad. You are probably not alone.

Let's sum up this poem. Frost sees in the song of the ovenbird a particular comment on life, one which the bird presents in the form of an unstated question. The question — what to make of a diminished thing — is one which is with us constantly. What happened to our youth? Where are the good old days? Aren't people honest any more? Questions of this sort are represented in the question sung by the bird in his comment on the decay and withering which follows spring.

Some persons, however, resist change. They dwell in their youth without being able to accept as reality the change from what was to what is now. A man can delude himself to disregard what is real in favor of what he wishes were real, in this example, spring.

But is this a satisfactory way out? Perhaps not, because very soon reality will intrude, and the products of the imagination will be seen as unsatisfactory, for they can produce only unhappiness.

So, the subject of this poem is reality and the imagination, discussed metaphorically by use of summer and remembered spring, commented on by a bird who knows "in singing not to sing"; in other words, he sings because he has to, not because he feels there is a particular season to praise or sing joyfully about. He is a part of nature and realizes it.

Man, on the other hand, is also a part of nature, but because of his faculty of imagination, he sometimes forgets his dependence on nature and tries to wish himself out of her. To do this, Frost tells us again and again in his poetry, is impossible.

Isn't this subject perhaps worth considering? I think so, and I would guess that you will see it discussed often by contemporary poets in one way or another. Look for it, and when you find a poem which uses an occasion and a controlling metaphor more to your liking, perhaps you'll find yourself agreeing with Frost more than you think.

Please accept reality and the imagination as the subject of this poem and go on to page 146.

[*from page 153*]

YOUR ANSWER: Animal life and vegetable life.

You are wrong. Doesn't this answer just define nature in a general way? Animal life and vegetable life are two elements of nature as we see her, and they are not shown in conflict here.

The bird is an animal, to be sure, and trees are vegetable, but where is the contrast?

Oh, I see. Trees shed their leaves while birds do not? Don't birds molt? No contrast here.

The bird is seen doing something, whereas the vegetable life is just there? Aren't you carrying this a little too far?

Regardless of the reasons for your seeing a conflict between animal and vegetable life (and I do not deny that there can be found *some* conflict *somewhere*), I think you are missing a much more important contrast. Your approach, if continued, might lead you to say that the conflict in Owen's "Arms and the Boy" is between bayonets and bullets, because bullets have a longer range and thus are more deadly.

Now return to page 153, reread the poem, and determine what the most *important* contrast in the poem is.

[*from page 158*]

YOUR ANSWER: Buffalo Bill.

Wrong. You have identified the occasion for the poem, but not much more. Buffalo Bill is described as "handsome" and "blueeyed"; then the poet asks "Mister Death" how he likes his new boy. In this way, Buffalo Bill is defined in and by the poem as succinctly and completely as necessary for the poet's purpose.

But isn't there more to this poem? Couldn't Cummings have used another example, another man? Suppose he were to have used Abraham Lincoln or Ernest Hemingway as the occasion, then posed the same question to "Mister Death." Would this have changed his subject? Not at all.

Return to page 158, reread the poem, and select another answer.

CHAPTER V

Tone and Style: The *How* of a Poem

Recognition of the subject of a poem, what the poet writes about, is important, but hardly an end in itself. Often we see poetry which almost succeeds — we note the fine use of metaphor; recognize the honesty, consistency, and completeness; agree that the subject is worthy of consideration — but the poem itself somehow fails to do anything for us at all. The letters of the alphabet, for instance, hardly stirred us, even though the arrangement met all the requirements for a poem.

Why do some poems succeed and others fail, often for no apparent reason? I think the answer lies in tone, how the author feels about his subject, and in style, the way the subject is presented.

Normally we think of style in terms of the author; the style of Hemingway, the style of Faulkner are both well known. But a poem is often seen to have its own distinctive style, tailored for the occasion and the subject. We saw an example of this in "Musée des Beaux Arts"; the way the subject was presented resulted from the subject itself, the relationship between art and life. Subject often determines style, just as subject is usually responsible for tone, the "attitude of the poet toward his subject."*

E. E. Cummings is one of the contemporary poets who uses a unique style in every poem he writes, and a Cummings poem is so immediately recognizable that we often tend to read his poetry, not for what it says, but for *how* it says it.

Please go on to page 168.

* Robert Penn Warren and Cleanth Brooks in *Understanding Poetry* extend this definition to include attitudes toward self and reader. But the poet himself (by our definition of the lyric) is usually part of the subject, and the attitude toward the reader will be considered in Chapter VII, "Meaning."

[*from page 167*]

Although Cummings often carries his style to what may seem ridiculous extremes (rarely using capital letters, omitting punctuation, separating words in odd places), this poem, "Portrait," exemplifies not only the better side of Cummings but also the predominant post-World War II poetry which has emerged from the influence of Ezra Pound, William Carlos Williams, and Cummings himself. In this poem we will see the great effect that style has on tone, and vice versa.

Read the poem again aloud, *not* as you would if the two sentences, separated by the ejaculatory word "Jesus," were written as a paragraph. Pause momentarily at the end of each line. Also pause, but not as long, wherever you see a double space between words in the same line, and speed up your reading when words are written together.

PORTRAIT

Buffalo Bill's
defunct
          who used to
          ride a watersmooth-silver
                                                  stallion
and break onetwothreefourfive pigeonsjustlikethat
                                                                                          Jesus

he was a handsome man
                                          and what i want to know is
how do you like your blueeyed boy
Mister Death

How would you describe the attitude of the poet toward his subject, death?

He is angry and bitter. page 173

He is contemplative. page 176

He merely accepts the incident and shrugs it off. page 179

[*from page 173*]

YOUR ANSWER: As a question.

Here we go. Is there a question mark at the end? No. But you just thought there should be?

Please, do not bring too much of your own experience into the reading of a poem. In this instance, your experience leads you to expect a question; therefore you automatically insert a question mark where there usually should be one. But is the final sentence really a question?

The final statement is ironic, seeming to be something (a question) which it really is not. The narrator does not want an answer; he speaks slowly, much as a parent who sees a child covered with mud would say, "What's going on here."

Cummings does not like the inevitability of death, but he accepts it. Notice that he does *not* wail or moan, asking why . . . why. Neither does he lament the death of a great man. He implies that there is no real answer to any question one might ask of death.

Be careful with modern poetry. By reading into a poem what you think should be there, you may arrive at a meaning just the opposite of what the author intends.

Return to page 173 and select the correct answer.

[*from page 178*]

YOUR ANSWER: Time.

I don't think so. Time functions in this poem much as in Frost's "Oven Bird." Without time, nothing will happen: no scrap, no rust, no ashes. But doesn't the poet accept this? The parenthetical comment is more of an aside than anything else; it reiterates something that is assumed to be true, and we find ourselves nodding in assent.

Look at the title, "Limited." At first you accepted this as perhaps the kind of train on which the poet is riding — but is there more to it? This is another example of the literary pun.

Is there something else "limited" besides the train? Certainly not time, because time as a concept is unlimited, existing forever. The subject of this poem can be called an attitude of man.

Return to page 178, reread the poem with the idea of limitation in mind, and select another answer.

[*from page 181*]

YOUR ANSWER: He is not particularly concerned.

Oh yes he is. Granted, there may be a fine distinction between lack of concern and placid acceptance, but this difference must be recognized for the poem to be understood.

Let me use a comparison. Isn't it possible for a man to be extremely concerned about something, yet accept it as a fact of life? What about an airline pilot, a mountain climber, or, for that matter, a sensible driver on our highways? Wouldn't each of these be "concerned" about danger? Yet doesn't each one accept the ever-present fact of danger? Granted, there are far too many drivers who are *not* concerned enough about traffic safety; these are the people who cause accidents. See the difference?

Now, apply this same distinction to the subject of understanding. You have probably said or thought often of another person, "That man really understands." How did you know? What did he understand that made him different from others? The passenger on the train understands only that he is going to Omaha, nothing more. He does not care about the causes of rust, scrap, and ashes, abstractions such as time, flux, or truth.

The poet does, and it is because of his concern that he has written this poem. Return to page 181, reread the poem, and select another answer.

[*from page 183*]

YOUR ANSWER: Past.

Careful. I'm not surprised that you misread the poem, because the time is unclear. But you should have no trouble identifying the time if you reread the poem closely. The past does not contain demon and lewd voices; rather, the past contains "the hope foresworn."

For the moment, imagine yourself standing on a Long Island beach or any beach that is deserted and swept by a cold, clammy wind. There are voices calling to you.

Return to page 182, reread the poem, paying particular attention to lines 5 and 6, and choose the right answer on page 183.

[*from page 168*]

YOUR ANSWER: He is angry and bitter.

I wonder. Don't anger and bitterness usually take different forms from what you see here? William Butler Yeats shows in one of his poems the legendary Cuchulain, angry and bitter at being deceived, striding into the ocean to do battle with the waves.

Yet, here, Cummings comments that Buffalo Bill is "defunct." Why *defunct*? Why not *dead*, *murdered*, *killed*, or any other word connoting death? And why does the author request only one favor from Mister Death, the answer to a simple question?

You have failed to see and read the poem *as it is*. Remember the suggestions I made earlier? About pausing and speeding up? Read the poem aloud again, this time attempting to show by your voice the peculiar arrangement of words on the page.

PORTRAIT

Buffalo Bill's
defunct
          who used to
          ride a watersmooth-silver
                                        stallion
and break onetwothreefourfive pigeonsjustlikethat
                                                            Jesus

he was a handsome man
                                        and what i want to know is
how do you like your blueeyed boy
Mister Death

How do you read the last line?

As a question. page 169

As a flat, ironic statement. page 180

[*from page 178*]

YOUR ANSWER: Death.

Perhaps my emphasis on this subject has conditioned you to see it too often. Here the death of men and machines, seen in the images of rust, scrap, and ashes, means inevitability, or that which must happen in the passage of time.

Look at the title. Could it suggest more than just a description of the train on which the poet is riding? If time exists as an unlimited something, mustn't we accept man's life and that of his creations as limited? Of course. But man possesses intelligence, imagination, knowledge. When Sandburg comments on what many men do with their minds, he expresses a thought very close to Frost's in "Oven Bird."

When you reread the poem, compare the attitude of the poet toward death, scrap, and rust with that of the unnamed stranger who says he is going nowhere but Omaha. How are the two men different? They are seen to possess differing degrees of what the poem is about. Return to page 178 and select another answer.

[*from page 193*]

YOUR ANSWER: The passage of time.

I don't think so. To be wailing about the passage of time, the voices need not restrict themselves to any specific subject. They would be like the aged man who despairs only because he is old, regardless of how happy and successful his life has been.

These voices do not seem to be concerned that time has passed; instead they wail about what has happened *during* the time before their present (our future). They decry the loss of something, implying that man could have prevented the terror that "needles the world heartbreak."

Forget the time element for a moment, and consider everything which follows the phrase "Crying out of the timid future," to be the subject of the crying itself. The comma at the end of this line precludes our thinking anything else.

Perhaps the comma is a typographical error and should have been a period? All right. Then what? Assume that the last lines are in fact a statement being made by the poet from the present. Then what on earth does the timid future have to do with the poem? Why couldn't the poem have disregarded the future entirely and remained in the present, talking only about what we see around us? And why is the future timid at all? Does the poet imply that the "shark-nosed bombers" will be manned by cowards who find the "tune Time plays" too hard to dance to?

Perhaps you can answer some of these questions. I cannot. Return to page 193, reread the poem literally, and select another answer.

[*from page 168*]

YOUR ANSWER: He is contemplative.

I think so. It is as if we watch and hear the poet writing his poem, perhaps like this: Buffalo Bill's (let's see, shall I say *gone, dead, passed away?*) defunct (so? now what? why does this matter? but he used to . . .) who used to (do what? *kill Indians? put on shows?* how?) ride a watersmooth-silver (*horse? cayuse?*) stallion (what else? how to represent what he was so well known for?) and (no, not do tricks with a gun, but) break (what? *targets? kewpie dolls? clay pigeons?*) onetwothreefourfive (now it comes) pigeonsjustlikethat (period — end of what he did; and he's dead) Jesus.

By writing the poem as he does, by using this particular style, Cummings forces the reader to ponder the situation just as Cummings himself does. The tone is a product of style.

Regardless of the many reasons which modern poets give for writing this way, one of the major appeals of modern poetry is the way a poem sounds, created first by a particular appeal to the eye, then to the ear. Punctuation, according to Charles Olson, an influential poet, creates an interruption of meaning as well as sound, while the other methods (longer spaces between words, syllables "hung" at the end of a line, the use of the mark / between words) demonstrate the need for pauses of varying lengths when a poem is read aloud.

Do you remember the historical definition of a lyric? A poem designed to be sung to the accompaniment of the seven-string lyre? Many of the moderns are attempting to produce a similar type of lyric, even though their accompaniment may be a seven-piece jazz group. If you have read any serious modern poetry which resembles Cummings' poem and it has baffled you, you have probably failed to understand it because you have not read it aloud. Try reading aloud. You will be on the way toward understanding. And remember, there is no such thing as a run-on line in many modern poems. If the poet wishes you to read more than one line without pausing, he will so indicate by writing in what appears to be prose, forcing you to pause only where he wants you to, either for meaning, sound, or both. We will return to an expanded discussion of this type of modern style later, but watch for this device from now on in every poem you read.

Please go on to page 177.

[*from page 176*]

Perhaps you can now see how the style of a poem, the method the poet uses to present his subject, affects the tone, the attitude of the poet toward his subject. In this poem, Cummings is contemplative, not wailing about the loss of a famous man, but musing on the fact that everyone dies, then posing a quasi-humorous question which cannot be answered.

The tone of the poem is often the most important single element to recognize if we are even to begin to understand what the poet is saying.

Please go on to page 178.

[*from page 177*]

Here is a poem by Carl Sandburg in which the lines contain not only a comment on the passage of time but also a study of what Sandburg sees as a particularly contemporary attitude.

Limited

I am riding on a limited express, one of the crack trains of the nation.
Hurtling across the prairie into blue haze and dark air go fifteen
    all-steel coaches holding a thousand people.
(All the coaches shall be scrap and rust and all the men and women
    laughing in the diners and sleepers shall pass to ashes.)
I ask a man in the smoker where he is going and he answers: "Omaha."

In this poem, the comment on time is fairly obvious. The "limited express, one of the crack trains of the nation," will eventually become "scrap and rust," and every one of the thousand people on board "shall pass to ashes." So far, there is little difference between this idea and that of Cummings in the preceding poem.

But what about the tone of the Sandburg poem, the attitude of the poet toward his subject? Four lines, each an apparent prose statement of an obvious idea: Line 1 — the poet is on board a train. Line 2 — the steel train holds a thousand people and is moving fast. Line 3 — time will pass and everything will die. Line 4 — the poet asks a fellow traveler where he is going.

That's all . . . but is it? Let us approach this poem first in the manner suggested in Chapter Four.

What is the subject of the poem?

Time. **page 170**

Death. **page 174**

Understanding. **page 181**

[*from page 168*]

YOUR ANSWER: He merely accepts the incident and shrugs it off.

It is time for reappraisal. I would agree that this poem, if written either conventionally or in the form of two prose sentences, might represent an attitude like the one you describe. Even then, however, the thought of asking "Mister Death" a question does imply a more pointed attitude, don't you think? This is hardly an ordinary occurrence.

I think you have failed to see the attitude of the entire poem, preferring instead to draw your conclusion only from the first, unpunctuated sentence, which ends with "pigeonsjustlikethat." Agreed, this segment does imply matter-of-factness, but suddenly the poet changes. "Jesus," he says, "he was a handsome man." Then the question. But is it really a question? Does the poet expect an answer from "Mister Death"? Note throughout the poem how the style, the arrangement of words, contributes to the tone. Why, for instance, might you pause between words when considering a certain subject? Would you be certain of what you wanted to think and say, or might you be making your mind up as you went along?

Return to page 168, reread the poem, and try again.

[*from page 173*]

YOUR ANSWER: As a flat, ironic statement.

Exactly. There is no question mark; nor is the narrator really asking anything. What he wants to know is apparently ridiculous: how Death "likes" his blue-eyed subject. There is no satisfactory answer, any more than the similar statement "Isn't it a hot day today."

If the statement is ironic, how, then, can there be anger? When you are angry you want to yell, fight, scream, moan, but when your rage is past, you confront the situation coldly and are capable of passing judgment. This is what the narrator is doing with "Mister Death." Notice the forced pause:

and what i want to know is
how do you like your blueeyed boy
Mister Death

I don't think the narrator of the poem knows *what* he wants to know from Mister Death; therefore he comes up with a sardonic, flat statement containing an implied, unanswerable question. "I like him fine, son," Death might answer to the narrator's retreating back, and nothing would be changed.

When you reread aloud, pay careful attention to the style, the way the material is presented. Imagine yourself considering a similar subject. How would your thoughts run? Keeping style in mind, return to page 168, reread the poem, and select the correct answer.

[*from page 178*]

YOUR ANSWER: Understanding.

Right. The poet, by commenting as he does in the first three lines, shows a much deeper understanding than does the other passenger in the smoker. In effect, both men eventually are going to the same place, but only the poet realizes it.

The tone of this poem is perhaps its most important single element, and again we see style helping to create the tone. Stylistically, there is no rhyme; the rhythm is that of everyday speech; the meter is obvious and unimportant; and there is little immediately apparent metaphor other than the image of the train hurtling toward its destination. In short, the poem reads like a newspaper excerpt. The style of the poem is deceptively simple; an incident is discussed, and the poem ends. But what about the parenthetical comment?

This comment is the focus of the poem, and in order to recognize tone, we must notice how each man reacts to the thought of inevitability expressed by the poet's aside. We see the second man paying little attention to the innuendoes of the question "Where are you going?" How does the poet differ? Read the poem again.

Limited

I am riding on a limited express, one of the crack trains of the nation.
Hurtling across the prairie into blue haze and dark air go fifteen
all-steel coaches holding a thousand people.
(All the coaches shall be scrap and rust and all the men and women
laughing in the diners and sleepers shall pass to ashes.)
I ask a man in the smoker where he is going and he answers: "Omaha."

What is the poet's attitude toward the thought that everything will eventually become scrap, dust, and ashes?

He is not particularly concerned. **page 171**

He accepts this necessity of life. **page 184**

He is sad. **page 187**

[*from page 185*]

YOUR ANSWER: Sardonically pessimistic.

Right, and even this description appears mild here. Wheelock is obviously distressed over what he sees as the impending doom of the world. His style is obvious: use adjectives to show what you feel.

Does he really transmit his distress? Certainly there are a few eye- and ear-catching phrases, and I do like the first four lines, the image of the "Autumnal wind, wailing the world sorrow." What about the rest of the poem? Is this overwhelming tone of despair justified by the poem itself? Let's examine the poem for tone and style.

The Timid Future

Wind in the eaves of the old house, wind over Russia
And the English coast, wind over the forelands
Of Europe, over the beaches of Long Island,
Autumnal wind, wailing the world sorrow,
With demon voices thronged, lewd voices
Crying out of the timid future,
Where now is paradise, the hope foresworn,
That could have been, had the heart stretched to hold it?
Where now lost Eden? Behind locked eyelids only
Glimmering a moment in the trance of love,
Recalled for a moment during the truce of music —
The hyssop sponge tendered in mercy
To the parched spirit, fretful in its torment —
Temporary assuagement. The tune Time plays
Grows harder to dance to now. Man's cleverness
Outwits itself; while round the watchful planet
The shark-nosed bombers wait to be unsheathed,
And terror needles the world heartbreak.

The poem falls into no recognizable category, nor does it contain any regular meter or rhyme scheme. But as we have seen, this fact is no bar to a poem's success. What about the use of metaphor; is our reaction to the poem triggered by what the poem says, or do we feel as we do because we happen to agree with the general premise that the world is in bad shape?

Please go on to page 183.

[*from page 182*]

In what time period are the “lewd voices” in line 5 calling from?

Past. **page 172**

Present. **page 190**

Future. **page 193**

[*from page 181*]

YOUR ANSWER: He accepts this as a necessity of life.

Of course he does; shouldn't we all?

The human condition — what we are, where we are, and why we are — is of great importance to thinking men, as is the consideration of where we are going and why. We know we are headed toward death, but are there not various ways of going there? The situation in this poem, an express train filled with laughing people, has made the poet pause and think of the insignificance of man and his creations when seen against the totality of time and the universe. This fact he accepts, but in the attempt to start a conversation with "a man" by asking an intentionally ambiguous question, he receives only the short answer, "Omaha."

There is no sadness on the part of the poet toward the thought of inevitable death and decay, but when he sees no one else even considering death, the tone of the poem becomes one of *infinite* sadness. The laughing people and the man in the smoker *think* they know where they are going, the poem tells us, but in reality they do not, and this lack of concern troubles Sandburg greatly.

But how does style contribute to the tone of sadness? Where are the tears, the wailing, the expressed sorrow? They are absent and therefore much more obvious. Who is more pathetic, the person who cries over the death of a friend, or the one who cannot cry but just sits quietly and vacantly? By presenting the subject of understanding unemotionally, crisply, apparently inconclusively (for it takes many readings to see what Sandburg is doing), the poet makes us feel as he does by poetic understatement of his sadness. His implied sadness shows that the poet understands other people's lack of understanding. Thoughtlessness, while necessarily a fact of life, need not be applauded.

Please go on to page 185.

[*from page 184*]

Before we study the next poem, let us further define our terms. Style consists not only of the form a poem takes but also of the poet's choice of metaphor. Cummings, in "Portrait," uses virtually no metaphor at all except for his personification of death, but when we read the poem in its entirety, we see Buffalo Bill as a representative of *all* men, and thus a symbol of mankind. Sandburg, too, uses one symbol, the train, and images of death. The man in the smoker becomes all men who care only about going to Omaha. A poet's choice of metaphor should be a logical product of his subject. When we see metaphor used strictly for its own sake, we see it used dishonestly.

Read the following poem by John Hall Wheelock, the subject of which is, according to the title, the world's future.

The Timid Future

Wind in the eaves of the old house, wind over Russia
And the English coast, wind over the forelands
Of Europe, over the beaches of Long Island,
Autumnal wind, wailing the world sorrow,
With demon voices thronged, lewd voices
Crying out of the timid future,
Where now is paradise, the hope foresworn,
That could have been, had the heart stretched to hold it?
Where now lost Eden? Behind locked eyelids only
Glimmering a moment in the trance of love,
Recalled for a moment during the truce of music —
The hyssop sponge tendered in mercy
To the parched spirit, fretful in its torment —
Temporary assuagement. The tune Time plays
Grows harder to dance to now. Man's cleverness
Outwits itself; while round the watchful planet
The shark-nosed bombers wait to be unsheathed,
And terror needles the world heartbreak.

What is the poet's attitude toward his subject, the world's future?

Sardonically pessimistic. **page 182**

Hopefully optimistic. **page 189**

Like Sandburg, he is sad. **page 192**

[*from page 193*]

YOUR ANSWER: Terror.

Again, this is an interesting answer. You have identified the element of terror which runs throughout the poem, but have misapplied it.

Isn't it true that what is terror to you might be nothing at all to someone else? In most terror stories, isn't there an evil villain who gleefully rubs his hands while the victim is being stretched on the rack? The demon and lewd voices seem to me like the villain.

You don't think so? Then why the word "demon"? The word "lewd"? You can make a case for your argument. *If* we assume that these voices which merely narrate the history of events from the present to the future appear demonic and lewd to the poet, then you are on solid ground. But you have missed something in the poem. Look at lines 4, 5, and 6:

> Autumnal wind, wailing the world sorrow,
> With demon voices thronged, lewd voices
> Crying out of the timid future,

The *wind* is "wailing the world sorrow"; it is *thronged* with the demon voices which cry out of the timid future.

I think we have no right to assume that something we do not like, something that frightens us, is produced only by demon voices. The poem, however, seems to imply that it is, and we must concern ourselves with what the poem says, nothing more. From the construction and punctuation of the poem, then, we must assume that all the words following the lines quoted above are spoken by the voices. Return to page 193, summarize these last lines, and select the right answer.

[*from page 181*]

YOUR ANSWER: He is sad.

By selecting this answer you have exemplified an interesting point: that it is possible to react the right way emotionally to a poem for the wrong reasons.

You have identified the element of sadness which permeates the poem, yet have justified it incorrectly. Perhaps psychologists will tell you why you do so, but let us not conjecture. Maybe we know too much about ourselves already.

Scrap, rust, and ashes do not make the poet sad. We all die, he says in a passing comment. But at least he has thought about the subject, showing more insight than the passenger does. The poet is thinking in metaphor, looking at the express train hurtling through the night. His immediate experience is the train, yet he thinks of the inevitability of death, perhaps with the desire to contemplate larger issues: where we exist and where we might be going. In answer to his question, the stranger on the smoker answers, "Omaha." No doubt Sandburg feels that Omaha is a nice place to go, but in this poem he is concerned with a far less temporary destination.

Sandburg is not sad that we will all die. His sadness results from the attitude of others. First, however, reread the poem and determine what his attitude toward the inevitability of death is. It is not profound.

Return to page 181 and try again.

[*from page 195*]

YOUR ANSWER: The effect of war on humanity.

I don't think so. You might say that *all* war poetry considers this subject: the death of human beings and vast destruction of property.

Jarrell, too, shows that war is terrible, but for a poem to be concerned with *all* humanity it must be capable of being projected against a universal backdrop, of being applicable to all places at all times, as was true of "Arms and the Boy."

In this poem, however, the lines specify combat in modern war.

> Six miles from earth, loosed from its dream of life,
> I woke to black flak and the nightmare fighters.

This situation is not applicable to the Civil War, for example, or the Crusades. Why not? If we regard as a function of style the selection of proper images, then the style of this poem requires our recognition of a strictly contemporary subject.

Return to page 195, reread the poem, and try again.

[*from page 185*]

YOUR ANSWER: Hopefully optimistic.

Good heavens, no! I hope you are here because of inquisitiveness rather than choice. If not, then there is still hope, but we have both just suffered a major setback.

What could Wheelock possibly be optimistic about? The timid future? The demon voices? The lost Eden? The shark-nosed bombers? The terror? Nothing, *nothing*, in the poem gives the slightest indication of optimism, and it is for this reason that I consider Wheelock another of the "demon voices . . . wailing the world sorrow."

There is no hope in this poem, unless you assume that the existence of a future, no matter how timid it may be, is at least something to look forward to. If you used this as a basis for your answer, then you are as guilty as Wheelock of unjustified emotion, of applying your own feelings to a poem which suggests only terror, playing on contemporary fears. We need only think of the possibility of nuclear war; the concepts of horror follow, and we are in tune with Wheelock.

In this poem, tone is applied not to the subject, the future of the world, but to the general condition of mankind as Wheelock sees it. I do not quarrel with Wheelock's hatred of war, only with his overwhelming and poetically dishonest inclusion of this attitude in a poem which appears much more limited.

Consider the *poem* again. Return to page 185 and select another answer.

[*from page 183*]

YOUR ANSWER: Present.

This is an interesting conclusion. The first time I read the poem, my reaction was the same. The repeated references to "now," coupled with our knowledge of alerted air forces, tend to make us think that Wheelock is bemoaning the present, not the future. But the demon voices are not calling from the present, even though we may think they should be.

Here is the poem again:

The Timid Future

Wind in the eaves of the old house, wind over Russia
And the English coast, wind over the forelands
Of Europe, over the beaches of Long Island,
Autumnal wind, wailing the world sorrow,
With demon voices thronged, lewd voices
Crying out of the timid future,
Where now is paradise, the hope foresworn,
That could have been, had the heart stretched to hold it?
Where now lost Eden? Behind locked eyelids only
Glimmering a moment in the trance of love,
Recalled for a moment during the truce of music —
The hyssop sponge tendered in mercy
To the parched spirit, fretful in its torment —
Temporary assuagement. The tune Time plays
Grows harder to dance to now. Man's cleverness
Outwits itself; while round the watchful planet
The shark-nosed bombers wait to be unsheathed,
And terror needles the world heartbreak.

Look at line 6. Read it closely, and you will have a direct statement of the time *from* which the voices call. But what are they saying? Technically, everything that follows is a summation of their comments. Or is it? Has Wheelock jumped from the voices to comments of his own? In line 14, is the "tune time plays" harder to dance to *now*, the present of the poem, or are the voices implying from the timid future that the tune *will be* (for us in the present) harder to dance to unless we mend our ways?

Please continue to page 191.

[*from page 190*]

I don't know. A further complication arises from the Eden reference mentioning a paradise which to us, in the present, is irretrievably lost. Do the "lewd voices" consider their plight so horrible that they look back on our time as paradise? I hope not. If they do, their sense of history is certainly warped.

All we have to go on is what the poem says, and line 6 tells us where the voices are calling from. Let's start from there. Return to page 183 and select another answer.

[*from page 185*]

YOUR ANSWER: Like Sandburg, he is sad.

I think there is a lot more than this. Sandburg's sadness was implied; we feel it when reading "Limited," but we cannot justify sadness until we determine what Sandburg is sad about: the lack of understanding of man.

Here the situation is entirely different. This poem is about as subtle as a brick wall: the poem's subject, the world's future, is obvious, and the style (the use of images, comments, and direct statements) precisely indicates how the poet feels about his subject.

Look at some of them:

> ". . . wailing the world sorrow,"
> "With demon voices thronged, lewd voices"
> ". . . the hope foresworn,"
> "Where now lost Eden?"
> ". . . the parched spirit . . ."
> ". . . Man's cleverness/ Outwits itself;"
> "And terror needles the world heartbreak."

Are all these merely expressions of sadness? Or is the tone of the poem just a bit stronger?

Return to page 185, reread the poem, and select another answer.

[*from page 183*]

YOUR ANSWER: Future.

Correct, but you had to do some digging to find out. The voices, according to the poet, are crying "out of the timid future." But what do they comment on? The future? Or the present? Here is the poem again. See if you can discover what makes the "lewd voices" cry.

The Timid Future

Wind in the eaves of the old house, wind over Russia
And the English coast, wind over the forelands
Of Europe, over the beaches of Long Island,
Autumnal wind, wailing the world sorrow,
With demon voices thronged, lewd voices
Crying out of the timid future,
Where now is paradise, the hope foresworn,
That could have been, had the heart stretched to hold it?
Where now lost Eden? Behind locked eyelids only
Glimmering a moment in the trance of love,
Recalled for a moment during the truce of music —
The hyssop sponge tendered in mercy
To the parched spirit, fretful in its torment —
Temporary assuagement. The tune Time plays
Grows harder to dance to now. Man's cleverness
Outwits itself; while round the watchful planet
The shark-nosed bombers wait to be unsheathed,
And terror needles the world heartbreak.

Assuming that the "lewd voices" are wailing *from* the future, what are they wailing about?

The passage of time. **page 175**

Terror. **page 186**

The loss of paradise. **page 196**

[*from page 197*]

YOUR ANSWER: His metaphors are inconsistent and dishonest.

Right. A friend of mine once said, "Let us stop cooling our heels in the melting pot of laziness." Thus he exhorted his students to work harder by use of an intentional mixed metaphor.

In this poem, however, inconsistent, mixed metaphors are not used (I hope) intentionally. First the heart is unable to stretch to hold hope; then it is needled by terror. The eyelids are locked, but during the "trance of love" they glimmer. The eye*lids* glimmer? Or does Eden glimmer? Music is seen as a "truce," then as Time's tune, which "grows harder to dance to now." And the reference to the "hyssop sponge" alludes to Christ on the cross, but there is no justification in the poem (or with reference to Christ, for that matter) of its being "tendered in mercy."

It is easy to tear down someone else's poem, just as it is simple to criticize another person for manners, dress, or belief. But it is best to be discreet and impersonal. In criticizing a person's manners, we assume that we have better ones; in objecting to his beliefs, we suggest ours are better.

The good poet, capable of self-criticism in every line, every word he writes, is able to control style and tone. Wheelock controls neither in this poem. The profusion of mixed metaphors, the hammering at the reader, the overblown style certainly help create a tone, but one which is not an honest product of the poem. The author completely forgets his subject, the future, and directs his invective against the condition of the world.

Certainly the poet shows a feeling for words and their sound, but does this in itself create good poetry? He is dismayed, as are most of us, by world crisis, but this does not justify his presenting the subject as he does, ridden with sardonic comments and hazy metaphor.

Let us look at a poem which approaches much the same idea in a far different manner. In discussing Randall Jarrell's poem, we should notice how its tone and style complement each other, how the attitude of the poet toward his subject gives it universality, and how the way the subject is presented becomes actually part of the subject itself.

Please continue on page 195.

[*from page 194*]

The Death of the Ball Turret Gunner

From my mother's sleep I fell into the State
And I hunched in its belly till my wet fur froze.
Six miles from earth, loosed from its dream of life,
I woke to black flak and the nightmare fighters.
When I died they washed me out of the turret with a hose.

Recognizing that the death of one man, an aircraft gunner, is the occasion for the poem, what is the poem's subject?

The effect of war on humanity. **page 188**

The terrors of aerial combat. **page 198**

The individual's identity in contemporary society. **page 202**

[*from page 193*]

YOUR ANSWER: The loss of paradise.

Right. This should not have been too difficult to recognize.

But — haven't people been wailing about this for years? The "demon voices" wail about "lost Eden," according to the poet, *from* the timid future. Why *demon* voices? And why is the future *timid*? Timid in the face of what? The "shark-nosed bombers" are hardly a symbol of timidity, and the loss of Eden, an accepted fact, does not seem particularly worth wailing about in the context of the poem.

Eve ate the fruit of the tree of the knowledge of good and evil; therefore mankind was thrust from paradise. What on earth does the threat of war have to do with this? And even if we assume that the future *is* timid, how does it differ from the present?

This poem is cheapened not for what it says so much as for the way it says it. Granted, the consideration of world peace is vital, but why hide in a corner and cry?

Read the poem once more. This time I would like you to evaluate the poet's style, here seen in his choice and use of metaphor. Pay particular attention to the underlined passages.

Please continue to page 197.

[*from page 196*]

The Timid Future

Wind in the eaves of the old house, wind over Russia
And the English coast, wind over the forelands
Of Europe, over the beaches of Long Island,
Autumnal wind, wailing the world sorrow,
With demon voices thronged, lewd voices
Crying out of the timid future,
Where now is paradise, the hope foresworn,
That could have been, had the heart stretched to hold it?
Where now lost Eden? Behind locked eyelids only
Glimmering for a moment in the trance of love,
Recalled for a moment during the truce of music —
The hyssop sponge tendered in mercy
To the parched spirit, fretful in its torment —
Temporary assuagement. The tune Time plays
Grows harder to dance to now. Man's cleverness
Outwits itself; while round the watchful planet
The shark-nosed bombers wait to be unsheathed,
And terror needles the world heartbreak.

Is there anything generally wrong with the poet's use of metaphor?

It is inconsistent and dishonest. **page 194**

There is nothing wrong that I can see. **page 200**

Hearts cannot stretch and bombers cannot be "shark-nosed." **page 203**

[*from page 195*]

YOUR ANSWER: The terrors of aerial combat.

Careful, your personality is showing. You have identified yourself with the ball turret gunner and are looking at everything through his eyes. Certainly aerial combat is terrible to him, but his death is only the occasion for the poem, nothing more. What about the other men involved: the ground crews, the pilots of the other "State"? Are they shown to react to the terrors of aerial combat? Not at all, and it is by recognizing this dichotomy that we approach the subject of the poem.

Look at the impersonal "they" in the last line. How does this group of unidentified men differ from the gunner? Do they care, or are they just doing a job which has been assigned to them?

Remember, we defined the subject of the poem as that facet of existence for which the occasion of the poem is a representative example. What is it here that concerns the poet so much that he has chosen the death of one particular man, a ball turret gunner (notice that he does *not* use the pilot of the plane), as the occasion for this poem?

Return to page 195, reread the poem, and select another answer.

[*from page 202*]

YOUR ANSWER: Every human being has a vital role in modern society.

Wrong. I wish this were true, and I think Jarrell does, too. Unfortunately, Jarrell sees and shows just the opposite. You have applied a fine, universal wish to a poem which shows the impossibility of individuality in the modern world.

Notice that the airplane returns safely, even though the ball turret gunner is dead. No mention is made of his having contributed anything to the combat, and after his death he is "washed out of the turret with a hose"; the act of cleaning up the airplane is wholly impersonal. Remember the position of the gunner, hunched in the airplane, alone in his turret. He may appear to be indispensable, but he is hardly treated as such.

Remember Wheelock's flamboyant and confusing metaphors in "The Timid Future"? What about Jarrell's metaphor (and there is really only one). Notice how the concept of mother, State, and the gunner's position in the ball turret (probably the poet means the belly turret on a B-17) all produce the same picture of the gunner's position. By presenting the subject by use of only one consistently developed metaphor, Jarrell's style is definitely controlled.

Read the poem again; note the use of the words *fell into*, *hunched*, and the impersonal *they*. These words hardly connote society's concern; they imply just the opposite.

Return to page 202, reread the poem, and choose another answer.

[*from page 197*]

YOUR ANSWER: There is nothing wrong that I see.

Thank you for being honest.

Remember the requirements of consistency and honesty? These apply throughout any poem, not only to the subject matter but to metaphor as well. There is nothing wrong with comparisons between any two parts of our experience or imagination so long as the metaphor which results is honest and consistent within the poem.

Let us look at one of Wheelock's images:

> . . . The tune Time plays
> Grows harder to dance to now.

This is an ancient metaphor. Unable to help ourselves, we all dance Time's tune. In effect, we are the playthings of Time, subject to Time's every whim, unable to release ourselves from our commitment to exist *in* and *by* Time.

It is conceivable that with world terror and trouble, existence in Time could become proportionately more difficult. So far so good.

But here Time is playing a tune, perhaps producing a wild dance which grows faster and faster, until . . . ? Where else is music mentioned in the poem?

Please continue to page 201 and read the poem again.

[*from page 200*]

The Timid Future

Wind in the eaves of the old house, wind over Russia
And the English coast, wind over the forelands
Of Europe, over the beaches of Long Island,
Autumnal wind, wailing the world sorrow,
With demon voices thronged, lewd voices,
Crying out of the timid future,
Where now is paradise, the hope foresworn,
That could have been, had the heart stretched to hold it?
Where now lost Eden? Behind locked eyelids only
Glimmering for a moment in the trance of love,
Recalled for a moment during the truce of music —
The hyssop sponge tendered in mercy
To the parched spirit, fretful in its torment —
Temporary assuagement. The tune Time plays
Grows harder to dance to now. Man's cleverness
Outwits itself; while round the watchful planet
The shark-nosed bombers wait to be unsheathed,
And terror needles the world heartbreak.

Is music mentioned anywhere else?

Yes. **page 204**

No. **page 207**

[*from page 195*]

YOUR ANSWER: The individual's identity in contemporary society.

Right. Beneath the apparently clear surface of the poem is a consideration of questions vital to man. What am I? Why do I exist? What am I here for? What is my role in society?

The subject of this poem must be concerned with the modern world simply because the occasion for the poem could not occur at any other time. Here the man is specifically a ball turret gunner who is seen as a casualty of *modern* war.

But the man is alone, confined in a tiny sphere, the ball turret, given the specific job of shooting down the aircraft of an enemy "State." He is an individual, yet he has an identity as one of the defenders of his airplane. How vital is he to the success of the bombing mission? This is the basic question the poet seeks to answer, using as his subject the role, the identity, of one single man in the modern world. Now reread the poem:

The Death of the Ball Turret Gunner

From my mother's sleep I fell into the State
And I hunched in its belly till my wet fur froze.
Six miles from earth, loosed from its dream of life,
I woke to black flak and the nightmare fighters.
When I died they washed me out of the turret with a hose.

In general terms, how does Jarrell see the individual against the universal backdrop?

Every human being has a vital role in modern society. **page 199**

The modern individual is a foetus; the world kills him before he is really born. **page 205**

Modern methods of warfare will bring an end to the human race. **page 210**

[*from page 197*]

YOUR ANSWER: Hearts cannot stretch and bombers cannot be "shark-nosed."

Why not? We allowed white mares to gallop in the sky. But remember, we questioned the golden hoofs and the green porcelain doors, didn't we? We should apply the same criteria here, demanding honesty and consistency in every metaphor.

Allow the poet to use any metaphor he wishes, as long as he uses it truly and not because he happens to like the sound, sight, or smell of a particular element which would not otherwise fit into the poem. Let him go as far out as he wants, but require that he knows why and where he is going.

Return to page 197, reread the poem, and select another answer.

[*from page 201*]

YOUR ANSWER: Yes.

Right. In line 11, when the "lost Eden" is seen to be

Recalled for a moment during the truce of music —

The *truce* of music? But this hardly fits in with the "tune Time plays." This kind of music, music as a truce, implies that we should lie back and relax, but wouldn't that be rather hard to do with Time supplying a counter-melody? No, I'm afraid this metaphor just won't do.

This is an example of a mixed metaphor, an inconsistent and contradictory use of comparison where there is a common basis — music — used in different and opposing ways. Had the poet used one or the other consistently in the poem, the result would have been better.

Look at the use of the heart in the poem. First it is stretchable, then needled by terror. Is this honest? Earlier we allowed Amy Lowell to let white mares gallop in the sky, but can you grant this poem even more license?

Finally (for the moment), what "glimmers" in line 10? The eyelids? Or lost Eden? Did you know right away, or did you have to decipher?

There are other examples of improper metaphor; I have noted only a few. Perhaps you have already puzzled over some of the others, but for now, return to page 197 and try again.

[*from page 202*]

YOUR ANSWER: The modern individual is a foetus; the world kills him before he is really born.

Exactly. This image is sustained by use of the concepts of *mother*, *hunched in its belly*, *wetness*, and the knowledge of the actual position of a ball-turret gunner, crammed in his round capsule with his head between his knees. To all intents and purposes, then, he has not been born; he is still in the foetal stage, undeveloped and dehumanized. But there is something wrong with this unborn child. The "I" falls *from* the mother *to* the State, where he hunches and freezes. Isn't this action paradoxical? We usually associate the mother with the recipient of the potential child, and within her there is warmth. Yet in the belly of the State there is coldness. And away from its (the State's) "dream of life" the "I" awakens to a nightmare. Reality is confused and he dies, unborn, to be "washed out" (also a pun on an Air Force term meaning "to be eliminated from flying training"), just as a dead foetus is removed from a womb. Rereading the poem with the paradox in mind, how would you describe the author's attitude toward his subject, the identity of the individual in the modern world?

The Death of the Ball Turret Gunner

From my mother's sleep I fell into the State
And I hunched in its belly till my wet fur froze.
Six miles from earth, loosed from its dream of life,
I woke to black flak and the nightmare fighters.
When I died they washed me out of the turret with a hose.

Ragingly angry. **page 208**

Bitter. **page 212**

Accepts as fate that which must be. **page 215**

[*from page 210*]

YOUR ANSWER: The "I" is a boy who is overwhelmed by the State.

Wrong. When approaching metaphor, don't forget that you must see its entire use within the poem. Certainly there is implicit in the poem a feeling of being overwhelmed, but it has nothing to do with the image used in these two lines. Where did you get the idea that a *boy* was being discussed?

Reread the two lines:

From my mother's sleep I fell into the State
And I hunched in its belly till my wet fur froze.

Mother? *hunched in its belly*? *wetness*? — what do these words connote to you? Translate them into an image, then return to page 210 and select the proper answer.

[*from page 201*]

YOUR ANSWER: No.

You are not reading the poem closely enough. Here it is again.

The Timid Future

Wind in the eaves of the old house, wind over Russia
And the English coast, wind over the forelands
Of Europe, over the beaches of Long Island,
Autumnal wind, wailing the world sorrow,
With demon voices thronged, lewd voices
Crying out of the timid future,
Where now is paradise, the hope foresworn,
That could have been, had the heart stretched to hold it?
Where now lost Eden? Behind locked eyelids only
Glimmering for a moment in the trance of love,
Recalled for a moment during the truce of music —
The hyssop sponge tendered in mercy
To the parched spirit, fretful in its torment —
Temporary assuagement. The tune Time plays
Grows harder to dance to now. Man's cleverness
Outwits itself; while round the watchful planet
The shark-nosed bombers wait to be unsheathed,
And terror needles the world heartbreak.

Reread the poem, attempting to answer the question "When is lost Eden recalled?" When you have done so, return to page 201 and select the correct answer.

[*from page 205*]

YOUR ANSWER: The author's attitude is ragingly angry.

I'm sorry, but Jarrell is not angry. Perhaps you are, or were, toward the situation he depicts; I know I felt frustration and anger when I first read this poem. Such is the power of words.

But Jarrell is past his anger, and his outward emotion is controlled. He does not lash out at the "State," nor does he criticize the ground crews or the enemy pilots who have killed the gunner. That the poem has a catalytic effect on you, the reader, is a mark in its favor, but you must not assume that the attitude of the poet is the same as yours.

How different the tone of this poem is from that of "The Timid Future." In the previous poem, the tone was blatantly obvious. In Jarrell's poem you are forced to become angry, but not because the poem itself is angry. The effect here is much like that of Sandburg's "Limited"; the tone assists the content of the poem to make you react in exactly the way the poet may have reacted when he first thought of the subject, not when he wrote the poem.

Return to page 205 and reread the poem aloud. Notice the regular rhythm, a loose pentameter, until the final line. Can you put this line into pentameter? I think not. It should be read slowly, coldly, impersonally, as if written not by a man who laments his own death, but by one who feels quite differently. When you have finished, select another answer.

[*from page 219*]

And fór | all thís | natúre | is né|ver spént

YOUR ANSWER: The line scans as shown above.

You are a traditionalist and have perhaps followed my instructions to the letter. Let me now say this: beware of anyone who tells you that you must react in such-and-such a way to contemporary poetry. Beware especially of anyone who tells you that you have to *like* contemporary poetry. You don't, you know. If this book does nothing more than help you to understand *why* you don't like anything written in this century, then it has succeeded.

Technically, the line can be scanned in the above manner, but I don't recommend it. Why? Because conventional scansion destroys not only the rhythm Hopkins intended but the pronunciation of a very familiar word. You don't hear the term as "naTURE loVERS," do you? The term is "NAture LOvers," stressed on the first syllable of each word.

Return to page 218 and reread the discussion of Hopkins' unique method of scansion. Try it out on the line at the top of this page, and then select another answer from those on page 219.

[*from page 202*]

YOUR ANSWER: Modern methods of warfare will bring an end to the human race.

Wrong. I have a feeling that you disagreed strongly with my comments on the previous poem, "The Timid Future." I will be honest. When I first read the poem, I was impressed by its tone of despair, but in thinking about the poem, I began to be disturbed about its faults. It is a valid question to consider: "Can a poem be bad even though it appears good at first?" I can't answer, but I do think that the reply should be conditional. Perhaps if the emotional effect on the reader is strong enough, then the poem has a qualified success in terms of the emotion alone.

But back to this poem. Would you not admit that the emotional effect is at least as great, if not greater, than that of "The Timid Future"? Jarrell demonstrates much more careful artistry. Your interpretation has been triggered by the poet's (and your) dislike of war, and you have applied an often-stated fear to a poem which considers primarily the *individual*, not the human race in general.

Let us examine Jarrell's use of metaphor in an attempt to see how he sees the individual in terms of modern society:

> From my mother's sleep I fell into the State
> And I hunched in its belly till my wet fur froze.

What is the image of the "I" the poet is using?

The "I" is a boy who is overwhelmed by the State. **page 206**

The "I" is unborn, being nurtured by the State. **page 217**

The "I" is shown as an animal. **page 222**

[*from page 229*]

YOUR ANSWER: Assonance.

You are right, but only partially so. I'd like to caution you again about making hasty appraisals, stopping short without recognizing all there is to a particular subject. Certainly assonance is important to Hopkins, not only in this poem but in all his others as well, but there are many other devices which should be noted.

What, for instance, do you make of the *s* and *t* sounds? The *m* and *s* sounds? The *f* repetition in the last line?

Return to page 229, reread the lines, and select another answer.

[*from page 205*]

YOUR ANSWER: The author's attitude is bitter.

Right. Whether or not you agree with Jarrell's point of view, the last line

When I died they washed me out of the turret with a hose

presents one of the most calculated, bitter comments on impersonality I have ever seen.

How is this achieved? First, because of closely controlled tone, second, because of style. The poet does not tell us what he thinks; he shows us, and this final line, with its broken rhythm forcing the reader to slow down and enunciate each of the short phrases, understates and underlines the poet's attitude.

As for style, notice how short the poem is? One metaphor contained in five lines certainly epitomizes the idea of brevity, doesn't it? This is a short poem about a short life.

An acquaintance of mine attacks this poem because he says the action shown in the last line did not happen and could never have happened to a crew member of an Army Air Forces aircraft. I agree with his statement as far as actual practice goes. Jarrell creates in this poem what he considers to be the ultimate in *not* caring, and we do not have to believe that it really did happen to receive the impact of his words.

By showing the utter disregard on the part of the gunner's own comrades, Jarrell underscores his belief that the individual has no role at all in modern society; in fact, once he has died he is treated as if he had never existed at all.

But how different Jarrell's approach is from that of Wheelock in the poem we looked at earlier! Here there is no moaning, no wailing, no invective against contemporary society. The controlling metaphor — the unborn child — is consistent throughout, moving from the concept of mother, through the belly of the State, and finally into the aircraft itself. You may possibly become ragingly angry at the condition of modern society which requires this unfulfillment and death-before-birth to exist, but not because the poet is angry in his poem. Rather his tone is just the opposite — cold and bitter — and it *produces* anger in the reader.

Please go on to page 213.

[*from page 212*]

Perhaps you are tired of war poetry. Perhaps we all are, not because of its quality as poetry, but because of its subjects. We cannot, however, avoid war and the threat of future war unless we know what war is and what it does, and by reading what some of our contemporaries have to say about war we increase our knowledge of the terrible scientific refinements of the twentieth century.

Recognizing that man has perfected his ability to destroy himself, many contemporary poets have turned to religion to seek a solution. We are experiencing a resurgence of religious poetry, a type which almost vanished after the seventeenth century. Many poets now feel that they must have faith *in spite of* what they see around them; religion is a recourse, not a requirement, but the faith of these men is just as strong as it was for the earlier poets. Conversely, many modern poets feel that to be committed to anything is to initiate one's own destruction; nevertheless, there are more good religious poems being written in the post-World War II period than there have been for years.

Few religious poets demonstrated greater faith and had more influence on poetry than did Gerard Manley Hopkins. Although a nineteenth-century poet, he was not published until 1918, and his style has affected many poets of this century. You saw the first two lines of this poem earlier; here is the complete work.

Please go on to page 214.

[*from page 213*]

God's Grandeur

The world is charged with the grandeur of God.
  It will flame out, like shining from shook foil;
  It gathers to a greatness, like the ooze of oil
Crushed. Why do men then now not reck his rod?
Generations have trod, have trod, have trod;
  And all is seared with trade; bleared, smeared with toil;
  And wears man's smudge and shares man's smell: the soil
Is bare now, nor can foot feel, being shod.

And for all this, nature is never spent;
  There lives the dearest freshness deep down things;
And though the last lights off the black West went
  Oh, morning, at the brown brink eastward, springs —
Because the Holy Ghost over the bent
  World broods with warm breast and with ah! bright wings.

First, what kind of a poem is this?

It is a Petrarchan sonnet. **page 218**

It is an irregular sonnet. **page 223**

It falls into no recognizable category. **page 225**

[*from page 205*]

YOUR ANSWER: The author accepts as fate that which must be.

Perhaps I should not have offered this answer, but let us discuss it. I think you are wrong, not because you noticed the poet's acceptance of what happens, but because you were not specific enough in your appreciation of tone.

Compare Jarrell's poem with Sandburg's "Limited" (page 178). Notice the different subject, metaphor, rhyme, and rhythm. How do they differ? We agreed that Sandburg regarded time and death as something to be accepted, yet showed his sadness at one man's refusal to understand. Doesn't Jarrell go far beyond Sandburg's sadness?

Be careful, however, that *you* don't go too far. Remember the discussion of anger before, and the necessary forms it takes. Perhaps we might say that Cummings in "Portrait" and Jarrell here seem alike at first, but that Cummings writes of natural death, while Jarrell is concerned with violent, unnatural death-before-birth. Therefore their reactions are different. How?

Return to page 205, reread the poem, and select another answer.

[*from page 231*]

YOUR ANSWER: *Regretful* describes the poet's attitude toward his subject.

I think we had better review the question. You were asked to determine the attitude of the poet toward his subject, the grandeur of God. Why don't men understand His power? Hopkins asks. For generations, trade, work, the dirtiness of human existence have served to divert men from God. Even man's feet, because they are shod, are separated from the natural earth on which they walk.

But look at the second stanza.

> And for all this, nature is never spent;
>   There lives the dearest freshness deep down things;
> And though the last lights off the black West went
>   Oh, morning, at the brown brink eastward, springs —
> Because the Holy Ghost over the bent
>   World broods with warm breast and with ah! bright wings.

Is this an expression of regret toward the grandeur of God, a grandeur which Hopkins sees continuously expressed by nature? Hardly. Return to page 231 and select another answer.

[*from page 210*]

YOUR ANSWER: The "I" is unborn, being nurtured by the State.

Right. The State has now assumed the role of the mother, and the "I" hunches in *its* belly, waiting to be born.

Is he ever born? Or does he become transferred yet again to another metaphorical belly, this time that of an airplane where his position, hunched with a machine gun between his knees, is unchanged. Is he ever allowed to live, or does he die before birth?

All of these questions point toward Jarrell's concept of the individual in the modern world, and the foetal image, sustained throughout this short poem, shows Jarrell's careful use of one honest, consistent, and complete metaphor. Stylistically, the way Jarrell has chosen to present his subject is excellent. He has not added anything superfluous, nor has he selected an image which cannot be developed precisely as he wants.

Recognizing the foetal image, you should have no difficulty seeing how Jarrell regards the individual in the modern world. Return to page 202, reread the poem, and choose the correct answer.

[*from page 214*]

YOUR ANSWER: It is a Petrarchan sonnet.

Right. I was just checking up on you. The octave and sestet, each with its own regular rhyme scheme, identify this poem.

I have a feeling, however, that you may have arrived here against your will. Perhaps you remembered my earlier statement that all sonnets must be written in iambic pentameter; then you tried to fit the lines of this poem into five-foot meter and failed. Technically, I suppose, you are right, but you probably are unaware that Hopkins, by revolutionizing scansion, created an entirely new approach to poetry.

Perhaps you are familiar with Thomas Gray's famous poem "Elegy Written in a Country Churchyard," which begins:

> The Curfew tolls the knell of parting day,
> The lowing herd winds slowly o'er the lea,
> The plowman homeward plods his weary way,
> And leaves the world to darkness and to me.

Now, *there* is iambic pentameter.

Perhaps you also opposed my refusal to use the ˘ sign over the unstressed syllables when scanning a line. All right. The quotation from Gray offers little problem; it has an alternating succession of stressed and unstressed beats, something like a series of Morse code A's: dit dah, dit dah, dit dah, dit dah, dit dah. But you don't read the poem *aloud* this way, not unless you want to put the listener (or yourself) to sleep. As I pointed out before, you should recognize the regularity of the line, but stress it to produce the emphasis and meaning you want. In effect, often the poet writes one way; you read another.

What Hopkins tried to do was write exactly as he wanted the poem to be read, and in many of his poems he added the accents and vertical pause lines to help the reader make the poem sound as Hopkins thought it should.

Please go on to page 219.

[*from page 218*]

In Hopkins' words, his poetry scans "by accents or stresses alone, without any account of the number of syllables" in a given foot.

It is this peculiar approach to scansion which identifies Hopkins' unique style. The "running foot," a necessary component of what he called "sprung rhythm," consists of one major stress with any number of unstressed beats. You might think this technique would produce haphazard rhythm. It does not; not when it is intentionally fused into preconceived, rigidly structured lines and forms. With most poets, the use of a regular form (such as the sonnet) is not readily apparent as a function of style; with Hopkins, just the reverse is true. As for his influence, it is the way he presents his material that has affected succeeding poets.

So, when reading Hopkins, consider his metrics and rhyme in terms of style and you will be better able to appreciate his poetic genius. Look, for instance, at the scansion of the sonnet's final line:

```
 /      /             //                /    /     /
World broods with warm breast and with ah! bright wings.
```

Count the major stresses. Five. Therefore, in Hopkins' language, the line is written in pentameter, and hence is in sonnet form.

Or look at line 9:

And for all this, nature is never spent;

How would you scan this line?

```
       /      /        /       /        /
And for | all this, | nature|is ne|ver spent.
```
page 209

```
 /              /    /          /       /
And for all this, nature is never spent.
```
page 230

Some other way. page 232

[*from page 233*]

YOUR ANSWER: Yes, the use of consonance does differ from anything we have seen before.

Right. Here is the line again:

World broods with warm breast and with ah! bright wings.

Notice the *b*'s and *w*'s, how they shift order in the last two words. Hopkins uses this technique often, achieving not only the effect of alliteration (here in *pairs* of similar consonants) but also a unique tonal effect when he reverses the consonants. Watch for this effect in all of his other poems, and perhaps you will begin to share with me the awe for the man's ability to fuse meaning and structure.

You should agree by now that there is much more to poetry than merely saying something which means something to somebody. Emotion often produces an explosion; we lash out, we shout, we grow red in the face, we cry. The creation of a poem demands just the opposite: implosion (to use the twentieth-century atomic term), if you will. A poem must be shaped; it must be structured; it must be the product of careful artisanship. The howl of a dog may be loud indeed, but, after all, it is only the howl of a dog. To be good, a poem must show its honesty by the use of metaphor and emotion in terms of the chosen subject; it must demonstrate consistency by remaining within limits selected by the poet in his use of structure, sound, and subject; and it must be complete, saying and showing exactly what the poet has intended.

Any other poem is no better than a good try, and we cannot praise an attempt, no matter how honest or heartfelt it may be, as highly as we can applaud a finished, perfect product.

Please go on to page 221.

[*from page 220*]

How do style and tone apply to what I have just said? Think back over the poems we have discussed. How do they differ from other poems you may have read on similar subjects? How do they differ from your best friend's latest summary of the mess this world is in, and why can't we do something about it? Style gives motion to subject; it makes what might seem commonplace alive and vibrant for the reader. But, like the girl with a curl on her forehead, when it is bad it is very, very bad.

And tone? Of course we are interested in how the poet feels toward his subject, but our primary concern is the subject itself. We are hardly satisfied with a friend's description of what he calls a great play or movie; we wish to see it ourselves, and we cannot bear having someone hovering near, telling us what he thinks. Tone, when overly stressed, can ruin our appreciation of a poem; but when it is properly used, it can make us as clay in the poet's hands. We react only the way he wants us to. Thus the tone of a poem, the attitude of the poet toward his subject, creates or complements our attitude toward the subject, and the poem succeeds.

Go on now to page 234.

[*from page 210*]

YOUR ANSWER: The "I" is shown as an animal.

Only partially true. You noticed the reference to fur, but you have perhaps forgotten that all living beings are animals, and in this poem Jarrell is concerned with the *human* animal, man. The "I" is not a dog, cat, or other household pet, but at one stage of man's life, he usually is covered with fine fur. This image appeals to the two senses, sight and touch, by reference to *mother*, *hunched in its belly*, and *wetness*. The cold, as we shall see later, creates a paradox, but it does not affect the image we are concerned with now.

Return to page 210, reread the two lines, and select another answer.

[*from page 214*]

YOUR ANSWER: It is an irregular sonnet.

This is a sticky one. I suppose you selected this because of the requirement I established earlier that all sonnets be written in iambic pentameter, and you did not identify the predominant foot in this poem as the iamb. You are both right and wrong. Hopkins rarely used traditional measurement (his scansion will be discussed later), but it is interesting that many of his poems do scan accurately in traditional terminology if, and only if, we distort sound and meaning. Watch.

Is báre | now, nór | can fóot | feel, bé|ing shód.
Be cáuse | the Hó|ly Ghóst | o vér | the bént

Isn't this iambic pentameter?

Yes, it is; but here you cannot read correctly with the stresses I have indicated above.

Hopkins devised his own method of scansion, based on what he called the running foot. He would measure lines only by the number of primary stresses, regardless of the number of secondary or unstressed beats involved. If you will look at the poem again and read it aloud, you will see that in every line there are five major stresses and a varying number of unstressed beats, and that many of the lines do not break down into standard feet.

Ironically, however, this poem contains only *one* line which cannot be warped into iambic pentameter (I'll let you find the line); hence, this requirement for the sonnet form is not abrogated. The pentameter has been mentioned, the poem has fourteen lines, and if you still don't know the correct answer, review page 49, then return to page 214 and select the right answer.

[*from page 231*]

YOUR ANSWER: *Pessimistic* describes the poet's attitude toward his subject.

Pessimistic toward what? God? Not at all. Look at the opening line of the second stanza:

And for all this, nature is never spent.

A simple, direct statement that, despite the all-smearing, all-blearing effect of man, nature (the expression of God's grandeur) is *never* spent. (There is a pun here. The word means both "exhausted" and "spent" in its financial sense.)

Why is nature never spent? Read the last two lines:

Because the Holy Ghost over the bent
World broods with warm breast and with ah! bright wings.

The grandeur of God is the poem's subject, and Hopkins hardly feels pessimistic about it. Return to page 231, reread the poem, and select another answer.

[*from page 214*]

YOUR ANSWER: It falls into no recognizable category.

Wrong.

There are times in every man's life when he must admit defeat. If, in the discussion of "Arms and the Boy" and "The Oven Bird," I could not help you to understand what a sonnet is, then I have no recourse but to admit failure.

The discussions of the sonnet are contained on pages 49, 134, and 137. Perhaps you missed these the first time through. Please review them, then return to page 214 and select another answer.

[*from page 229*]

YOUR ANSWER: Consonance.

You are right, but only partially so. Again, be careful about using a first impression as a final answer. You recognized, I'm sure, the repeated *s* and *t* sounds, as well as the *f* and *m* examples of consonance. But look at the lines again:

Generations have trod, have trod, have trod;
And all is smeared with trade; bleared, smeared with toil;
And wears man's smudge and shares man's smell: the soil
Is bare now, nor can foot feel, being shod.

What do you see in the underlined word segments? Haven't you overlooked something?

Return to page 229, and select the correct answer.

[*from page 233*]

YOUR ANSWER: No, the use of consonance does not differ from anything we have seen before.

You have overlooked a use of consonance which is unlike anything we have discussed so far.

Let's review. We defined consonance on page 51 as the use in slant rhyme of similar consonant sounds. If you are uncertain of the term, mark this place and return to page 51 and 48 for review. When you are sure of the definition, read on.

This line:

And for all this, nature is never spent

is fairly commonplace in its use of consonance. The *s* and *n* sounds are repeated in an orderly fashion, much like the examples we have seen earlier.

But what about this line:

It will flame out, like shining from shook foil;

Do you see any progression, any pattern? Look at the last four words: *sh*ining *f*rom *sh*ook *f*oil. See how the *sh* and *f* sounds are repeated in pairs?

The same pattern is seen in the sixth line:

And all is seared with trade; bleared, smeared with toil.

The *s* and *t* sounds are repeated in pairs, just as above.

This is one of Hopkins' favorite devices, one which has produced some of the most interesting sound patterns in contemporary poetry. And patterns they are, consciously contrived and flawlessly executed.

Look at the last line now, trying to identify the patterned consonance.

World broods with warm breast and with ah! bright wings.

Return to page 233 and select another answer.

[*from page 231*]

YOUR ANSWER: *Jubilant* describes the poet's attitude toward his subject.

Of course. Hopkins exults in the grandeur of God, and in almost every one of his poems he praises, extols, and champions the revelation of God to man by His works. Look at the first line again:

The world is charged with the grandeur of God.

What more can he say? There is a vitality, an effervescence in this statement. Then in line 2 he gives us a shimmering image which makes us *see* the grandeur he is talking about.

Remember the definition of tone: the attitude of the poet toward his subject. Don't be misled if the poet appears to vary his attitude toward specific elements of his poem, as Hopkins does here when talking about man. When he says,

And all is seared with trade; bleared, smeared with toil;
And wears man's smudge and shares man's smell:

he is not changing his attitude toward the grandeur of God at all. The second stanza, rising to the high point of jubilation (and notice his return to the image of brightness he began with), underscores his faith in God.

So the tone is one of jubilation; the style, basically a contemporary version of the Petrarchan sonnet. There is more, much more.

Style, the way the author chooses to present his subject, is not produced merely by the form or shape of the poem. We have seen how style is a function of metaphor, that the selection of images can add to or detract from emphatic presentation of material. But what about sound? That is where Hopkins excels, for sound becomes a part of his style.

Please go on to page 229.

[*from page 228*]

We have mentioned the rhythmic structure; now let's look at the finer points. Here are lines 5, 6, 7, and 8 again. Read them aloud, pronouncing each word exactly.

> Generations have trod, have trod, have trod;
> And all is seared with trade; bleared, smeared with toil;
> And wears man's smudge and shares man's smell; the soil
> Is bare now, nor can foot feel, being shod.

What is used here to create startling sounds?

Assonance. **page 211**

Consonance. **page 226**

Both assonance and consonance. **page 233**

[*from page 219*]

And for all this, nature is never spent;

YOUR ANSWER: The line scans as shown above.

Right. This is the way Hopkins would scan it. Notice, however, that you could technically scan (and read) the line in iambic pentameter:

And FOR all THIS naTURE is NEVer SPENT

But why do it, when both meaning and sound are demolished?

This brings us back to the topic of unaccented syllables. Why mark them at all? Marking unaccented feet is usually justified by the ease in determining the types of feet used, but what do you do when a poet such as Hopkins writes a line which contains four or five unaccented beats in a row? The obvious answer is: invent new terms to fit the situation. This, however, is an unsatisfactory alternative. You tend to forget the poem itself in favor of the way you want to talk about it.

Since each line of this poem contains five major stresses and in other respects the form is traditional, it is a contemporary Petrarchan sonnet. The iambic requirement has been dropped, but the five-foot line remains. Perhaps it too will go soon, but it has not yet done so.

The subject of the poem is obvious, told us by the title. Read the poem again.

Please go on to page 231.

[*from page 230*]

God's Grandeur

The world is charged with the grandeur of God.
It will flame out, like shining from shook foil;
It gathers to a greatness, like the ooze of oil
Crushed. Why do men then now not reck his rod?
Generations have trod, have trod, have trod;
And all is seared with trade; bleared, smeared with toil;
And wears man's smudge and shares man's smell: the soil
Is bare now, nor can foot feel, being shod.

And for all this, nature is never spent;
There lives the dearest freshness deep down things;
And though the last lights off the black West went
Oh, morning, at the brown brink eastward, springs —
Because the Holy Ghost over the bent
World broods with warm breast and with ah! bright wings.

What is the attitude of the poet toward his subject, the grandeur of God?

Regretful. **page 216**

Pessimistic. **page 224**

Jubilant. **page 228**

[*from page 219*]

YOUR ANSWER: The line scans some other way.

More power to you. If you will not change your mind, if your scansion appeals to you more than either of the two examples, if you are happy, fine. I agree with you completely, for there are a dozen different ways to scan any Hopkins poem, and each with its merits. As long as you have five major stresses, you're probably just as right as the next man.

If you don't have five stresses, however, I suggest a revaluation of your method. Hopkins *wrote* five stresses; perhaps you haven't examined the line closely enough.

In any event, return to page 218, reread the material on Hopkins' method, and try to select what you think is *my* answer.

[*from page 229*]

YOUR ANSWER: Both assonance and consonance.

Yes, and alliteration, onomatopoeia, cacophony, euphony, sibilance, and practically any other poetic term of sound you wish to apply. It is interesting to recognize the similarity between Hopkins and Wilfred Owen ("Arms and the Boy") with respect to tonal quality; and it is interesting to note that Owen, writing twenty years later, had never heard of the religious poet. Owen died the year the first Hopkins poem was published (1918).

The droning repetition "have trod, have trod, have trod" symbolizes, by the way it is written, the plodding, day-to-day existence of persons who do not recognize the grandeur of God.

Notice, too, the progressive slant rhyme from *trod* to *toil*, then to *soil*, which finally resolves into *shod*. Each word is linked not only with its rhyming counterpart but with the words immediately surrounding it as well.

Let's look closely at the second stanza.

And for all this, nature is never spent;
  There lives the dearest freshness deep down things;
And though the last lights off the black West went
  Oh, morning, at the brown brink eastward, springs —
Because the Holy Ghost over the bent
  World broods with warm breast and with ah! bright wings.

Hopkins was a Jesuit priest and a scholar, and his use here of the Holy Ghost as a dove (brooding, with wings) is historically consistent, as are the flame and oil used as symbols of God.

Look particularly at the last line. Does this use of consonance differ from anything we have seen so far?

Yes. **page 220**

No. **page 227**

CHAPTER VI

Theme: What the Poem Says

Subject can be called the *what* of the poem, style and tone the *how*, and theme the *why*. I won't discuss the various definitions of the word "theme," but I will recall for you some of its many uses. You write a *theme*; you notice the *theme* of a symphony, of a modern housing development, and of a work of art.

What do these uses of the word have in common? Specifically, the intention of the artisan who in each case made the thing we are talking about. The creator wants to communicate an idea to somebody, and in a work of art the theme is seen when we apply the subject to the universal, actually creating a symbol of the poem itself. Thus a boy playing with weapons can tell us that war is predatory, a painting by one of the Old Masters that art, to succeed, must be selective, and a man riding on a train that lack of understanding is a sad thing indeed.

I won't try to tell you which comes to the mind of the poet first, subject or theme. One of the great mysteries of life is the process of creation, and I am enough of a conservative to accept it without further examination. Our interest lies in why the poem says what it does.

How does the poet show the importance of his subject? What is he trying to prove? What application does all this have to life? To death? To truth? To time? In answering these questions, we determine what a poem says, and we recognize its theme.

Please go on to page 235.

[*from page 234*]

Here is a poem by Thomas Hardy.

The Oxen

Christmas Eve, and twelve of the clock,
  "Now they are all on their knees,"
An elder said as we sat in a flock
  By the embers in hearthside ease.

We pictured the meek mild creatures where
  They dwelt in their strawy pen,
Nor did it occur to one of us there
  To doubt they were kneeling then.

So fair a fancy few would weave
  In these years! Yet, I feel,
If someone said on Christmas Eve,
  "Come; see the oxen kneel

"In the lonely barton by yonder coomb
  Our childhood used to know,"
I should go with him in the gloom,
  Hoping it might be so.

First, what is a *coomb*?

A narrow valley enclosed on all sides but one. **page 239**

A cattle shed, opening into a pasture. **page 243**

A large haystack, usually containing a salt-lick. **page 245**

[*from page 250*]

YOUR ANSWER: Children have a deeper faith than adults.

I am glad you chose this answer, because it gives me the opportunity to make a general comment about the lyric.

Suppose I were to say, "All men are dishonest." What would your reaction be? Wouldn't you ask me to prove my statement?

Would your reaction differ if I said, "*I think* all men are dishonest"? Would you require proof then, or might your interest lie in finding out why I thought so?

The two statements are different. If you agree with the first statement, you are accepting what you consider to be a *fact*, but if you affirm the latter belief, you side with an *opinion* — in this case, mine.

If you challenged either statement, you would refute the first by presenting evidence; but you would refute the second by attempting to make *me* see the error of *my* ways.

The lyric poet writes opinion, not fact. If you agree with him, you are not necessarily swayed by his logical presentation of evidence; rather, you identify yourself with him, actually forgetting what he uses as proof.

By selecting this answer, you have demonstrated that you concur with Hardy's point of departure, that a child's faith is stronger than that of an adult. This you can see from the first two stanzas. But you have not noticed the personality of the poet, the "I" intruding in the last two stanzas, commenting on what is to many an accepted fact.

Look at the conclusion again.

  Yet, I feel,
If someone said on Christmas Eve,
  "Come; see the oxen kneel

. . . .

I should go with him in the gloom,
  Hoping it might be so.

How does Hardy react to the change in faith? Does he shrug his shoulders and say, "Too bad; that's life"? What does he say he will do if someone *else* suggests going to see the oxen?

By answering these questions, you will arrive at what I think is the theme of this poem. Return to page 250, reread the poem, and select another answer.

[*from page 244*]

YOUR ANSWER: *Memory* is the occasion for "On Dwelling."

I'm sorry. Memory, as was pointed out earlier in the discussion of "A Woman Too Well Remembered," is never the occasion for the poem. Memory of what? Of whom? The occasion for the poem is the person, place, thing, or incident defined in and by the poem. It is what we see happening, for instance, or what we see described. The occasion for the poem is the event which exemplifies what the poet is concerned with.

Return to page 244, reread the poem, and select another answer.

[*from page 260*]

YOUR ANSWER: He does not believe reality exists.

Oh yes he does, although he never describes it. Look at the title, "On Dwelling." The poet tells us that dwelling in the town is ghostly, that the country too has become vague. Where does the poet dwell? Look at stanza 2.

> Here I too walk, silent myself, in wonder
> At a town not mine though plainly coextensive
> With mine, even in days coincident:
> In mine I dwell, in theirs like them I haunt.

His reality is the town which is "plainly coextensive" with the one in which he walks. Regardless of what or where it is, the poet haunts "their" town (unreality), but in *his* he dwells. Everything else has become unreal, even the country which he has left behind. What he sees now is unreal, and what he remembers is unreal also.

Return to page 260, reread the poem, and select another answer.

[*from page 235*]

YOUR ANSWER: A narrow valley enclosed on all sides but one.

Right. Most dictionaries carry this word. If yours does not, then look up *combe*, the earlier and more nearly correct spelling. Often, references are difficult to pinpoint, yet somewhere there is an answer which is worth while to find.

Barton is more obscure, so I'll help you to the extent that the word means "demesne" (which you *can* look up), and by extension it means "farmyard" or "farm outbuildings."

We are talking about theme — what the poem says — and often the theme is obvious. I think it is apparent here. The theme is suggested by the occasion, the kneeling of oxen, and the subject, faith. If we could all believe, Hardy implies, we might be a lot better off.

Please go on to page 240.

[*from page 239*]

Why, we might ask ourselves, does a treatment of a familiar theme appeal to us as it does? Watch how Hardy handles time. Here is the poem again.

The Oxen

Christmas Eve, and twelve of the clock,
  "Now they are all on their knees,"
An elder said as we sat in a flock
  By the embers in hearthside ease.

We pictured the meek mild creatures where
  They dwelt in their strawy pen,
Nor did it occur to one of us there
  To doubt they were kneeling then.

So fair a fancy few would weave
  In these years! Yet, I feel
If someone said on Christmas Eve,
  "Come; see the oxen kneel

"In the lonely barton by yonder coomb
  Our childhood used to know,"
I should go with him in the gloom,
  Hoping it might be so.

Which time period(s) is (are) evident in the poem?

The past. **page 242**

The past and future. **page 246**

The past, present, and future. **page 250**

[*from page 250*]

YOUR ANSWER: Christmas is for the young.

Wrong.

You are far away from the poem itself. You have concurred in a truism, but this is not what Hardy says. A child's belief in kneeling oxen is certainly akin to a belief in Santa Claus, but isn't there more to this poem than just Christmas? Is Christmas only one of many examples of faith, or do you really think Hardy advocates that children should believe only that oxen kneel once a year?

The subject of this poem, faith, is discussed by the demonstration of two approaches: the first, that of the child; the second, that of the adult. There is no doubting by the child; but the poet, as an adult, states that he might like to believe, even though he now doubts. He hopes: "It might be so."

In this comparison, the poet expresses a subtle wish for something. Why does he say that he is willing to go and see if the oxen are really kneeling? Doesn't he seem to doubt his own doubting? Return to page 250, reread the poem, and select another answer.

[*from page 240*]

YOUR ANSWER: The past.

You are only partially right.

You have read the poem too hastily. True, the opening scene is remembered by the poet, but you have overlooked both the time in which the poet writes and the other time which he contemplates, "hoping it might be so." Try to visualize the poet creating this poem: there is one time period. His memories constitute another, his wishes still a third.

Return to page 240, reread the poem, and select another answer.

[*from page 235*]

YOUR ANSWER: A cattle shed, opening into a pasture.

Wrong. Let me caution you again about guessing. You're wrong here, even though this answer might have seemed correct from the context.

Use your dictionary. You will have to do so with later poems.

Return to page 235, look up the word, and select the correct answer.

[*from page 249*]

YOUR ANSWER: *Urbanization* is the subject of "On Dwelling."

You are halfway there. Urbanization, while important to the poem, is not its true subject any more than suffering is the subject of Auden's poem "Musée des Beaux Arts." Urbanization may have started out as the subject when Graves wrote his first draft, but it was soon overshadowed by a much larger and more important concept.

Would the poem be altered drastically if it considered industrialization instead of urbanization? Or sexual mores? Would either affect the last stanza, which considers the poet's memory of what used to be? I doubt it.

Let us retreat slightly and attack from another angle. Reread the poem.

On Dwelling

Courtesies of good-morning and good-evening
From rustic lips fail as the town encroaches:
Soon nothing passes but the cold quick stare
Of eyes that see ghosts, yet too many for fear.

Here I too walk, silent myself, in wonder
At a town not mine though plainly coextensive
With mine, even in days coincident:
In mine I dwell, in theirs like them I haunt.

And the green country, should I turn again there?
My bumpkin neighbours loom even ghostlier:
Like trees they murmur or like blackbirds sing
Courtesies of good-morning and good-evening.

What is the occasion for the poem?

Memory. **page 237**

A man walking in a city. **page 247**

Rural versus city life. **page 251**

[*from page 235*]

YOUR ANSWER: A large haystack, usually containing a salt-lick.

Wrong.

This is indeed an original answer. You must have guessed. Try looking up the word in the dictionary; if you tried and failed, look under the word *combe*, the older spelling. In any event, don't settle for a guess when you have the facts available. You will need reference help to approach much of contemporary poetry; so get into the habit of using it.

Return to page 235, look up the word, and select another answer.

[*from page 240*]

YOUR ANSWER: The past and future.

You are only partially right.

You have overlooked something. True, the past is represented by the poet's memory of what he used to do, the future by what he wishes might be so, but what about the time period in which the poem is written? Try to imagine where the poet is when he thinks forward and back. The transition from past to conditional future is made in stanza 3, but isn't there a definite indication of tense in the lines:

So fair a fancy few would weave
In these years!

What years? Answer this question and you will have a full appreciation of Hardy's use of time.

Return to page 240 and select the correct answer.

[*from page 244*]

YOUR ANSWER: *A man walking in a city* is the occasion for "On Dwelling."

Precisely. The "I" is walking in a city, thinking, but much more than urbanization concerns him. Look at the poem.

On Dwelling

Courtesies of good-morning and good-evening
From rustic lips fail as the town encroaches:
Soon nothing passes but the cold quick stare
Of eyes that see ghosts, yet too many for fear.

Here I too walk, silent myself, in wonder
At a town not mine though plainly coextensive
With mine, even in days coincident:
In mine I dwell, in theirs like them I haunt.

And the green country, should I turn again there?
My bumpkin neighbours loom even ghostlier:
Like trees they murmur or like blackbirds sing
Courtesies of good-morning and good-evening.

Notice that the first stanza is an impersonal statement about the effect of urbanization. In the second stanza, the poet sees ghosts walking in a town which is itself vague and unreal, a town which is "plainly coextensive" with his. Is anything he sees real to him? What about his memory of the country? How do his former neighbors appear to him? Solid? Meaningful? Or ghostlike, hence unreal?

If this poem were an invective against the unreality of the city, don't you think the poet would have extolled the merits of the country, answering his question "Should I return there?" with an emphatic "yes?" But he does not, and it is his failure to do so which identifies the true subject of this poem. Having recognized the unreality of the city, the poet searches for something real. What has he found?

What concerns the poet so much that he has chosen a man walking in a ghostly town as the occasion for this poem? Return to page 249, reread the poem, and select another answer.

[*from page 250*]

YOUR ANSWER: The desire for faith never really dies, despite outward appearances.

I think so. In arriving at this as the theme of the poem, we appreciate the lyric temper of much modern poetry. Hardy is not attempting to create impersonal, absolute truths but is saying honestly, "This is how *I* feel." Those who can agree do so, not because of logical proof, but because of identification with the "I" of the poem. The lyric is not persuasive; it will never change anyone's convictions, but what it can do is help us recognize something about ourselves that we have either never known or have managed to forget.

Notice, for instance, how the child in this poem pictured the oxen as "meek mild creatures" in a "strawy pen." Is this correct, or is the adult description, using the words *lonely* and *gloom*, more nearly true? The scene has changed drastically in the poet's mind, even though he might have wished otherwise.

Perhaps the lack of apparent emphasis and vitality has made this poem less attractive to you than others you have seen. No problem, but some would like it far better than the rest. I think you would agree that it is honest, consistent, and complete, and, although much more placid than "Arms and the Boy," for instance, still worthy of praise. Remember, as long as you know *why* you do or do not like something, you are in a better position to understand it.

Please go on to page 249.

[*from page 248*]

By being honest in their poetry, poets often reveal their personalities to their readers. Hardy does so in "The Oxen," showing what cynics would call a sentimental streak. Sometimes, however, the revelation of self which we see in the works of a contemporary poet is hardly as obvious as Hardy's, yet nonetheless striking. See what you can do with the following poem by Robert Graves.

On Dwelling

Courtesies of good-morning and good-evening
From rustic lips fail as the town encroaches:
Soon nothing passes but the cold quick stare
Of eyes that see ghosts, yet too many for fear.

Here I too walk, silent myself, in wonder
At a town not mine though plainly coextensive
With mine, even in days coincident:
In mine I dwell, in theirs like them I haunt.

And the green country, should I turn again there?
My bumpkin neighbours loom even ghostlier:
Like trees they murmur or like blackbirds sing
Courtesies of good-morning and good-evening.

Let us begin by reviewing. What is the subject of this poem?

Urbanization. **page 244**

Reality. **page 260**

Progress. **page 262**

[*from page 240*]

YOUR ANSWER: The past, present, and future.

Right. The past and conditional future are discussed, and the present exists in the poet's mind as he thinks about what was and what might be.

Note the setting. The poet remembers an early Christmas Eve when he and others "sat in a flock," accepting as truth the story of the kneeling oxen. Why in a "flock"? Should we not recognize that this word differentiates the child from the adult, that once maturity is reached, a man is no longer a member of the flock, but able to decide for himself?

Let's arrive at a statement of theme for this poem. Read it once more.

The Oxen

Christmas Eve, and twelve of the clock,
  "Now they are all on their knees,"
An elder said as we sat in a flock
  By the embers in hearthside ease.

We pictured the meek mild creatures where
  They dwelt in the strawy pen,
Nor did it occur to one of us there
  To doubt they were kneeling then.

So fair a fancy few would weave
  In these years! Yet, I feel,
If someone said on Christmas Eve,
  "Come; see the oxen kneel

"In the lonely barton by yonder coomb
  Our childhood used to know,"
I should go with him in the gloom,
  Hoping it might be so.

What is the theme of this poem?

Children have a deeper faith than adults. **page 236**

Christmas is for the young. **page 241**

The desire for faith never really dies, despite outward appearances. **page 248**

[*from page 244*]

YOUR ANSWER: *Rural versus city life* is the occasion for "On Dwelling."

You have forgotten the definition of *occasion*. The occasion is the person, place, thing, or incident defined in and by the poem. Normally, the occasion is the basic image, something which appeals immediately to the senses.

When searching for the occasion, ask yourself, "What does the poet see?" Try to determine what obvious action he describes; or if the poet is the main character, ask yourself what he is physically doing in the poem. You saw a boy playing with weapons in an earlier poem; you saw a poet's former lover; you saw a night sky. What do you see happening in this poem?

Return to page 244, reread the poem, and select another answer.

[*from page 260*]

YOUR ANSWER: He is afraid of reality.

I think not. Tone is the attitude of the *poet* toward his subject, not the attitude *you* might have in a similar situation. Furthermore, he states definitively that he sees too many ghosts for fear.

I will not deny that his attitude might lead to fear, but there is, within the limits set by the poem, no indication that he is afraid.

Return to page 260, reread the poem, and try again.

[*from page 258*]

YOUR ANSWER: Reality is exemplified by the town in which the poet says he "dwells."

Certainly. His reality, his dwelling, contrasts with the ghostly town of the others, which the poet, "like them," haunts.

Where is his dwelling? Think for a moment. Do you have goals? ideals? beliefs? principles? wishes? Is there anything you consider real which you cannot see around you but nevertheless exists for you as definitely as if it were tangible? Can you see faith? love? honor?

Does the poet try to establish a reality of his own? The "courtesies of good-morning and good-evening" seem real at first, and we think, upon quick reading, that something traditionally pleasant has been lost as a result of urbanization. But nothing has really been lost. Graves feels that the "rustic lips" have themselves forgotten the true meaning of "good-morning" and "good-evening."

What has Graves created which replaces the unreality he sees about him?

Return to page 271, reread the poem, and identify the theme.

[*from page 287*]

YOUR ANSWER: *A battle* becomes the basis for the controlling metaphor.

I think not. Who is fighting whom? Is there really a conflict shown or did you infer that strife is inevitable? When we speak of the controlling metaphor, we are concerned only with what is in the poem.

Remember the definition of an image: a verbal impression which appeals to one or more of the senses. In this poem there is a major image which appeals to sight, an image which becomes the controlling metaphor.

Do not think that understanding of the controlling metaphor immediately gives you both subject and theme. Remember Lowell's "Night Clouds"? The controlling metaphor in that poem was built on the image of white mares galloping through the night sky, but discovering this was just the beginning of understanding the poem.

A good image is honest, consistent, and complete within the framework of the poem. When you reread "Return to Ritual," decide what scene the poet describes in all *three* stanzas. When you can see the image which acts as setting for the poem, you should have no difficulty in answering the question.

Return to page 287, reread the poem, and select another answer.

[*from page 271*]

YOUR ANSWER: The theme of "On Dwelling" is *memory is fallible, therefore untrustworthy.*

I don't think the poet would disagree, but I would guess that he might be rather disappointed at your stopping here. You have taken his comment on "bumpkin neighbors," fastened upon it, and excluded the rest (and actually more important portion) of the poem.

How, for instance, do you account for the ghosts, for the "town . . . plainly coextensive with mine"? If memory is the only fallible faculty present in this poem, why does the city in which the poet walks seem as ghostly as the country?

Join me in what I will call the game of counter-assumption. You probably rejected the first answer, "City dwellers become ghosts," because you thought it too limited and not encompassing the entire poem. I hope you agree by now that your answer is no broader, considering as it does no more than that which the other answer excludes.

Keep in mind that the theme of a poem must result honestly, consistently, and completely from *all* the material within it and that you took the other, equally limited view. Assume you selected the answer "City dwellers become ghosts," and go on to page 258.

[*from page 264*]

YOUR ANSWER: Those of the men marching on the road.

You are partly right, but you have not recognized the participation of the poet and the reader in the action of the poem. You should assume, from the "drumming phalanx" and the presence of dust, that the men on the road are *already* marching when you and the poet arrive on the scene, having stopped your futile exploration of the "lone paths that narrow into peace." You stand there, watching, remembering the "clean moss ways and the tamaracks," but then something happens. What changes? Do you infer from the poem that you and the poet will return to your previous environment, or will you join the marching men? Pay particular attention to the last stanza, to the poet's invocation of the "mother of marches."

Return to page 264, reread the poem, and select the correct answer.

[*from page 287*]

YOUR ANSWER: *A wide road with a fence beside it* becomes the basis for the controlling metaphor.

Right. Notice the dust which is present on roads when men are marching.

I mentioned earlier that most lyric poetry contains no characters except the "I" of the poem, the poet (or his representative). What about this poem? Read it again, noticing the impersonality of the first stanza, then the increasing subjectivity of the next two.

Return to Ritual

The mother of life indulges all our wandering
Down the lone paths that narrow into peace.
She knows too well the gradual discovery
And the slow turning round until we cease:
Resolved upon the wide road once again
Where dust hangs over day and mantles men.

Here is the drumming phalanx, here is the multitude;
Listen, and let us watch them over the stile.
We that remember clean moss ways and the tamaracks,
Let us be timorous now and shudder awhile.
We shall be early enough, no matter when,
Mother of dust, O mother of dust and men.

How time passes, here by the wall of eternity!
Even so soon we summon her; we are prepared.
Already these feet are lifting in a wild sympathy;
Who can remember the cool of a day unshared?
Mother of marches, mother, receive us then.
Listen! The dust is humming a song to the men.

The poet is obviously present, standing on the opposite side of the fence from the road containing the "multitude." But he uses the term "we," saying "let us watch them over the stile." To whom does he make this suggestion?

The reader. **page 264**

The "mother of life." **page 273**

One of the marching men. **page 279**

[*from page 271*]

YOUR ANSWER: The theme of "On Dwelling" is *City dwellers become ghosts.*

I'm afraid you are looking for the wrong material. You should let your mind make more associations than you have allowed it so far.

City dwellers become ghosts is not the theme of this poem.

Let's try to prove this by reference to the poem. You have recognized the occasion for the poem, a man walking and thinking in a city, and have correctly determined the poem's subject, reality. Keep these in mind. Now, accept the statement *city dwellers become ghosts* as only *part* of a comment on people in general. Recognizing this, aren't you restrictive to apply this comment only to city people? Here is the poem again.

On Dwelling

Courtesies of good-morning and good-evening
From rustic lips fail as the town encroaches:
Soon nothing passes but the cold quick stare
Of eyes that see ghosts, yet too many for fear.

Here I too walk, silent myself, in wonder
At a town not mine though plainly coextensive
With mine, even in days coincident:
In mine I dwell, in theirs like them I haunt.

And the green country, should I turn again there?
My bumpkin neighbours loom even ghostlier:
Like trees they murmur or like blackbirds sing
Courtesies of good-morning and good-evening.

If city dwellers *and* "bumpkin neighbours" are vague and ghostly, therefore unreal, what does exemplify reality to the poet?

The town in which he "dwells." **page 253**

The town which, like "them," he haunts. **page 263**

Courtesies of good-morning and good-evening. **page 267**

[*from page 264*]

YOUR ANSWER: Those of the reader and the poet.

Right. I have emphasized this because the urge to action is an important part of the structure of the poem. First you see the impersonal, direct statement; then you become part of the scene; finally (once you have read stanzas 1 and 2) you are forced to feel exactly what the poet feels, the "wild sympathy," and you even begin to hear the song the dust is humming to the men.

Return to Ritual

The mother of life indulges all our wandering
Down the lone paths that narrow into peace.
She knows too well the gradual discovery
And the slow turning round until we cease:
Resolved upon the wide road once again
Where dust hangs over day and mantles men.

Here is the drumming phalanx, here is the multitude;
Listen, and let us watch them over the stile.
We that remember clean moss ways and the tamaracks,
Let us be timorous now and shudder awhile.
We shall be early enough, no matter when,
Mother of dust, O mother of dust and men.

How time passes, here by the wall of eternity!
Even so soon we summon her; we are prepared.
Already these feet are lifting in a wild sympathy;
Who can remember the cool of a day unshared?
Mother of marches, mother, receive us then.
Listen! The dust is humming a song to the men.

We have established the scene: the fence, the wide road, and the marching men, an image which I have called the basis for the controlling metaphor.

What does this scene become symbolic of?

Haste. **page 266**

Death. **page 277**

Time. **page 283**

[*from page 249*]

YOUR ANSWER: *Reality* is the subject of "On Dwelling."

Right. The occasion for the poem, a man walking in a city, makes the reader consider urbanization, a concept which Graves accepts just as Auden accepts suffering in "Musée des Beaux Arts." The town, "plainly coextensive" with the town in which he walks, exists only in the poet's imagination; everything else that he senses and remembers appears ghostlike.

Notice his choice of words. The town encroaches. On what? Obviously the country, but how? The town absorbs, not necessarily by illegal or forceful means, but stealthily, gradually. Property is encroached upon, but so are customs and the habits of country people.

The eyes of the city dwellers "see ghosts, yet too many for fear." One might become frightened at the sight of one ghost, but a group of ghosts is ludicrous. The scene reminds me of a ghostly convention, replete with parades and meetings.

Understanding of this poem depends in great part on recognition of tone. Read the poem again.

On Dwelling

Courtesies of good-morning and good-evening
From rustic lips fail as the town encroaches:
Soon nothing passes but the cold quick stare
Of eyes that see ghosts, yet too many for fear.

Here I too walk, silent myself, in wonder
At a town not mine though plainly coextensive
With mine, even in days coincident:
In mine I dwell, in theirs like them I haunt.

And the green country, should I turn again there?
My bumpkin neighbours loom even ghostlier:
Like trees they murmur or like blackbirds sing
Courtesies of good-morning and good-evening.

What is the poet's attitude toward his subject, reality?

He does not believe it exists. **page 238**

He is perplexed. **page 271**

He is afraid. **page 252**

[*from page 265*]

YOUR ANSWER: He understands humanity.

Before I can accept this answer, I must ask you to expand upon it slightly. If you mean that the poet demonstrates a "keen understanding of the human situation," I must challenge you on the grounds that you haven't really said anything. *What* does he understand about humanity?

Graves does not imply in this poem that he, as artist, understands more than the common, ghostlike crowd does. Rather, he *starts* with this attitude, commenting that courtesies fail among the ghosts of the town, and including himself in the common fold. He describes his urban neighbors as having "eyes that see ghosts," but states, "In mine I dwell, in theirs *like them* I haunt." Finally, even the courtesies from the "rustic lips" degenerate into a vague murmur. It hardly appears to be humanity which he understands; everything has become unreal.

Return to page 265, reread the poem, and select another answer.

[*from page 249*]

YOUR ANSWER: *Progress* is the subject of "On Dwelling."

Wrong.

Do you consider the "encroachment" of the city upon the country a sign of progress? Perhaps it is, but even the term *progress* is strictly modern in scope. Previous centuries did not use the word to mean "getting better"; people preferred to think in terms of a progression, something which merely moved from one place to another.

To Graves, however, the growth of a city is neither improvement nor tragedy; it just happens. Yet in considering the effects of this urban expansion, the poet contemplates a much more abstract situation, one which might be defined as the nature of ghostliness itself. First determine the occasion for the poem; use it as a point of departure for deciding what concerns the poet so much that he has chosen this occasion for his poem. There will be time later to bring his comments upon his subject into your interpretation.

Return to page 249 and try again.

[*from page 258*]

YOUR ANSWER: Reality is exemplified by the town which, "like them," he haunts.

Wrong. You have misread either the poem or the question. The poet's reality is *not* seen in what he calls "their" town, simply because it is vague and ghostly. The town in which he walks may appear real to one of the ghosts, but definitely not to the poet.

Look at the title, "On Dwelling." Three types of dwelling are mentioned: first the country, second the city, and third what the poet calls *his* town.

Graves shows the first two, the city and the country, as vague and ghostly, therefore unreal. He does not regard them as concrete, tangible places in which to dwell; or, at any rate, he has discarded them in favor of something strictly his own, something more real to him than the city and country of others.

Keeping this last statement in mind, return to page 258 and select another answer.

[*from page 257*]

YOUR ANSWER: The poet makes the suggestion to the reader.

Right.

You apparently noticed that the first stanza is impersonal and that the second introduces the "we" concept. The poet has his metaphorical arm around the reader's shoulder and is pointing out what is going on in front of them, thus including the reader in the occasion for the poem.

Does the poet incite the reader to action? Let's see. Read the poem again.

Return to Ritual

The mother of life indulges all our wandering
Down the lone paths that narrow into peace.
She knows too well the gradual discovery
And the slow turning round until we cease:
Resolved upon the wide road once again
Where dust hangs over day and mantles men.

Here is the drumming phalanx, here is the multitude;
Listen, and let us watch them over the stile.
We that remember clean moss ways and the tamaracks,
Let us be timorous now and shudder awhile.
We shall be early enough, no matter when,
Mother of dust, O mother of dust and men.

How time passes, here by the wall of eternity!
Even so soon we summon her; we are prepared.
Already these feet are lifting in a wild sympathy;
Who can remember the cool of a day unshared?
Mother of marches, mother, receive us then.
Listen! The dust is humming a song to the men.

In stanza 3, whose feet "are lifting in a wild sympathy"?

Those of the men marching on the road. **page 256**

Those of the reader and the poet. **page 259**

[*from page 271*]

YOUR ANSWER: The theme of "On Dwelling" is *nothing is real except the imagination.*

Right. It was a long leap.

Remember Frost's "The Oven Bird"? It's helpful to notice the difference between what Frost recommends and what Graves says here. In this poem the poet walks silently in a ghostly town, one which is coextensive with his own and exists in his imagination. Frost, recognizing the power of imagination, attacks the habit of existing in an ideal, imaginary world, much preferring to live according to limitations defined in and by nature.

On Dwelling

Courtesies of good-morning and good-evening
From rustic lips fail as the town encroaches:
Soon nothing passes but the cold quick stare
Of eyes that see ghosts, yet too many for fear.

Here I too walk, silent myself, in wonder
At a town not mine though plainly coextensive
With mine, even in days coincident:
In mine I dwell, in theirs like them I haunt.

And the green country, should I turn again there?
My bumpkin neighbours loom even ghostlier:
Like trees they murmur or like blackbirds sing
Courtesies of good-morning and good-evening.

Assuming that this poem tells us there is nothing real except the imagination, what is revealed to us about the poet himself?

He understands humanity. **page 261**

He dislikes country life. **page 272**

He has become a ghost himself. **page 276**

[*from page 259*]

YOUR ANSWER: The scene becomes symbolic of haste.

Look at this word again. Can you really say that the *entire* poem symbolizes haste? Haven't you reacted only to the increasing tempo at the end and forgotten all about the "lone paths" and the "slow turning round" of the first stanza?

There is certainly an increase of pitch, intensity, and tempo throughout the poem, but is this in itself the controlling metaphor? What part does dust play here? Once excited to action, where is everyone going? Why must anyone go at all? Why is there contrast between "lone paths, . . . clean moss ways, . . . cool of a day unshared," and the scene of the poem — the wide, dusty road filled with marching men?

When you reread, look at the whole poem, not just at the beginning or end. When you answer the questions above and recognize the presence of dustlike inevitability, you should be able to see what the scene symbolizes.

Return to page 259, reread the poem, and select the correct answer.

[*from page 258*]

YOUR ANSWER: Reality is exemplified by courtesies of good-morning and good-evening.

Your answer poses an interesting problem. Are you really wrong, or have you actually reacted to the poem correctly and gone far beyond the obvious meaning? I don't know. Let's see.

When I first read this poem, I immediately thought of the sad loss of traditional niceties, beliefs, and customs. I expected this poem to be just another condemnation of our modern lack of values. But I was wrong, and I began to doubt my interpretation when I examined the last stanza. Why, for instance, should the poet conclude that even country dwelling is ghostly? Why the mention of "bumpkin neighbors" who sound like murmuring trees or blackbirds?

By equating the ghostliness of town and country, the poet forces a consideration of something else: reality itself. If neither town nor country is real to him, then what is? I think he might agree that a good morning or good evening is real, but what about the *terms* "good-morning" and "good-evening" (notice the hyphen) when they are used only as "courtesies"? Is it not possible that the "rustic lips" have already lost the true meaning of these words *before* the town "encroaches"? This is a distinct possibility, and should be considered.

Perhaps you see now why I questioned your answer. This poem discusses the very nature of reality itself. Where does a person really dwell? Is anything external at all real, or is everything that we experience merely droning courtesy or ghostlike unreality?

Return to page 258 and select the obvious example of reality as expressed by the poet.

[*from page 287*]

YOUR ANSWER: *Marching men* becomes the basis for the controlling metaphor.

I think you have failed to reread the poem closely enough. You have reacted only to the sense of the last stanza, without regarding the controlling metaphor.

Here is the poem again.

Return to Ritual

The mother of life indulges all our wandering
Down the lone paths that narrow into peace.
She knows too well the gradual discovery
And the slow turning round until we cease:
Resolved upon the wide road once again
Where dust hangs over day and mantles men.

Here is the drumming phalanx, here is the multitude;
Listen, and let us watch them over the stile.
We that remember clean moss ways and the tamaracks,
Let us be timorous now and shudder awhile.
We shall be early enough, no matter when,
Mother of dust, O mother of dust and men.

How time passes, here by the wall of eternity!
Even so soon we summon her; we are prepared.
Already these feet are lifting in a wild sympathy;
Who can remember the cool of a day unshared?
Mother of marches, mother, receive us then.
Listen! The dust is humming a song to the men.

Do you see now that the sight of marching men is part of a larger image? *Marching men* does not include the watchers, the "stile," or even the road itself. Where does the marching take place? What surrounds the marchers? Is everyone marching throughout the poem?

The controlling metaphor is seen as a product of simile, image, and symbol, and may be quite unlike any of its parts. The image we are concerned with gives us the setting for the poem and is the basis for the controlling metaphor which will be discussed later.

Reread the poem; then return to page 287 and select another answer.

[*from page 277*]

YOUR ANSWER: The "mother of men" is *Time.*

I don't think so. Time functions differently in this poem, as I suggested on page 283.

Whatever the "mother of life" (also referred to as "mother of dust and men" and "mother of marches") is, I think we must agree that the poet shows her to be responsible for all the action in the poem. She has indulged all our "wandering down the lone paths that narrow into peace"; she is prophetic; and when summoned, she receives her supplicants. She is presented as mother, and everything has begun with her. She knows what will happen to her children (men), yet does not take any action to protect or save them.

But what about time? In this poem, time functions only as the medium in which everything must happen. Time is responsible for nothing; indeed, it only "passes." How, then, could the "mother of men" represent time?

Return to page 277, reread the poem, and select another answer.

[*from page 282*]

YOUR ANSWER: *War* is the subject of "Return to Ritual."

Precisely, and it is interesting to note that at no time is there a reference to war, nor is there the slightest hint, other than the connotation of the word "phalanx," that war is what the poet is concerned with.

We arrive at this subject by recognizing not so much what is pointed *at* but what is ignored. Fate indulges man's wanderings down the paths "that narrow into peace." There are many of these, perhaps broad at first, but quickly narrowing and becoming metaphorically impassable. There is only one wide road to this poet, that which leads to *un*peace, or war. The masses move on this road, covered with dust, marching.

Now it should be an easy step to the theme of this poem.

Return to Ritual

The mother of life indulges all our wandering
Down the lone paths that narrow into peace.
She knows too well the gradual discovery
And the slow turning round until we cease:
Resolved upon the wide road once again
Where dust hangs over day and mantles men.

Here is the drumming phalanx, here is the multitude;
Listen, and let us watch them over the stile.
We that remember clean moss ways and the tamaracks,
Let us be timorous now and shudder awhile.
We shall be early enough, no matter when,
Mother of dust, O mother of dust and men.

How time passes, here by the wall of eternity!
Even so soon we summon her; we are prepared.
Already these feet are lifting in a wild sympathy;
Who can remember the cool of a day unshared?
Mother of marches, mother, receive us then.
Listen! The dust is humming a song to the men.

What is the theme?

War means death for mankind. **page 278**

Man is controlled by destiny. **page 286**

War is inevitable. **page 292**

[*from page 260*]

YOUR ANSWER: He is perplexed by reality.

Exactly.

He questions his inability to provide answers to his own queries. Complicated? Of course, and this is one of the reasons that a poem differs from an annual report on urban progress by the town council.

Let me paraphrase the poem: The poet comments that the rustic courtesies are no longer practiced by ghostlike city people who pass each other without comment or recognition. He dwells in one town, and walking in another ghostly town he wonders if he should return to the country. Finally, he decides that his "bumpkin neighbours" in the country are even ghostlier than those in the city. Their courtesies seem to him like the murmur of trees or the song of blackbirds.

Straightforward? Let's see. Here is the poem again. Read it closely.

On Dwelling

Courtesies of good-morning and good-evening
From rustic lips fail as the town encroaches:
Soon nothing passes but the cold quick stare
Of eyes that see ghosts, yet too many for fear.

Here I too walk, silent myself, in wonder
At a town not mine though plainly coextensive
With mine, even in days coincident:
In mine I dwell, in theirs like them I haunt.

And the green country, should I turn again there?
My bumpkin neighbours loom even ghostlier:
Like trees they murmur or like blackbirds sing
Courtesies of good-morning and good-evening.

What is the theme of this poem?

City dwellers become ghosts. **page 258**

Memory is fallible, therefore untrustworthy. **page 255**

Nothing is real except the imagination. **page 265**

[*from page 265*]

YOUR ANSWER: He dislikes country life.

Not at all. The poem tells us that nothing is real except the imagination, yet there is no indication that the poet *dislikes* that which is unreal.

It might appear to you that the poet expresses a *preference* for the country. He does show, however, that he is uncertain about *what* he prefers. He has been away from the country, and is unable to answer the question "Should I return there?" simply because the country, too, has become ghostly to him.

I think you should reread the poem, looking for a change in the poet's attitude. He does seem to express a preference in the beginning, but by the end we see him equating country and town. Why? What has happened to him? Can you see any difference between him and the ghostly people he points to?

Return to page 265, reread the poem, and choose the correct answer.

[*from page 257*]

YOUR ANSWER: The poet makes the suggestion to the "mother of life."

Wrong.

You have made a bad guess.

The "mother of life" is not present in this poem, and is referred to only in the third person until the next to last line, where she is called to by the "we" of the poem. Notice also in the second line of the last stanza the phrase "Even so soon we summon her." If your answer was correct, then the "we" would be summoning part of itself.

The identity of the "mother of life" will be discussed later; but for now, realize that she cannot be included in the "we." Return to page 257, reread the poem, and select another answer.

[*from page 293*]

YOUR ANSWER: The poet sees *nature.*

I believe this is too general an assumption here. Here is stanza 1 again:

The hovering and huge, dark, formless sway
That nature moves by laws we contemplate
We name for lack of name as order, fate,
God, principle, or primum mobile.

Let's explicate, this time by diagramming. Here is what Bowers is saying:

NATURE

moves
(by laws which men can only contemplate)
"the hovering and huge, dark, formless sway"
which men call
"order, fate, God, principle, or primum mobile."

In context, then, the words *order*, *fate*, *God*, *principle*, and *primum mobile* are names given by men to what Bowers calls the "hovering and huge, dark, formless sway." Man has no real knowledge of nature's laws, Bowers tells us; he can only "contemplate" them.

What we must do first is define as best we can what the "hovering and huge, dark, formless sway" is. Does this phrase sound at all familiar? It should. It is a paraphrase of similar descriptions seen in literature from its beginning, descriptions used by men attempting to define what existed before the creation of the earth. Regardless of your personal beliefs about creation, you should be able to find one answer on page 293 which adequately describes, *according to the poem*, what the "hovering and huge, dark, formless sway" means to the poet.

Reread the four lines quoted above, then return to page 293 and try again.

[*from page 282*]

YOUR ANSWER: *Death* is the subject of "Return to Ritual."

Not this time. Death, like time, is a necessary part of the poem but not the subject. Subject is the *what* of the poem, that which the poet writes about. Does death fit this definition? Is Van Doren writing about death, showing differing concepts, discussing it, analyzing it? Or is he possibly using death symbolically, to suggest a finality which is not spelled out for us.

We know that death is inevitable, just as we know that without time, nothing happens. What kind of death does Van Doren hint at? Natural? Hardly. We should not miss the marchers' destination shown us *by* (not in) the poem; of course it is death, but why? What have a wide road and fate to do with death?

The answer lies in the first stanza, in which we see the "mother of life" *indulging* our travels down the "lone paths that lead to peace." Notice the contrast; *lone* as opposed to the multitude. Why peace? You should be beginning to see the contrast. The subject of this poem is not mentioned, but its opposite is established early as that which man (according to the poet) cannot have, even though he strives for it. Metaphorically speaking, the poet tells us that our desire for narrow roads will not produce success; we are required, perhaps because of something in us which only fate understands, to travel the wide, dusty road to . . . ? Of course death is the result, but how? Because of what? The answer is the subject of the poem.

Return to page 282, reread the poem, and select another answer.

[*from page 265*]

YOUR ANSWER: He has become a ghost himself.

Of course he has. Look at lines 3 and 4:

> Soon nothing passes but the cold quick stare
> Of eyes that see ghosts, yet too many for fear.

Can we assume that Graves dislikes cities? I don't think so. If we consider his unanswered question "And the green country, should I turn again there?" we might conjecture further that the poet felt much the same way about the country before he became a city dweller.

Some contemporary poets agree with Graves that everything we see around us is unreal, ghostly, illusory; and some suggest a solution. In Auden's poem "Musée des Beaux Arts," the answer is the reality of art, and this theme runs throughout modern literature. Unfortunately (for our purposes), few of the great poems on this subject are short. Read Yeats's "Among School Children" or "Sailing to Byzantium" for a further expansion, or "Notes toward a Supreme Fiction," by Wallace Stevens.

Please go on to page 287.

[*from page 259*]

YOUR ANSWER: The scene becomes symbolic of death.

"Dust thou art; to dust returneth." Dust images are common in poetry; they are a favorite device used to suggest death.

I think we can sense the feeling of being manipulated in some way by forces beyond our control. What we see happening is *not* of our own doing; we are forced to participate in a deadly game, something alien to our remembrance of "clean moss ways and the tamaracks."

Read the poem once more.

Return to Ritual

The mother of life indulges all our wandering
Down the lone paths that narrow into peace.
She knows too well the gradual discovery
And the slow turning round until we cease:
Resolved upon the wide road once again
Where dust hangs over day and mantles men.

Here is the drumming phalanx, here is the multitude;
Listen, and let us watch them over the stile.
We that remember clean moss ways and the tamaracks,
Let us be timorous now and shudder awhile.
We shall be early enough, no matter when,
Mother of dust, O mother of dust and men.

How time passes, here by the wall of eternity!
Even so soon we summon her; we are prepared.
Already these feet are lifting in a wild sympathy;
Who can remember the cool of a day unshared?
Mother of marches, mother, receive us then.
Listen! The dust is humming a song to the men.

Let us make the last major identification. Who or what is "the mother of men"?

Time. **page 269**

Fate. **page 281**

Eve. **page 288**

[*from page 270*]

YOUR ANSWER: The theme of "Return to Ritual" is that *war means death for mankind.*

Wrong. When you accept a general treatment of a subject such as war, you preclude the limitation of this subject by time. Remember Jarrell's poem "The Death of the Ball Turret Gunner"? He used contemporary aerial war to show the effect of the "State" on the individual, but did we not agree that some would survive? The victors, perhaps? Of course, and in this poem there is even less evidence that everyone will perish.

There will always be those who wander, alone, down the "paths that narrow into peace." Perhaps idealistically, maybe because they know no better, these people will try to find a warless condition which the poet in this poem does not admit exists. What happens? They fail, then are drawn to the wide, dusty road which leads to war. The dust (death) hums a song to the men, and the multitude marches.

Mankind, however, continues to exist, regardless of the toll taken by war, and there is no indication that the race will ever end.

The theme of this poem should be obvious by now; return to page 270, reread the poem, and choose the correct answer.

[*from page 257*]

YOUR ANSWER: The poet makes the suggestion to one of the marching men.

I'm afraid not. You have misunderstood the setting. When the poet says, " Let us watch them *over the stile*," the marching men ("them") are on the *other* side of the fence separating the poet and his companion from the wide road.

Again, this poem differs from others we have seen so far, but how? Let's review. To whom was "The Timid Future" addressed? To anyone in particular, or to all readers in general?

In "The Death of the Ball Turret Gunner," did you feel personally included in the poem, as if Jarrell were talking directly to you alone or to everyone about the effects of the State on modern man?

In most of the poems we have seen, the poet speaks to man in general, not addressing any specific person.

"Return to Ritual" is more direct. Determine whom the poet addresses and you will also recognize the identity of the "we" within the poem.

Return to page 257, reread the poem, and select another answer.

[*from page 293*]

YOUR ANSWER: The poet sees *chaos*.

Right. The "hovering and huge, dark, formless sway" is the original chaos which existed before the universe was created. Perhaps you have read Milton, especially books II and VII of *Paradise Lost*. If so, then you should recognize the similarity in tone and style — deep, somber, heavy, and often inverted. Milton's stated purpose in his great epic was "to justify God's ways to man," and I cannot help feeling that Bowers has a similar purpose in this poem, one which we might summarize as a justification of *man's* ways toward God.

Paraphrasing, then, we see that the poem so far tells us that we place names upon the chaotic flux of nature, but we can only contemplate nature's ways, not understand them.

Let's move on. Here are the next five lines:

> But in that graven image, word made wood
> By skillful faith of him to whom she was
> Eternal nature, first and final cause,
> The form of knowledge knowledge understood
> Bound human thought against the dark we find.

What is the "graven image" the poet describes?

The Virgin Mary. **page 294**

A work of art. **page 298**

A pagan statue. **page 304**

[*from page 277*]

YOUR ANSWER: The "mother of men" is *Fate*.

Yes. Van Doren alludes to Fate (or Fortune) as the "mother of life."

The "mother of life" reference is, however, vague, and my interpretation of the poem is based on a passing knowledge of classic Greek and Roman thought. The Fates are traditionally pictured as old women, spinning the threads of life, and once they were considered also to be spirits of birth. Perhaps Van Doren had one of them in mind; perhaps he means something else entirely. Though the poem may seem to you hopelessly confused and ambiguous, I think that Fate, Fortune, or Destiny personify the mother of life, making the poem meaningful to me. Ironically, here she also is seen as the mother of death.

Perhaps you question my reference to classic thought? You remember in our discussion of "The Death of the Ball Turret Gunner" that I did not think the poem concerned anything except modern society and "States." Van Doren's poem is much more general. First, the men are not described, the scene is purposely vague, and there is an aura of timelessness and death. Look at the word *phalanx*. Have you ever read a contemporary news report which talks of a "phalanx of men"? Of course not. The word is ancient, specifically meaning in ancient Greece a well-formed body of heavy infantry. "Here," the poet says, "is the phalanx, here is the multitude." I can't help feeling that this scene could have taken place outside the gates of Troy as well as in modern times.

Reread the poem, keeping in mind the reference to the phalanx and the comment that Fate, the mother of life, *indulges* all our wanderings down narrow paths.

Please go on to page 282.

[*from page 281*]

Return to Ritual

The mother of life indulges all our wandering
Down the lone paths that narrow into peace.
She knows too well the gradual discovery
And the slow turning round until we cease:
Resolved upon the wide road once again
Where dust hangs over day and mantles men.

Here is the drumming phalanx, here is the multitude;
Listen, and let us watch them over the stile.
We that remembers clean moss ways and the tamaracks,
Let us be timorous now and shudder awhile.
We shall be early enough, no matter when,
Mother of dust, O mother of dust and men.

How time passes, here by the wall of eternity!
Even so soon we summon her; we are prepared.
Already these feet are lifting in a wild sympathy;
Who can remember the cool of a day unshared?
Mother of marches, mother, receive us then.
Listen! The dust is humming a song to the men.

What is the subject of this poem?

War. **page 270**

Death. **page 275**

Fate. **page 284**

[*from page 259*]

YOUR ANSWER: The scene becomes symbolic of time.

Again . . . once more . . . *still*: Look at the *entire* poem. Time is certainly present; how can we ever be without it? But, while time contributes to everything in the poem, it is not itself symbolized by anything we can identify here.

Perhaps you have confused the concept of time with that of inevitability. Inevitability is (as are motion, haste, speed, pursuit, and the like) a function of time, not time itself. Marching, or any progression, depends on time but differs from it.

Certainly there are comparisons between differing elements of time. The poet says that he and the reader *wander* down "lone paths"; then we see the "drumming phalanx." Feet which are at first still begin to lift in a "wild sympathy," and "time passes." But what does all this mean? Where is everyone going, and why? Consider these questions, return to page 259, and when you have reread the poem carefully, select the correct answer.

[*from page 282*]

YOUR ANSWER: *Fate* is the subject of "Return to Ritual."

Wrong. We have established that fate equals the "mother of life"; therefore if the poem is about fate, it must be about the "mother of life." I think you will agree that this is not the case. Fate acts in this poem as an overseer, perhaps causing, definitely affecting, but only contributing. To be *about* fate, the poem would have to discuss what fate is, how we see it, perhaps whether or not it exists, as well as mention what fate *does*.

Despite our "wandering down the lone paths that narrow into peace," Van Doren tells us, we are inevitably drawn to the wide road, to the dusty march toward . . . death? Is this all? We all will die, certainly, but why? How? What is it about the dusty road and the "multitude" which is quite different from a natural approach to death?

Think about this question, try to recognize the contrast the poet establishes between the lone, narrow way and the "drumming," wide road; then ask yourself, "Why is the multitude headed toward an early death?" The answer is the subject of this poem.

Return to page 282, reread the poem, and select another answer.

[*from page 295*]

YOUR ANSWER: "He" accomplishes this by Divine inspiration.

Not here. Bowers is more interested in looking at the creation of the Virgin Mary with respect to *man's* role, not God's. He is briefly considering one facet of empiricism, the belief that nothing is real except that which is perceived.

Bowers assumes that chaos does exist, defining it metaphorically as the absence of light and form. In the attempt to give order to this lack of order, he says, man tries to name it, applying terms such as God, fate, or primum mobile. This solution is not enough for the poet. Bowers recognizes man's inability to understand that which is nameless.

Bowers shows that a glorified image such as the Virgin Mary is meaningless to any man who is unable to create for himself its expression of "bound human thought." The existence of God for someone else is not enough, he implies. We must assist in His creation within and by our own minds.

You should now understand the approach Bowers is using here. When you reread, ask yourself, "What does the 'he' of the poem have that the 'we' do not? How does he differ from the rest?" You should then be able to select the right answer. Return to page 295 and try again.

[*from page 270*]

YOUR ANSWER: The theme of "Return to Ritual" is that *man is controlled by destiny.*

Wrong. Remember the definition of theme, "what the *poem* says." We understand what fate does from two or three lines; the rest of the poem is concerned with a more specific application: war. What does fate have to do with war? Can fate prevent war? Or does the poet show just the opposite? Return to page 270, reread the poem, then choose the right answer.

[*from page 276*]

That problems exist is no revelation, but the belief that there are no ready solutions to certain problems *is* an important contemporary topic. Some poets offer religion, some suggest art, and others even yearn for death; but the poems about apparently insoluble problems continue to be written.

Here is one of these, by Mark Van Doren.

Return to Ritual

The mother of life indulges all our wandering
Down the lone paths that narrow into peace.
She knows too well the gradual discovery
And the slow turning round until we cease:
Resolved upon the wide road once again
Where dust hangs over day and mantles men.

Here is the drumming phalanx, here is the multitude;
Listen, and let us watch them over the stile.
We that remember clean moss ways and the tamaracks,
Let us be timorous now and shudder awhile.
We shall be early enough, no matter when,
Mother of dust, O mother of dust and men.

How time passes, here by the wall of eternity!
Even so soon we summon her; we are prepared.
Already these feet are lifting in a wild sympathy;
Who can remember the cool of a day unshared?
Mother of marches, mother, receive us then.
Listen! The dust is humming a song to the men.

What image becomes the basis for the controlling metaphor?

A battle. **page 254**

A wide road with a fence beside it. **page 257**

Marching men. **page 268**

[*from page 277*]

YOUR ANSWER: The "mother of men" is *Eve.*

You may have a point here, but I think you would have to do some heavy explaining to justify it. True, both Eve and the Virgin Mary are often referred to as the "mother of mankind," but the phrase as used in this poem does not seem to imply that either Eve or Mary is being considered. I will not deny the possibility, but I don't read the poem that way.

Rather than see the "mother of men" as a person, I prefer to envision her as a personification of a controlling force, one which understands and affects the destiny of her children: men. She is shown as not only the mother of *life*, but also of the end of life: death.

Don't discard the possibility of an Eve or Mary connotation, but try to see "mother of life" in more general terms. Imagine that she could have existed long before Christianity, perhaps even have been deified at one time, and you will then be able to receive the full implications of this symbol.

Return to page 277, reread the poem, and select another answer.

[*from page 293*]

YOUR ANSWER: The poet sees *divinity.*

Wrong. Perhaps you misread the question, or maybe you are just being human. We are trying to discover what the *poet* sees behind the names *man* invents. Bowers is playing a dual role here: first, a normal man; second (and more important for our purposes), a commentator on the human race. He does not say that "men" do the naming; rather he says "we."

Let's review. All four lines constitute one inverted sentence. Look at them again:

> The hovering and huge, dark, formless sway
> That nature moves by laws we contemplate
> We name for lack of name as order, fate,
> God, principle, or primum mobile.

Don't be misled by the poet's intricate sentence structure. The subject is "we"; the verb is "name." We must ask ourselves, "What, in the poem, do we name?" Answer: "The hovering and huge, dark, formless sway." What do we call it? Answer: "order, fate, God, principle, or primum mobile."

Look at this list of names. Each one suggests something constant, fixed, definite, but each one connotes an extraterrestrial, intangible concept. Bowers is trying to go behind the words which have been created by men. He claims no superunderstanding, but he does feel that the standard words are inadequate.

What existed in the universe before the earth was created? What may *still* exist, according to many men, beyond the limits known to modern science? Think about this, then reread the first four lines, return to page 293, and select another answer.

[*from page 295*]

YOUR ANSWER: Through recognition and fear of chaos.

This is not enough. Most men recognize and fear the "hovering and huge, dark, formless sway," Bowers says, and attempt to apply names such as "order, fate, God, principle, or primum mobile." How can you name something whose existence you do not recognize?

The poem is concerned, not with unsuccessful attempts at naming, but with the Virgin Mary. Hers is not a futile name applied to laws "we contemplate"; she is shown to be a "congruent form" created in what is otherwise chaos.

How is this accomplished by the "he" of the poem? Certainly "he" must recognize chaos, but in this respect "he" is no different from the rest of humanity, the "we" of the poem. What makes the "he" unique? Return to page 295, reread the poem with this last question in mind, and select another answer.

[*from page 297*]

YOUR ANSWER: Because she, unlike order, fate, principle, etc., is both created and understood by human intellect.

Right. To this poet, the Virgin Mary has been created from chaos by skillful faith, and consists of an "image of the mind" become a congruent, equal combination of glorified will and matter. Why? Because of faith. Faith in the need for order, and faith in the power of the intellect.

Simple? Hardly. We have come a long way since we first saw mares galloping against a night sky.

Read the poem again.

The Virgin Mary

The hovering and huge, dark, formless sway
That nature moves by laws we contemplate
We name for lack of name as order, fate,
God, principle, or primum mobile.
But in that graven image, word made wood
By skillful faith of him to whom she was
Eternal nature, first and final cause,
The form of knowledge knowledge understood
Bound human thought against the dark we find.
And body took the image of the mind
To shape in chaos a congruent form
Of will and matter, equal, side by side,
Upon the act of faith, within the norm
Of carnal being, blind and glorified.

Do you think the *poet* glorifies the Virgin Mary?

Yes. **page 296**

No. **page 307**

[*from page 270*]

YOUR ANSWER: War is inevitable.

Right. It's not a pretty thought, but perhaps plausible. Rejecting man's responsibility for war, Van Doren appears to blame powers beyond man's control.

Or does he? Have you been led into an interpretation which you cannot justify to yourself? Have I read too much into this poem, making a great deal more of it than I should? If I have done so and you have agreed with me without knowing why, where do we both end up? Perched precariously on the proverbial limb? Right.

Why not take one more look at the poem on page 270? Accept the "mother of life" as the earth itself, the Earth-Mother. Interpret the marching as the return to the clay from which man was originally made. Peacefulness exists, Van Doren may be saying, in the "clean moss ways and the tamaracks," but modern man is ever forced to hurry, join the crowd, and participate in the metaphoric mass-march which leads inevitably toward death. Thus man is denied idyllic, rural peace. When you have finished reading, return here.

Never allow anyone to impress his beliefs upon you without your consent. No matter what you now believe to be the theme of this poem, be certain your understanding results from the poem itself, not from what I try to make you believe. Commonly, those who appear most sure of themselves may have little justification for their confidence.

Either of the two themes is satisfactory, and arguing over the merits of one instead of of the other illustrates some of the fun of poetry.

Please go on to page 293.

[*from page 292*]

Although some poems appear easily understood at first reading, others seem immediately baffling. This sonnet by Edgar Bowers is obviously concerned with religion, but for you to understand exactly *what* about religion will take some effort. When you read this poem, try to determine what use Bowers is making of commonly accepted beliefs.

The Virgin Mary

The hovering and huge, dark, formless sway
That nature moves by laws we contemplate
We name for lack of name as order, fate,
God, principle, or primum mobile.
But in that graven image, word made wood
By skillful faith of him to whom she was
Eternal nature, first and final cause,
The form of knowledge knowledge understood
Bound human thought against the dark we find.
And body took the image of the mind
To shape in chaos a congruent form
Of will and matter, equal, side by side,
Upon the act of faith, within the norm
Of carnal being, blind and glorified.

Bowers has omitted every unnecessary word (and perhaps, for some readers, a few necessary ones); therefore, his sentence structure, while grammatically correct, is too complex to be understood at once. First, mentally insert the word *which* after "laws" in line 2. Now read the first four lines again. Nature has laws, the poet says, but because ultimate understanding is impossible, men can only contemplate the ways of nature.

Assuming man's true ignorance, what does the poet see behind the "names" *God*, *order*, *fate*, *principle*, or *primum mobile*?

Nature. **page 274**

Chaos. **page 280**

Divinity. **page 289**

[*from page 280*]

YOUR ANSWER: The "graven image" is the Virgin Mary.

Right. The clue lies in the line which introduces "him" to whom *she* was "eternal nature, first and final cause." The unnamed "he" (significantly not capitalized) has made the "word" into "wood"; in other words, he has given permanence and solidity to what would otherwise be only an insufficient definition such as order, fate, primum mobile.

How did "he" manage to accomplish this? By using his knowledge to understand the "form of knowledge," he was able to create what Bowers calls a "graven image," binding human thought *against* the dark chaos mentioned in the beginning.

Perhaps we should pause over "form of knowledge." Bowers' intricate, compressed sentences (a contrast to the style of Cummings, isn't it?) are often hard for the reader to decipher. Let us recast one such phrase. Speaking of the Virgin Mary, Bowers says:

> In that graven image, the knowledge of the creator understood the form of knowledge and managed to bind together all human thought against the dark that we normal people see.

Better? Perhaps as a traditional English sentence, yes, but not necessarily as poetry.

It is interesting that Bowers does not tell us exactly what the "form of knowledge" is, but he has told us what it is *not*. The "form of knowledge" is not order, fate, or primum mobile; actually it is chaos itself, apprehended by the intellect. The Virgin Mary is also, in opposition to the first list of names, the only satisfactory form *for* knowledge. The knowledge of the "he" has understood what form true knowledge must take, and the result is the "blind and glorified" Virgin Mary.

Please go on to page 295.

[*from page 294*]

Here is the poem again:

The Virgin Mary

The hovering and huge, dark, formless sway
That nature moves by laws we contemplate
We name for lack of name as order, fate,
God, principle, or primum mobile.
But in that graven image, word made wood
By skillful faith of him to whom she was
Eternal nature, first and final cause,
The form of knowledge knowledge understood
Bound human thought against the dark we find.
And body took the image of the mind
To shape in chaos a congruent form
Of will and matter, equal, side by side,
Upon the act of faith, within the norm
Of carnal being, blind and glorified.

The poet includes himself in the "we" who place labels on chaos in the attempt to define what is undefinable. He shows a certain "he" who has succeeded in creating, in the form of the Virgin Mary, a measure of stability. How does the "he" manage to accomplish this in the poem?

By Divine inspiration. **page 285**

Through recognition and fear of chaos. **page 290**

By a combination of faith and skill. **page 297**

Through an act of faith. **page 300**

[*from page 291*]

YOUR ANSWER: Yes, I think the poet glorifies the Virgin Mary.

I would enjoy talking with you. A Jesuit told me once, "Everyone is a Catholic; some are better than others, and some don't know it yet." He said this jocosely, of course, but behind this statement is the basis for your belief that the poet himself glorifies the Virgin Mary. In this poem he does not. If he glorifies anything, it is the human mind and the power of the intellect, skillfully used to produce an object which can be glorified.

I cannot say your answer is wrong, however, if you infer that the poet is unintentionally glorifying the Virgin. I do not think I have the right to tell *you* what *he* does or does not believe. Neither can I say definitely that he would like to glorify the Virgin, because I would be thinking for someone else, a dangerous process.

When you return to page 291 and select the other answer, take a look at the question. I did not ask, "Does the poet glorify the Virgin Mary?"; instead, I asked you what *you thought* about this possibility. You have told me; thus your reaction to the poem has been established and the poem, in this respect, has succeeded. Return now to page 291 and choose the other answer.

[*from page 295*]

YOUR ANSWER: By a combination of faith and skill.

Right. Notice the comparison between the name of the Virgin Mary and the earlier list which resulted from man's inability to find the proper name (and I do not think we should place much significance here on the capitalization of the word *God* — if it were not just first in the sentence . . . ?). These names are not shown to have resulted from faith; rather they come about because of man's futile attempt to "contemplate" the laws of nature. The creation of the Virgin Mary differs from all these, primarily because of the faith and skill of the "he" who originated the concept.

Let us study the last five lines; then we will attempt to put everything together and arrive at the theme.

> And body took the image of the mind
> To shape in chaos a congruent form
> Of will and matter, equal, side by side,
> Upon the act of faith, within the norm
> Of carnal being, blind and glorified.

The poet is discussing his idea of what the Virgin Mary is, a "congruent form of will and matter." The "body" belongs to the "he" mentioned earlier, and the "act of faith" echoes the "skillful faith" suggested before. Faith in what? Faith that chaos is not an end in itself, that there must be order. Finally, the poet suggests that the Virgin Mary is "blind (because he thinks of her as a "graven image") and glorified."

A final question on content. Why is the Virgin Mary "within the norm of carnal being"?

Because she, unlike order, fate, principle, etc., is both created and understood by human intellect. **page 291**

Because she is both a human being and a deity. **page 299**

[*from page 280*]

YOUR ANSWER: The "graven image" is a work of art.

I think you are wrong, but I would not like to bet. If you read the poem as a discussion of art, the act of creation itself and the justification for skillful, faithful artisanship, you have an interpretation which is difficult to disprove. But I ask this: what do you make of the requirement of faith placed on the man who creates? Faith in what? Art? Himself? Something else? Divinity, perhaps? And once you introduce Divinity, you must admit that Bowers is telling us that, without faith in God, no artist can create a good work. I cannot accept this.

As for faith in "something else," I feel that Bowers is being more specific. Look at these lines again. Speaking of the "graven image," the poet describes its creation by a man

. . . to whom she was
Eternal nature, first and final cause,

thereby defining the image in terms of the title of the poem. Not just any created thing at all will do here. Try again. Return to page 280, reread the lines, and select another answer.

[*from page 297*]

YOUR ANSWER: Because she is both a human being and deity.

You may believe this view, but it is not expressed in the poem. You are applying either what you believe or what you would like to believe in a dishonest manner. (Remember our early definition of honesty. Regardless of the importance or validity of your belief, you are introducing into your interpretation of the poem some material *not* directly a part of the poem; hence you are being poetically dishonest. And please note: I am not calling you a liar.)

There are no indications that the Virgin Mary is considered divine by the poet, or, for that matter, by the "he" who created her in the poem. She is "glorified," but do not several Christian denominations do this without admitting her divinity?

She exists within the "norm of carnal being" because she was created by man and must exist in this world, as all man-made creations do. But the poem does not tell us that she is a god. Return to page 297 and try the other answer.

[*from page 295*]

YOUR ANSWER: He accomplishes this through an act of faith.

I'm afraid not.

That's the way "we" might try to "shape in chaos a congruent form" — we who place labels on chaos and try to name the unnamable. But the "he" of the poem is an artisan, a maker of images. He doesn't rely on faith in the learned disquisitions of Aristotle, Aquinas, and Augustine. He has faith, all right, but he doesn't try to justify his faith with mere words; he makes it into a real and concrete image: the Virgin Mary.

"He" doesn't create the image "within the norm/Of carnal being" simply by recognizing that men cannot comprehend chaos, or by listening to the advice of someone else. He makes it by a combination of qualities which he finds within himself — qualities which Bowers not only discusses but exemplifies in this poem.

Return to page 295 and choose the correct answer.

[*from page 306*]

YOUR ANSWER: He thinks it is a waste of time because he cannot believe in divinity himself.

Wrong. Nothing in the poem justifies this view.

Do not equate sympathy with tolerance. (Again, use your dictionary.) We can dislike yet tolerate, but it is difficult to sympathize with a belief, person, or way of life in which we see no value. I do not mean that the poet yearns for faith. But I do not believe we can rule out this possibility by seeing his attitude toward the creation of Virgin Mary as a "waste of time."

Furthermore, we are not really concerned with his attitude toward the Virgin. We are interested in his attitude toward the creation by the intellect of a "graven image, . . . blind and glorified." Contrast his approach to the names "we" place on the chaos for "lack of name." How does he show this process to differ from the "skillful faith" which created the Virgin Mary? Once established, this difference will show you his attitude toward her creation.

Return to page 306, reread the poem, and select another answer.

[*from page 307*]

YOUR ANSWER: The poet believes in God.

Do you really think so? I don't think his belief is demonstrated here. Because Bowers equates God with "order, fate . . . principle, or primum mobile," he appears to consider the existence of divinity as but one more name we apply because of our lack of real understanding of nature's laws. When examined individually, the terms can be seen to include practically all known attempts to understand the laws of nature. Order — for the scientists; fate — for the determinists; God — for the religious; principle — for the humanists; and primum mobile — for any who still subscribe to the Ptolemaic universe with its spheres and four elements, earth, water, air, and fire.

Bowers prefers to accept what lies *behind* the names, what first causes all names to be invented. Pay particular attention to the first few lines, and you should have the answer. Return to page 307, reread the poem, and try again.

[*from page 306*]

YOUR ANSWER: He tolerates this process.

It is time to define terms. Look up *tolerance* in your dictionary.

If you still believe that Bowers merely tolerates the creation of the Virgin Mary by the intellect, then you are saying only that the poet is a nice man who puts up with something he sees little value in. I see no justification for this view.

Why write a poem about something you only tolerate? Consider this, then return to page 306, reread the poem, and try again.

[*from page 280*]

YOUR ANSWER: The “graven image” is a pagan statue.

Careful, you’re narrowing your approach. You have by reflex linked the terms *pagan statue* and *graven image*, but you have not investigated the latter phrase as it is used in the poem.

Let’s get back to the poem. When you reread, look for the obvious. Everything between the words *image* and *form* define by apposition what the “graven image” is. Read in context. Look for what the poet says, not for what you would like to see. Return to page 280, reread the lines, and select another answer.

[*from page 307*]

YOUR ANSWER: The poet believes in chaos.

Right. It would be going too far, however, to say that he worships chaos. Notice in the first four lines the repeated reference to "we." People who glorify the Virgin Mary are another breed to this poet, for he classes himself with those who only "contemplate" nature's laws.

Despite his acceptance of chaos, however, he is different from those who try to pin labels upon it. First, he recognizes the existence of faith, then demonstrates a strong belief, not in a being, but in a process. He has faith in the power of the intellect to create an object worthy of glorification. It is fine, he implies, to have faith in miracles, but this is not enough. To this poet, true faith results from intellectual investigation of faith; it is not something given to a person, but something arrived at by extreme effort. "Skillful faith" is capable of giving *form* to knowledge; therefore only a combination of skill, belief, and knowledge can bind "human thought against the dark" — the chaos which most people see.

This is his subject — the creation of the Virgin Mary by the intellect. He does not discard any possibility of divine origin, but implies that divinity in itself is not requisite to glorification unless man's mind is able to understand as well as to accept on faith.

Please go on to page 306.

[*from page 305*]

We should examine tone; then we can proceed to theme. Here is the poem for reference.

The Virgin Mary

The hovering and huge, dark, formless sway
That nature moves by laws we contemplate
We name for lack of name as order, fate,
God, principle, or primum mobile.
But in that graven image, word made wood
By skillful faith of him to whom she was
Eternal nature, first and final cause,
The form of knowledge knowledge understood
Bound human thought against the dark we find.
And body took the image of the mind
To shape in chaos a congruent form
Of will and matter, equal, side by side,
Upon the act of faith, within the norm
Of carnal being, blind and glorified.

What is the attitude of the poet toward his subject, the creation of the Virgin Mary by the intellect?

He thinks it is a waste of time because he cannot believe in divinity himself. **page 301**

He tolerates this process. **page 303**

He is highly respectful. **page 309**

[*from page 291*]

YOUR ANSWER: No, I think the poet does not glorify the Virgin Mary.

I agree. He seems to accept this belief by those who *do* have skillful faith, but as we shall see later, he insists upon a much more justifiable faith than many people possess.

Now, assuming that the poet does not glorify the Virgin Mary, reread the poem and try to see if he does appear to glorify anything.

The Virgin Mary

The hovering and huge, dark, formless sway
That nature moves by laws we contemplate
We name for lack of name as order, fate,
God, principle, or primum mobile.
But in that graven image, word made wood
By skillful faith of him to whom she was
Eternal nature, first and final cause,
The form of knowledge knowledge understood
Bound human thought against the dark we find.
And body took the image of the mind
To shape in chaos a congruent form
Of will and matter, equal, side by side,
Upon the act of faith, within the norm
Of carnal being, blind and glorified.

What does the poet believe in?

God. **page 302**

Chaos. **page 305**

Nothing. **page 308**

[*from page 307*]

YOUR ANSWER: The poet believes in nothing.

Semantics, semantics, semantics. Do you mean by this answer that Bowers appears not to believe in anything, or do you say that Bowers believes in "nothing" as a concept in itself. In either case, I don't think you are justified by evidence in the poem.

Notice, I did not ask you to identify what Bowers worships, rather, what he believes in, what he accepts as definitely existing. I think we agree that he admires the power of the intellect, but there is something else which he accepts, the recognition of which started him thinking about this poem in the first place.

You have overlooked the obvious. Bowers does not believe in "nothing," but he does not subscribe to the infallibility of any name "we" place on what he *does* accept.

Think about this, then return to page 307, reread the poem, and try again.

[*from page 306*]

YOUR ANSWER: He is highly respectful.

Of course he is. Perhaps the most striking evidence of his respect is seen in his inclusion of himself among those who "name for lack of name." Then, by discussing a successful attempt to give form to chaos, he shows his respect for those who are able to do what he cannot. Could we call the tone also one of wistful admiration, shown by one who would like to have faith, but as yet is unable? Perhaps, but we should realize that all we are doing is guessing. Had the poet started with "they" who believe something, then shown one person who differed, he would have created quite a different tone. The poet would then have been excluded from both approaches, perhaps regarding each in an equal light. As it is, he favors the "he."

I think the theme of this poem should now be obvious, but I do recognize the problem in stating it concisely. Here is my wording:

> The existence of the Virgin Mary is a monument
> to the power of intellectual faith.

Agree? If you don't, but have sufficient reasons for an interpretation of your own, then no effort has been wasted. Even if you are still slightly confused (as I am, even after reading the poem at least fifty times), we have still accomplished a great deal, even though you may not think so now. Wait a while, then reread this poem and see what happens.

We have formally discussed theme, what a poem says, but it should be obvious that we have been concerned with it long before the beginning of this chapter. After all, the theme of a poem is really the reason for its existence. Poetry is one form of communication, and to be worth while, the poem must say something to the reader. Speaking and writing without communication are meaningless.

Are we guilty of oversight? What have we forgotten? What about *meaning*? This is an important word. We have not overlooked it, but we have discussed all the basic terms we need to approach contemporary poetry. (There is one minor exception, as you will find out later.)

Please continue to page 310.

[*from page 309*]

Meaning is the theme of a poem as it relates to you, the reader. Once you determine what a poem says, then your reaction to it creates the meaning. Perhaps some of you readers see little meaning in Bowers' complex poem, possibly because you thought it contained irreligious content. Why shouldn't you? Perhaps some of you took issue with Van Doren's theme that war is inevitable, or perhaps you disagree strongly with me that the poem even considers such a theme. Or maybe you agree so firmly that you are disappointed at the poem's shallow treatment of such an important subject.

No matter. The meaning of a poem depends on the reader, and a poem can mean many things to many readers. With this thought in mind, go on to page 311.

CHAPTER VII

Meaning: The Reader and the Poem

What I will say in this chapter may offend some of you. I cannot, however, subscribe blindly to any of the existing poetic and critical theories, even though most of them are held by critics much more learned than I. Here are just a few:

A critic can conclusively determine what a poet means.
A poem should mean the same to everyone.
A poem must have paraphrasable content.
There is a limit to a poem's meaning.
To be good, a poem must be obscure.
Criticism is an art form in itself.
Only poets make good critics.
Only critics make good poets.
There is a formula for the creative process.

The list could be much longer, but everything it contains, if considered as absolute doctrine, is hokum.

This view has been expressed often, even by the instigators of the dogmas listed above. I differ from many critics in my refusal to invent a theory of my own, which would only add to the general store of superfluous knowledge (interesting as some of it may be). I offer no justification for art. Good art sells itself. I exalt no art form above another. I will never insist that I alone am right. I require only that the finished product be honest, consistent, and complete, regardless of how or why it was created. I will never insist that had *I* written the poem, it would have been better. If I could do so, others would be writing about my poetry, not I about theirs.

Please go on to page 312.

[*from page 311*]

Am I trying to say that a poem can mean anything at all, that there are no bounds whatsoever? No. The effect of a poem should be justified by the poem. The poem can be a catalyst for emotion; it can put you to sleep; it can make you think; it can do almost anything to you, its effect limited by what is in the poem itself.

We are going to discuss four poems, one of which you have seen briefly before. The purpose will be to establish what the poem means to you as an individual reader. What the poem means to me will be offered as a springboard to your own interpretation.

Let's begin. Here is the poem by Stephen Crane. Read it again, carefully.

> I saw a man pursuing the horizon;
> Round and round they sped.
> I was disturbed at this;
> I accosted the man.
> "It is futile," I said,
> "You can never — "
>
> "You lie," he cried,
> And ran on.

What is the tone of this poem?

Pessimistic. **page 314**

Sardonic. **page 317**

One of puzzlement. **page 322**

[*from page 315 or 325*]

YOUR ANSWER: Yes. The poem symbolizes imperfection.

Right. Wouldn't the tone, therefore the theme, have been entirely different if the poem had ended thus:

> "You lie," he cried,
> And ran on.
> Fool!

Not only the length but the meter as well is seen to diminish as the poem progresses, but because a final, single beat is missing, the poem appears to hang at the end, intentionally incomplete, as if the poet were not at all certain of his attitude toward the man and his determination. Thus the poem, as an organic unity, shows Crane's reaction to an unanswerable question: "Why strive for the impossible?"

The shape of a poem is not only symbolic; it is also functional. I promised earlier, when discussing E. E. Cummings, to make a further inspection of the recent emphasis on projected sound. The next poem you will see is by Lawrence Ferlinghetti. Read it aloud, pausing at the end of each line, imagining if you can some form of modern music as background. Let the sound and rhythm predominate at first; then read it again aloud, concentrating on meaning.

Please go on to page 316.

[*from page 312*]

YOUR ANSWER: The tone of this poem is pessimistic.

Do you really think so? Tone, you remember, is the attitude of the poet toward his subject, and I think you have failed to apply this definition to the poem.

We established early that the main symbol, the man chasing the horizon, represented futile determination; this is also the subject. Look at the poem again:

I saw a man pursuing the horizon;
Round and round they sped.
I was disturbed at this;
I accosted the man.
"It is futile," I said,
"You can never — "

"You lie," he cried,
And ran on.

Do not confuse the attitude of the "I" in the poem with that of the poet later; the two men are poles apart. The "I" says that the runner's determination is futile, expressing the all-too-common attitude toward that which man fails to understand. One might accuse the "I" of being pessimistic (and make certain you know what the word means), but not the poet looking at the entire scene much later. The poet sees both the runner and the "I" (perhaps himself at an earlier time), showing by his handling of both men a much broader understanding than he possessed before. The attitude of the poet toward himself (the "I") is not the same as his attitude toward the subject: futile determination.

Notice what the poem shows the "I" doing. He watches, is disturbed, accosts the runner, tells him his chase is futile, and is rebuffed. The subject, futile determination, results from what we see happening, but the tone of the poem is a product of the poet's attitude, not only toward the runner, but toward himself as well.

Return to page 312, reread the poem, and select another answer.

[*from page 325*]

YOUR ANSWER: No. In modern poetry the shape is incidental.

I'm afraid we part company here.

When I talk of shape, I refer to the impression the poem makes on my eye, nothing more. If you say that in modern poetry all shape is incidental, you may be missing something important. There is much "pictorial" poetry in our time: thin poems, round poems, poems about Christmas which look like a Christmas tree, and so on. Any element of a poem which adds to its meaning is worth considering. The shape of Crane's poem is, you must admit, not standard. Stephen Crane was one of the first American users of the French symbolist technique, which derived from Mallarmé, Valéry, Rimbaud, and others. Many Crane poems have interesting shapes, punctuations, and word placements.

I would guess that Crane might have intended a final, ironic comment in this poem, but may have realized that he was attempting to define the undefinable, to limit the infinite. It is as if the poet, recognizing his own inability to understand man's incessant pursuit of the unattainable, understood at the same time the impossibility of anyone's ever defining it. So he stopped writing, leaving a poem which is roughly the shape of an incomplete, unfinished right triangle. Thus the poem becomes a visual symbol as well, and as such it pleases me more.

So accept for the moment that there may be meaning in the shape and go on to page 313.

[*from page 313*]

I cannot help but think
that their 'reality'
was almost as real as
my memory of today

when the last sun hung on the hills
and I heard the day falling
like the gulls that fell
almost to land

while the last picnickers lay
and loved in the blowing yellow broom
resisted and resisting
tearing themselves apart

again

again

until the last hot hung climax
which could at last no longer be resisted
made them moan

And night's trees stood up

Let's first approach it conventionally. What two elements are being compared?

Life and death. **page 318**

Sunrise and sunset. **page 321**

Paintings and an experience. **page 324**

[*from page 312*]

YOUR ANSWER: The tone of this poem is sardonic.

You have missed a very important distinction made between the attitude of the "I" and the runner. You may not be certain of the meaning of the word "sardonic," so look it up now.

Here is the poem again:

I saw a man pursuing the horizon;
Round and round they sped.
I was disturbed at this;
I accosted the man.
"It is futile," I said,
"You can never — "

"You lie," he cried,
And ran on.

Notice how the "I," disturbed, accosts the runner. Does he yell at the man? Sneer at him? No, the poet tells us, the "I" *says* to the runner, "It is futile, . . . you can never — " perhaps with an all-knowing shrug of the shoulders. We might call this attitude of the "I" pessimistic, but only toward what he sees the runner doing. Following this, the runner cries out, hurrying on. See the difference? The "I" says; the runner cries. Thus an important distinction is made.

Do not, however, accept either of these attitudes as that of the poet, the creator of the poem. He stands apart, looking at the entire scene: the chase, the dialogue, and yes, perhaps at himself as a younger man. He may now perhaps accept futile determination, but I doubt if he understands it better. Do you? Why do some men strive against the impossible, reach for the inaccessible, hope for the unattainable? How do you feel toward a man whose quest (you think) is futile? Can you admire his effort? Do you envy him? Or are you like the "I" of the poem, unaccepting, pessimistic, and aloof, preferring only that which is within easy reach?

When you reread the poem, analyze your answer to the above questions; then you should be able to see the attitude of the poet toward his subject.

Return to page 312 and try again.

[*from page 316*]

YOUR ANSWER: *Life and death* are being compared.

Life, yes, but where is death?

You have jumped to a conclusion which is in no way justified by the poem, one which perhaps appeals to you but which is hardly the concern of the poet.

When you reread, imagine that the poet is pointing at two different scenes: the first he describes, then questions; the second he talks of as having happened "today."

Return to page 316, identify the two scenes, and select another answer.

[*from page 325*]

YOUR ANSWER: I don't know whether the shape contributes to the meaning.

Many years ago I learned of an answer a famous poet is reported to have given to the question "What did you mean by the rock you used in such-and-such a poem?" The poet replied, "A rock." Likewise, Ernest Hemingway once said (with regard to *The Old Man and the Sea*) that even though he tried to create real things and real people, if he made them "real enough and true enough, then they could mean many things."

Mean many things to whom? You, of course, the reader. How? Simple. You must first accept art for what it is: something made by man. See it this way in the beginning, not considering purpose or theme or even subject, but as the work of an artisan, put in front of you for appraisal.

I ask the above questions to introduce this point: to appreciate any work of art you must accept it as it is, letting your emotion and intellect react in any way they want to. A horror movie, seen again and again, loses the appeal of shock and surprise. Yet it still has value to persons who wish to investigate why and how it affected them the first time.

I did not even consider shape in Crane's poem until after I had read it perhaps thirty times, so don't feel left out if you cannot see the relationship between shape, theme, and tone. To me, the poem looks like a rough, incomplete right triangle.

XXXXXXXXXXXX
XXXXXXXXXX
XXXXXXXX
XXXXXX
XXXX
XX

Perhaps you might call it a spearhead with a broken tip. In either instance, the shape implies incompleteness.

Can the poet offer an answer to the obvious question, "Is the runner's determination futile?" The "I" of the poem thinks so, but by the time he, as poet, writes the poem, he is not quite so sure of himself.

We will see shape complementing meaning in the next poem as well. Go on to page 313.

[*from page 322*]

YOUR ANSWER: He is disturbed.

Wrong. You read too fast. We are interested here in the *initial* attitude of the "I," not in his final one. Reread the first two lines again:

I saw a man pursuing the horizon;
Round and round they sped.

How many times do "they" speed around before the "I" acts? Just once? Or isn't it true that the "I" stands still for a while, watching, before he accosts the runner. I hardly think we should assume the "I" is immediately disturbed.

Return to page 322, reread the poem, and choose another answer.

[*from page 316*]

YOUR ANSWER: *Sunrise and sunset* are being compared.

Sunset is discussed in the poem, but not sunrise.
Return to page 316, reread the poem, and try again.

[*from page 312*]

YOUR ANSWER: The tone of the poem is one of puzzlement.

Right, but I cannot help feeling that you may have arrived here with distinct reservations. Perhaps a review is in order. Unless you can recognize that there are actually *three* characters in this poem, I suggest you turn to page 314 and read the discussion before continuing. (Don't forget to mark your place.)

Still a bit confused? I'm not surprised. Do me a favor, after which you should be able to see how subject, tone, style, and theme all contribute to meaning. Begin by visualizing the action: the "I" is watching the runner, and the poet observes both men as if through the wrong end of a telescope.

Put yourself in the place of the "I." Have you not at least once attempted to set someone straight, someone you knew to be wrong? Did you succeed in convincing him of his error, or did he perhaps comment on your ignorance of the facts or tell you to keep your nose out of his business? How did you feel?

The "I" undergoes a similar experience. Rebuffed, he sees the runner speed away on his futile chase. By understanding why the poet presents the action as he does, we approach the meaning of the poem.

Read the poem again.

I saw a man pursuing the horizon;
Round and round they sped.
I was disturbed at this;
I accosted the man.
"It is futile," I said,
"You can never — "

"You lie," he cried,
And ran on.

How does the "I" react to his *first* sight of the man running after the horizon?

He is disturbed. **page 320**

He does nothing. **page 325**

He tries to stop the runner. **page 333**

[*from page 329*]

YOUR ANSWER: Sorolla belonged to the Realist school of painting.

Before you read another line, define *realism.*

Can you do it?

Now — here is my definition. Realism denotes an attempt to reproduce faithfully what the author believes most men usually see, feel, hear, taste, or touch. Notice the emphasis on the majority. A realistic writer identifies his impressions with those of everyone else; hence he writes for others, trying to create for them what he thinks they sense all along.

Remember my earlier comments on realism? A work can technically be realistic even if each character does not brush his teeth every morning, does not have breakfast, or is not shown coming home from work at the usual time. But what the art does show must not distort what the majority sees. William Dean Howells, considered one of the great American "realists," never used a love scene. "There'll be no fumbling on my couches," he is supposed to have said. Is this realism?

Regardless of your definition, remember that any example of it must conform. Is there any evidence in Ferlinghetti's poem that Sorolla is a realist? You have chosen one word in the poem — the poet's comment on "reality" — and come to an unjustified conclusion. Return to page 329, reread the poem, and select another answer.

[*from page 316*]

YOUR ANSWER: *Paintings and an experience* are being compared.

Right. The paintings? According to Ferlinghetti, they are beach scenes by Sarolla [sic]. (Ferlinghetti seems to be referring to the many paintings of similar scenes by Joaquin Sorolla y Bastida, a Spaniard who lived from 1863 to 1923.)

And the experience? The poet's "memory of today," the sight of picnickers making love in the late afternoon.

We should begin to look at more than one poem at a time, so I ask you to remember (and, if necessary, refresh your memory by rereading the poems) the views of Auden in "Musée des Beaux Arts" (page 111) and Graves in "On Dwelling" (page 249). Both of these poems consider illusion and reality, one discussing the selectivity of art and its rendering of truth, the other deciding that what we see around us is illusion, what we have in our intellect, reality.

The same considerations are apparent in Ferlinghetti's poem, but how different the approach and appearance are!

What Ferlinghetti does is create a poem which requires an additional ingredient, the sound of the human voice. Watch. I'll rearrange the words into what we might call conventional order.

> Sarolla's women in their picture hats,
> Stretched upon his canvas beaches,
> Beguiled the Spanish Impressionists.
> And were they fraudulent pictures of the world,
> The way the light played on them,
> Creating illusions of love?

You can't help noticing the difference.

I will not attempt to define what it is that causes this poem to lose its vitality when rearranged; I will point out, however, the obvious shifts in emphasis produced when the poem is compressed. We habitually tend to stress the words which begin and end a line, often overlooking what lies in between. Ferlinghetti will not tolerate this, forcing us by internal pauses to emphasize only what he wants us to.

Please go on to page 326.

[*from page 322*]

YOUR ANSWER: He does nothing.

Right. The dialogue occurs after the "I," as if viewing an automobile race on a circular track, has watched the man and the horizon speeding "round and round."

Notice how the "I" reacts after watching for a while. He is "disturbed." Again, he is not particularly upset at *what* the man is doing but at the reason behind the chase. He "accosts" the man. He makes a straightforward, unemotional statement. Contrast his "It is futile" with the runner's "You lie." Is there not a difference between the two men, one stating what to him is fact, the other crying out emotionally?

Here is the poem again.

I saw a man pursuing the horizon;
Round and round they sped.
I was disturbed at this;
I accosted the man.
"It is futile," I said,
"You can never — "

"You lie," he cried,
And ran on.

Study the shape of the poem. Notice how it tapers off, starting with a long line and ending with a short one. Does this suggest anything to you? If we assume that the poet does not become puzzled until after the experience, does the shape of the poem contribute in any way to its meaning?

Yes. The poem symbolizes imperfection. **page 313**

No. In modern poetry the shape is incidental. **page 315**

I don't know. **page 319**

[*from page 324*]

Many poets use the *caesura*, but, as I have mentioned before, punctuation creates not only a break in sound but one in meaning as well, definitely destroying continuity when overused. Ferlinghetti avoids over-punctuating, preferring to let shape and size of the lines determine the sound. Furthermore, notice when reading this poem aloud how your breathing is controlled for you. You are not forced, as you may have been elsewhere, to take a required breath because you are turning blue in the face, thereby breaking the flow of meaning or sound. Your breathing has been established for you by the required pauses. Pleasing sounds are nice, but lest I be accused of exalting this poem dishonestly, let me initiate a comparison. Read stanza 2 of "Musée des Beaux Arts" (page 111), then reread the beginning of Ferlinghetti's poem.

Sarolla's women in their picture hats
stretched upon his canvas beaches
beguiled the Spanish
Impressionists

And were they fraudulent pictures
of the world
the way the light played on them
creating illusions
of love?

Whose art can you see more clearly, Brueghel's or Sorolla's? (From now on I'll use the correct spelling.)

Brueghel's. **page 328**

Sorolla's. **page 334**

[*from page 329*]

YOUR ANSWER: Sorolla belonged to the Impressionist school of painting.

You are here for one of two reasons: either you know who Sorolla is or you jumped to a conclusion which can be refuted by reference to the poem. Can you define *Impressionism?* If not, how can you identify anyone as a member of this school? Everyone seems to have a slightly different approach, but all definitions seem to begin with the *impression* of reality as apprehended by the artist. To me, an Impressionist is primarily concerned with what *he* sees, not with what anyone else tells him he is supposed to see. I hinted at this term on page 27; perhaps you might review my comments there. The term *Impressionist* was imposed from without by those who did not agree with what the artist accepted as reality.

The artist may see the object of his art in a manner we might call impressionistic, but to him what he sees is real. Even though each medium of art, sculpture, painting, poetry, fiction, amends this initial approach according to its special needs, the basic requirement is unchanged. An Impressionist is concerned with reality as *he* sees it, not as he is told he should see it.

Look at the poem again. Perhaps you made a decision which is not justified by the evidence shown in the poem itself. Forget what you might like to see in the poem and concentrate on what is there. Return to page 329, reread the poem, and select another answer.

[*from page 326*]

YOUR ANSWER: I can see Brueghel's art more clearly.

I agree. Sorolla's paintings appear only as commented upon; Brueghel's art is described for us.

Think for a minute: would the technique used by Auden have been more satisfactory here? Or are we being dishonest in even considering the question? Do you think Ferlinghetti should have made us see Sorolla's art, or has he shown us just enough? Consider your answer carefully, then continue.

Two of the critic's worst vices are suggesting improvements and name-calling. I indulge in the first when I say, "The poet should have done this or that"; I use the second when I imply that the artist must be stupid not to have asked my advice. I don't especially admire either view. Why? Because I am concerned only with the poem, not the personality of the author. I might, for instance, say that Ferlinghetti is a better poet than he is an art critic, but here I would have to justify my belief only from the evidence in the poem.

Please go on to page 329.

[*from page 283*]

Would I be justified? Forget the poet as a personality; concentrate on the "I" of the poem.

Sarolla's women in their picture hats
stretched upon his canvas beaches
beguiled the Spanish
Impressionists
And were they fraudulent pictures
of the world
the way the light played on them
creating illusions
of love?

I cannot help but think
that their 'reality'
was almost as real as
my memory of today

when the last sun hung on the hills
and I heard the day falling
like the gulls that fell
almost to land

while the last picnickers lay
and loved in the blowing yellow broom
resisted and resisting
tearing themselves apart

again

again

until the last hot hung climax
which could at last no longer be resisted
made them moan

And night's trees stood up

To what school of painting did Sorolla belong?

Realist. **page 323**

Impressionist. **page 327**

I don't know. **page 337**

[*from page 337*]

YOUR ANSWER: *Beguile* means "deceive."

You are right, but you are using the original meaning, not the one I think Ferlinghetti intends. Gradually the word has lost the early connotation of deception in favor of *delightful* deception. Nowadays a beguiling little girl is one who delights us with her coquetry, her vivacity, even though we know her motives are fraudulent. As for women? I think Louis Simpson, in "A Woman Too Well Remembered," answered this question for us.

Actually, we have three possibilities inherent in this one word; it can mean "deceit," "delight," or both, and I would applaud the poet's cleverness if he used both meanings simultaneously. I cannot do so, however, because of the context. Everything points to Sorolla's having *delighted* the Spanish Impressionists, even though members of an opposing school of art might have called his paintings fraudulent and unreal.

Remember the word "context," and read accordingly from now on. Your dictionary reflects primarily what was, not what now may be. Dictionaries are hard-pressed to keep up with connotative changes, and by the time a word has been assigned a formal, dictionary meaning, common usage may have altered it still further.

We must not, however, excuse a poet who fails to use the particular word which precisely denotes what he wants the reader to sense or imagine. A great poem is as flawless as a perfect gem.

Please go on to page 331.

[*from page 330 or 335*]

Back to the poem.

Sarolla's women in their picture hats
stretched upon his canvas beaches
beguiled the Spanish
Impressionists
And were they fraudulent pictures
of the world
the way the light played on them
creating illusions
of love?
I cannot help but think
that their 'reality'
was almost as real as
my memory of today

when the last sun hung on the hills
and I heard the day falling
like the gulls that fell
almost to land

while the last picnickers lay
and loved in the blowing yellow broom
resisted and resisting
tearing themselves apart

again

again

until the last hot hung climax
which could at last no longer be resisted
made them moan

And night's trees stood up

What is the poem's subject?

Reality versus illusion. **page 339**

Art and life. **page 343**

Love. **page 350**

[*from page 351*]

YOUR ANSWER: Modern love is tender and meaningful.

'Twould be nice, if 'twere so. Unfortunately, the poem does not show this at all. We cannot help wishing, though, and perhaps this quality of love is what we most desire. Maybe the poet himself wishes along with us, but again, not in this poem.

Let the words of a poem, not your imagination, tell you what the poem says. What are the lovers seen doing? Are they gazing quietly into each other's eyes, lost in the dewy essence of a spring morning? Hardly. They are seen "resisted and resisting/ tearing themselves apart." Just once? No — "again . . . again," and when finally they are unable to resist, what happens? Cries of pleasure? Not at all. They moan.

What do their moans signify to you? There is a word which fits.

Return to page 351, reread the poem, and select another answer.

[*from page 322*]

YOUR ANSWER: He tries to stop the runner.

Perhaps *you* might, but the "I" does not, at least at first. By reading into the poem an action which is not there, you make too hasty an interpretation.

When you reread the poem, try to establish its time sequence.

Return to page 322, reread the poem, and try again.

[*from page 326*]

YOUR ANSWER: I can see Sorolla's art more clearly.

I hesitate to challenge your impressions of art, but I must at least tell you why I see Brueghel's painting more clearly than I do Sorolla's.

Ferlinghetti gives us only a passing glimpse of beaches and women, hardly describing Sorolla's art but merely mentioning that such scenes exist. The paintings are presented; they do appear to be "fraudulent pictures of the world." Notice, I am not comparing Sorolla's art with Brueghel's, rather, Ferlinghetti's and Auden's methods of presentation.

Now look at *The Fall of Icarus*. You can see the ship, the ploughman, the boy disappearing into the sea. Auden has discussed suffering; his description underlines it. We not only see the painting; we know what it is supposed to mean.

If you believe that impressionism better depicts reality, more power to you (I agree, by the way). But we are concerned here with what the poets describe, not with schools of painting.

Return to page 326 and select the other answer.

[*from page 337*]

YOUR ANSWER: *Beguile* means "delight."

You have selected the definition I think Ferlinghetti is using, but technically you are wrong. Although *beguile* does have as a primary definition in many dictionaries the connotation of "delight," this meaning is rather new (and perhaps unfortunate). Actually, *beguile* means "deceive." Louis Simpson wrote of a beguiling woman in "A Woman Too Well Remembered."

Thus we have the word *beguile* with two meanings, each of which sends the poem in a different direction. Or is Ferlinghetti being extremely clever and consistent in using both meanings simultaneously? We have observed this technique before. Can you see an intentional pun here? I cannot, and for this reason consider Ferlinghetti's use of the word unnecessarily confusing.

Please go on to page 331.

[*from page 342*]

YOUR ANSWER: The tone of the poem is *ragingly angry.*

Right. This is the last definite assumption you will be asked to make about this poem. Read it aloud again, this time imagining that you have been slighted by a person you love, that this person has abruptly refused you something you considered extremely important. Growl out the words, sneer, show as much hate as you can, and listen to what results.

Not from This Anger

Not from this anger, anticlimax after
Refusal struck her loin and the lame flower
Bent like a beast to lap the singular floods
In a land strapped by hunger
Shall she receive a bellyful of weeds
And bear those tendril hands I touch across
The agonized, two seas.

Behind my head a square of sky sags over
The circular smile tossed from lover to lover
And the golden ball spins out of the skies;
Not from this anger after
Refusal struck like a bell under water
Shall her smile breed that mouth, behind the mirror,
That burns along my eyes.

Now what? We agree that the poet is angry at a woman, but we are not certain why. Perhaps you already think you understand the poem, too, but you really don't. By the time we are done with this poem you should be thoroughly confused, as I think Thomas intended you should be. Is there any possibility that the "I" is standing in a bathroom or bedroom?

Yes. **page 354**

No. **page 352**

[*from page 329*]

YOUR ANSWER: I don't know what school of painting Sorolla belonged to.

I don't know, either, from the context of this poem, and this may be a detriment to an excellent poem. Ferlinghetti knows (I hope), but he has not communicated this knowledge to the reader. (If you wish definitions of impressionism and realism, see pages 323 and 327.)

I am not really bothered by the use in the poem of the term *Impressionist*, followed by the word *reality*. These are conventional, even if they are subject to violent argument. What bothers me is the poet's use of *beguiled*, and I wish to pause over this one word in order to point out a characteristic of contemporary poetry which must be understood before we go any farther.

You will remember my earlier remarks on the modern poet's distrust of many traditional absolutes: faith, science, God, peace, truth, reality, and so on. We live in a period of constant change (analyze the paradoxical effect of the two previous words), and we must understand that not only things and concepts change but also the means of discussion — the words themselves. If you have never consulted the Oxford English Dictionary (available in most public and school libraries) and discovered the history of a word or phrase, you have missed a fascinating experience. Pick any common word and see how its meaning has varied through the years. You will be astonished, I assure you. Look up *baggage*, for instance.

No matter what the original meaning of a word, however, a poet normally adheres to the meaning accepted by his age, and this why I have trouble with *beguile*. Look it up. What does the word mean?

"Deceive." **page 330**

"Delight." **page 335**

[*from page 342*]

YOUR ANSWER: The tone of the poem is *regretful.*

Wrong.

Isn't this comment mild? Or did you choose it as a last resort. Perhaps you are having difficulty with the tone because you cannot pin down the subject of the poem. If this is the case, you are not alone.

When reading Thomas, don't try to paraphrase. Usually, you just can't. I doubt seriously if many of his poems will ever be understood once and for all, mainly because they contain conflicting impressions, disparate images, and references which at first seem obvious, then become vague and obscure.

Look at stanza 1 again:

> Not from this anger, anticlimax after
> Refusal struck her loin and the lame flower
> Bent like a beast to lap the singular floods
> In a land strapped by hunger
> Shall she receive a bellyful of weeds
> And bear those tendril hands I touch across
> The agonized, two seas.

Notice that there are only two commas in the first seven lines. Read the stanza aloud again, pausing only (and taking a deep breath) after the word *anger*. Try various inflections, determining which one best fits the use of the words *anger*, *refusal*, *struck*, *lame*, *beast*, *strapped*, *bellyful*, and *agonized*.

When you have finished, return to page 342 and try again.

[*from page 331*]

YOUR ANSWER: *Reality versus illusion* is the poem's subject.

The poem may be about reality versus illusion if you wish. But read what follows.

Robert Graves discussed reality by showing first what was unreal, then by suggesting a "dwelling," his imagination, which by contrast became more real than anything sensible. Does Ferlinghetti do this? Certainly he uses the word *real* in various ways throughout the poem, but isn't he usually commenting on something else? He mentions the "reality" of Sorolla's possible illusions of love, adding that the paintings were "almost as real" as the memory he then describes.

The subject of a poem can be thought of as the subject of a sentence; in the sentence, the verb and all other words tell you something about the subject. Here I regard reality as a modifier, but not what the poet is writing about.

For my sake, return to page 331, reread the poem, and try again.

[*from page 351*]

YOUR ANSWER: Modern love is frustrating.

Right. So Ferlinghetti believes. The lovers are seen "tearing themselves apart, . . . resisted and resisting," at last unable to resist any longer. There is a frustrating urgency present here which must be recognized.

Does "love" exist for Ferlinghetti? Is it "real"? I think so, but not perhaps as the picnickers see it. Why picnickers, by the way? Would you consider a picnic an escape from something — the city, everyday life, or perhaps reality itself? Do the picnickers understand the nature of their love?

Ferlinghetti talks of rather commonplace subjects, giving them new life through the way he presents them. In this poem, for instance, he first shows his subject, love, as a possible illusion seen in an Impressionist painting; then he comments that the "reality" of the paintings was "almost as real" as his "memory of today." Finally, by describing his memory of picnickers making love, he implies that there is, after all, an inescapable, urgent, frustrating love which much be recognized, even if not always understood.

But look *how* he presents it.

Here is the last section again, the description of his "memory of today."

when the last sun hung on the hills
and I heard the day falling
like the gulls that fell
almost to land

while the last picnickers lay
and loved in the blowing yellow broom
resisted and resisting
tearing themselves apart
again
again
until the last hot hung climax
which could at last no longer be resisted
made them moan

And night's trees stood up

Please go on to page 341.

[*from page 340*]

If you could not accept my belief that shape contributes to meaning in Crane's poem, perhaps you will at least agree now that Ferlinghetti not only talks about the falling day, but also shows it. Again we have an imperfect triangle, this time containing the discussion of day's end. But does any day really end, once and for all? Perhaps to us, standing in one place, it appears to. Actually you could consider one day as an unchanging absolute, moving over the face of the earth, showing itself to everyone at different times. The sun appears to be hung on the hills, much like the permanently fixed gulls which fall "almost to land" in Sorolla's painting. (Compare this with the "hung climax" at the end.) Ferlinghetti suspends motion for us, just as the painter does. And the shape suggests precisely what the poet is talking about — something (day) which becomes less . . . less . . . and less, but never reaches the ultimate of nothing.

Read more Ferlinghetti. He is an important contemporary voice.

Go on to page 342.

[*from page 341*]

Critics who insist upon concrete, paraphrasable content in poetry are just as misled as those who require obscurity. I mentioned earlier that a poem can be a catalyst, something which creates a reaction. Dylan Thomas' poetry acts this way, suggesting but never defining, evoking but not limiting. When you read the following poem, try first to determine the tone; then we will be able to discuss further.

Not from This Anger

Not from this anger, anticlimax after
Refusal struck her loin and the lame flower
Bent like a beast to lap the singular floods
In a land strapped by hunger
Shall she receive a bellyful of weeds
And bear those tendril hands I touch across
The agonized, two seas.

Behind my head a square of sky sags over
The circular smile tossed from lover to lover
And the golden ball spins out of the skies;
Not from this anger after
Refusal struck like a bell under water
Shall her smile breed that mouth, behind the mirror,
That burns along my eyes.

First, what is the tone of this poem?

Ragingly angry. **page 336**

Regretful. **page 338**

Bitter and resentful. **page 345**

[*from page 331*]

YOUR ANSWER: *Art and life* is the subject of the poem.

I don't think a distinction is made between the two, certainly not like the one Auden made in "Musée des Beaux Arts." The discussion of Sorolla's art is primarily an introduction to what really concerns the poet, his "memory of today." When you reread the poem, concentrate on the latter part first. Identify what the basis of the "memory" is, then see if there is any similarity between this memory and the illusion created by Sorolla's art. The subject of this poem is common to both.

Return to page 331, reread the poem, and select another answer.

[*from page 354*]

YOUR ANSWER: Giving up, as in *striking the colors.*

Why not? Something has been refused the poet, thereby causing his anger. Look at the line in which the word occurs:

Refusal struck her loin and the lame flower

Perhaps the concept of refusal itself caused her loin to give up, to surrender its function, thereby denying the poet what he most wanted. If a man desires a fight and his opponent refuses to fight, would this not be cause for anger?

Return to page 354 and try again.

[*from page 342*]

YOUR ANSWER: The tone of the poem is *bitter and resentful.*

Wrong.

Perhaps the main reason I like Thomas so much is his ability to affect each reader differently. Certainly there is an element of bitterness here, and obviously the poet resents something or someone. But is this all? Perhaps you have identified a bitter and resentful tone either from a silent reading or by dwelling too long on stanza 2.

I'd like you to reread the poem, this time aloud. Forget about the subject (whatever it may be) and concentrate on the words.

Please go on to page 348.

[*from page 354*]

YOUR ANSWER: Hitting, like a boxer *striking his opponent.*

I think this connotation is entirely possible. When talking of the effect of a hurricane, would we not be concerned with what happened after the storm struck the mainland? The poet is angry; this we know, and isn't it conceivable that he is furious at the act of refusal itself, a refusal which struck the woman who appears to be the object of his anger, thereby preventing her from satisfying his desires? If a person cheats you of something, is not your ire also directed at the act of cheating itself? Of course it is.

Return to 354, reread the word in context, and try again.

[*from page 351*]

YOUR ANSWER: Modern love is free love, and Ferlinghetti believes in it because he is a member of the Beat Generation.

Wrong, I'm afraid.

Ferlinghetti does not consider himself a member of the Beat Generation; neither does he subscribe to the Beat poets' apparent conviction that atomic destruction is inevitable, that the world is in a sorry state, and that drugs and sensual experience provide an escape from everyday horrors.

Ferlinghetti is a serious artist. Perhaps he is also just beginning to show what he is capable of writing. As for "free love," I'm afraid this term does not exist in the contemporary vocabulary. I have not heard or read it for years. It is a link with the past. Concentrate on the poem, please, not on hearsay.

Return to page 351, reread the poem, and try again.

[*from page 345*]

Not from This Anger

Not from this anger, anticlimax after
Refusal struck her loin and the lame flower
Bent like a beast to lap the singular floods
In a land strapped by hunger
Shall she receive a bellyful of weeds
And bear those tendril hands I touch across
The agonized, two seas.

Behind my head a square of sky sags over
The circular smile tossed from lover to lover
And the golden ball spins out of the skies;
Not from this anger after
Refusal struck like a bell under water
Shall her smile breed that mouth, behind the mirror,
That burns along my eyes.

Now read it again. Note that the presence of only two commas in the first stanza forces you to read most of the lines in one burst. The poem does slow down slightly in stanza 2, becoming less violent, but when we look for tone we should consider the entire poem, not just part of it. Here I would not agree that there is a difference between the attitude of the "I" toward the cause of his anger and the attitude of the poet toward the "I."

Whom does he snarl at? Someone who has made him angry. *She* — a woman is making him furious. She is the subject, and the tone should now be obvious.

Return to page 342, reread the poem, and try again.

[*from page 354*]

YOUR ANSWER: Ringing, like a clock *striking the hour*.

Careful, you are not considering the word in the context of stanza 1. In stanza 2, the poet says:

Not from this anger after
Refusal struck like a bell under water

This repetition of word and idea is a favorite Thomas device. Not apparent at first, the implication of bell-ringing is obvious in stanza 2; when we reread, we see that the refusal Thomas mentions could also have "struck like a bell under water" in stanza 1, permeating "her loin" and causing the act of refusal which angers the poet.

Return to page 354, reread the word in context, and try again.

[*from page 331*]

YOUR ANSWER: *Love* is the subject of the poem.

Right. This poem is about love and man's understanding of it. Read the poem again.

Sarolla's women in their picture hats
stretched upon his canvas beaches
beguiled the Spanish
Impressionists
And were they fraudulent pictures
of the world
the way the light played on them
creating illusions
of love?
I cannot help but think
that their 'reality'
was almost as real as
my memory of today
when the last sun hung on the hills
and I heard the day falling
like the gulls that fell
almost to land
while the last picnickers lay
and loved in the blowing yellow broom
resisted and resisting
tearing themselves apart
again
again
until the last hot hung climax
which could at last no longer be resisted
made them moan
And night's trees stood up

Please go on to page 351.

[*from page 350*]

You should be able to see the difference between Auden's use of suffering in his poem and Ferlinghetti's approach to love here. Remember what we decided about suffering in the Auden poem, that it was not investigated or discussed, but merely accepted and used as a vehicle for an inspection of the creative process? And didn't we see Graves, in his poem "On Dwelling," using urbanization only as a springboard to the subject, reality itself?

Let's presume for the moment that Sorolla presents a "picture of the world" which has in it "illusions of love." Accepting Ferlinghetti's belief that the "women . . . stretched upon . . . canvas beaches" may represent illusions of love, what does the poet show to be an inescapable reality of modern love?

Modern love is tender and meaningful. **page 332**

Modern love is frustrating. **page 340**

Modern love is free love, and Ferlinghetti believes in it because he is a member of the Beat Generation. **page 347**

[*from page 336*]

YOUR ANSWER: No, there is no possibility that the "I" is standing in a bathroom or bedroom.

Why not? In order to say that a person is not doing something, shouldn't you be required to offer an alternative? Can you do this from the poem? Do you have any idea where the poet definitely is?

Again, the problem with most Thomas poems is precisely their frustrating, kaleidoscopic inconclusiveness. You feel that there must be something concrete behind the poem, yet you rarely can identify just what it is. You see a little part of everything at once. And you often feel that Thomas is leaving out perhaps the one word which would create the perfection you can identify in many other poems.

For all I know, the poet might be standing on his head under water. I mentioned the bathroom or bedroom because of the mirror reference in stanza 2. If I were to think and say what the poet appears to be doing, there might be a mirror in front of me. Return to page 336, reread the poem with this possibility in mind, and select the other answer.

[*from page 354*]

YOUR ANSWER: Quitting, as in *striking for higher pay.*

You should not miss this connotation. How does management feel when labor walks off the job without notice? Happy? Hardly, and this meaning of the word should be recognized if you are to appreciate how deftly Thomas manipulates meaning.

Return to page 354, reread the word in context, and try again.

[*from page 336*]

YOUR ANSWER: Yes, there is a possibility that the "I" is standing in a bathroom or bedroom.

Of course there is. In Thomas' poetry, anything is possible. My impression is that he is standing in front of a mirror, and most mirrors are seen in either bathrooms or bedrooms, and he is speaking for the benefit of his reflection.

Something about a woman, and the poet is angry. In the first line he says, "Not from this anger . . ." will anything happen. You may stress any word; the meaning is still basically the same. His anger is anticlimactic, occurring after "Refusal struck her loin . . ."

Lines 2 through 4 appear to describe what caused his anger.

Not from this anger, anticlimax after
Refusal struck her loin and the lame flower
Bent like a beast to lap the singular floods
In a land strapped by hunger

Which of the following is not a possible connotation of the word *struck* when seen in context?

Giving up, as in *striking the colors*. **page 344**

Hitting, like a boxer *striking his opponent*. **page 346**

Ringing, like a clock *striking the hour*. **page 349**

Quitting, as in *striking for higher pay*. **page 353**

All of the above are correct. **page 356**

[*from page 356*]

All of which brings up the question, "What was refused?" Read the poem again.

Not from This Anger

Not from this anger, anticlimax after
Refusal struck her loin and the lame flower
Bent like a beast to lap the singular floods
In a land strapped by hunger
Shall she receive a bellyful of weeds
And bear those tendril hands I touch across
The agonized, two seas.

Behind my head a square of sky sags over
The circular smile tossed from lover to lover
And the golden ball spins out of the skies;
Not from this anger after
Refusal struck like a bell under water
Shall her smile breed that mouth, behind the mirror,
That burns along my eyes.

Assuming first that the woman was responsible, what did she refuse the "I" of the poem?

Sexual love. **page 360**

Truthfulness. **page 362**

I haven't the slightest idea. **page 365**

[*from page 354*]

YOUR ANSWER: All of the above are correct.

Right. Here is where Thomas excels. His ability to create consistent interweaving of meaning and sound is rarely surpassed in contemporary poetry. As soon as you think you have grasped one meaning, another suggests itself.

For example, whose "refusal" is it, the woman's or the poet's?

> Refusal struck her loin . . .

If you read the meaning of *hitting* into the word, then the refusal may have been administered from without to the woman. But if you subscribe to the *giving-up* connotation, then it was the woman herself who refused.

You wonder about the bell-ringing? Look at the use of the word later:

> Not from this anger after
> Refusal struck like a bell under water
> Shall her smile . . .

Is the refusal being "struck like a bell," or is the poet talking about anger resulting from refusal which itself did the striking? Reread carefully, and you should see that both interpretations work.

Go on to page 355.

[*from page 368*]

YOUR ANSWER: He will never see the woman again.

You may be thinking too specifically, but I would not say that this answer is impossible. I doubt if the poet wants to see her again on the same basis as before, but I don't think he is definitely ruling out the possibility. Do you recall Simpson's "A Woman Too Well Remembered"? We assumed that his physical relationship with her no longer existed, yet he ended by saying, "When I think of her, other faces fade." For Thomas, has not the thought of what happened served to create as well as intensify his rage? What good would not seeing the woman be if memory could produce such a reaction?

When you look at the lines again, try to extend your thinking as far as possible, keeping in mind the pomposity of the pronouncement. How far is as angry a man as this one willing to go in vowing for the future? Return to page 368, and select another answer.

[*from page 360*]

YOUR ANSWER: "She" will not become pregnant by him.

Right. Isn't this a rather ridiculous idea? How can she, if either he is incapable or she is unwilling? One should never overlook the humorous element in Thomas' poetry. There are few great artists who cannot laugh at themselves. I think Thomas may be laughing here over his initial rage and is able to see himself in perspective.

Perhaps we do see a further extension of tone, this time in the attitude of the poet toward himself.

The woman will not "bear" (give birth to or carry away with her) what the poet refers to as "those tendril hands I touch." What are the "tendril hands"? Perhaps we can see them as his own hands, clasped in anger. Maybe they are the hands of an unborn child. The word *tendril* suggests a twining growth which sometimes supports the stalk of another flower. Certainly there is a connection between the hands and the "lame flower" which thirsts for what little water there is in a barren land. (Think about this image for a moment; it is quite packed.) And what about the "bellyful of weeds"? This obviously suggests pregnancy, but do not miss another meaning derived from the slang expression "get a bellyful of something." Thomas loves the rancorous growth, the weed, the tendril to use as symbol, because it is simultaneously life and death, growth and decay, and can mean either or both.

The "agonized, two seas"? Frankly, I don't have the slightest idea. There is the implication of vastness and great distance, but just why there are two seas I cannot say. Could one be the "sea of life," the other the "sea of eternity"? Maybe.

Let's move on to stanza 2. We might assume that the poet is less raging; at least he notices his surroundings ("behind my head") and is able to consider something other than the woman herself.

Please go on to page 359.

[*from page 358*]

Read the stanza again.

> Behind my head a square of sky sags over
> The circular smile tossed from lover to lover
> And the golden ball spins out of the skies;
> Not from this anger after
> Refusal struck like a bell under water
> Shall her smile breed that mouth, behind the mirror,
> That burns along my eyes.

What is the "square of sky"? Is it the reflection of the mirror on a wall behind him? It may be a window seen in the mirror, a window which contains the "golden ball" of the sun. Is his metaphorical sun setting, spinning out of the skies?

But the square is sagging. Does this represent surrealistically the loss of order in his world, the refusal of love having produced chaos where before there was order?

One image in this stanza can be tentatively identified, however. What do you sense from the "circular smile tossed from lover to lover"?

Nothing. **page 363**

This symbolizes the reciprocity of love. **page 366**

He may be describing the act of blowing a kiss. **page 368**

[*from page 355*]

YOUR ANSWER: The woman refused the "I" sexual love.

This answer is probably correct, if one judges not only from this poem but also from other Thomas poems. William York Tindall effectively sums up in two words Thomas' range of subject matter by calling it "wombs and tombs" — birth and death. The sexual imagery throughout this poem backs up this interpretation. *Bellyful*, *bear*, *loin*, and the act of refusal itself are examples.

This poem is obviously steeped in sexual imagery. The poet is ragingly angry, either because he has been refused or because he is impotent, therefore refusing both himself and the woman.

Maintaining the sexual emphasis by loaded imagery, Thomas then discusses what will not happen.

Not from This Anger

Not from this anger, anticlimax after
Refusal struck her loin and the lame flower
Bent like a beast to lap the singular floods
In a land strapped by hunger
Shall she receive a bellyful of weeds
And bear those tendril hands I touch across
The agonized, two seas.

Behind my head a square of sky sags over
The circular smile tossed from lover to lover
And the golden ball spins out of the skies;
Not from this anger after
Refusal struck like a bell under water
Shall her smile breed that mouth, behind the mirror,
That burns along my eyes.

We can understand the "lame flower/Bent like a beast" any way we wish, but we must recognize the pun in lines 5 and 6. "Not from this anger," the poet says, describing the basis for his rage. Then he tells us what will not happen. What is your reaction to these lines?

"She" will not become pregnant by him. **page 358**

"She" will not take the "tendrils hands" away. **page 364**

I don't particularly like this poem. **page 367**

[*from page 369*]

YOUR ANSWER: The death of Agamemnon results from Zeus' rape of Leda.

Of course. The poem tells you this, but now what? Could you perhaps have seized on the literal statement "Agamemnon dead" and decided to go no farther in your investigation, hoping that the sources would be revealed as you read on?

If you selected this answer honestly, you have not looked closely enough at the poem. The death of Agamemnon is a result of the rape in the sense that one of the begotten children, Clytemnestra, later murdered her husband, Agamemnon. But the death of Agamemnon — which occurred in later history, that is, after the fall of Troy — is used as a symbol for history itself. Decide now whether you have overlooked something or just do not know; then return to page 369, reread the poem, and try again.

[*from page 355*]

YOUR ANSWER: The woman refused the "I" truthfulness.

"Look not for truth in woman," another poet once said, but I don't think Thomas is particularly concerned here. Not with the objective truth, anyway.

I agree that the poet appears to have expected something quite different from what he received, but is there any indication that the woman had ever lied to him? Perhaps what was refused existed as a promise only in his own mind. If this were so, wouldn't the anger be doubly intense, directed first at the woman and then at himself for his own stupidity? Have you ever done just this?

Perhaps the woman was truthful. How would you feel toward a woman who said you were the scum of the earth, adding that she never wanted to hear your name again? It would hardly be pleasant.

When you reread, analyze the images Thomas uses: the "lame flower," the "bellyful of weeds," the concept of bearing and breeding. What connotations do you see, and why should the poet use this particular series of images?

Return to page 355, reread the poem, and select another answer.

[*from page 359*]

YOUR ANSWER: I sense nothing from the image described.

Could you have misread the question, inferring that I asked you to *make* sense out of the image? I did not ask this at all. Remember the appeal of an image to the senses: sight, hearing, feeling, taste, and touch. To sense, therefore, is merely to apprehend by means of the senses, not to understand through the intellect.

If you sensed nothing from this image, then you would not be able to see the "circular smile" or sense the motion implied by the "tossing from lover to lover." Haven't you ever seen a circular smile? I'll bet you have and also that you have seen it tossed many times. Think about this. Try to visualize a circular smile on the face of your wife, husband, lover, or anyone of the opposite sex. What is this person doing if he or she tosses this smile to you?

Return to page 359, reread stanza 2, and try again.

[*from page 360*]

YOUR ANSWER: "She" will not take the "tendril hands" away.

You are right, but only partly so. What you have done is extract only one action which the poet obviously says will not happen. Do you know what the "tendril hands" are? If not, how can you justify your answer?

Perhaps the above comment was unfair. I don't know what the "tendril hands" are. That is, I could not point them out to you as a physical feature of someone you know. I can, however, sense the impression I think Thomas is trying to convey, that of twining, grasping, tendril-like hands which wish to clasp and hold. Whose hands? Your guess is as good as mine.

Whatever the "tendril hands" really are, they should be seen as only a part of the metaphoric structure. "Not from this anger," Thomas tells us,

> Shall she receive a bellyful of weeds
> And bear those tendril hands I touch across
> The agonized, two seas.

By interpreting the word *bear* only to mean "carry away," you have limited the possible meanings of the word. Doesn't it also mean "to give birth"? Doesn't this connotation follow directly from the idea of a "bellyful"? I do think both meanings are present, and you should not insist so strongly on one that the other is necessarily excluded.

Return to page 360, reread the poem, and select another answer.

[*from page 355*]

YOUR ANSWER: I haven't the slightest idea what the woman refused.

I don't blame you; neither did I at first reading, many years ago. But the reason for my discomfiture is now obvious: I was attempting to discover exactly what Thomas was talking about, a process which I now recognize as futile. Normally the approach to a poem consists of determining what the poet is writing about, then of investigating what he says. With Thomas this procedure is impossible.

Try this: begin with two or three quick readings and attempt only to hear the poem. Don't worry about subject or theme; concentrate only on sound. Then investigate metaphor in the poem, attempting to identify which images and symbols appear to be repeated or developed. If you are familiar with other works by Thomas, look for images which he has used before. Try to establish continuity in both metaphor and sound.

Thomas is a sensuous writer. His poetry appeals much less to the intellect than it does to sight, smell, hearing, taste, and touch, and we should overcome our desire to find out exactly what is being talked about.

Assume you are angry at someone, without being certain why. Keep reading and rereading the poem until thoughts begin to form from the mass of sensual imagery. Return to page 355, look at the poem again and again, then try once more. Guess only as a last resort.

[*from page 359*]

YOUR ANSWER: I sense that the image symbolizes the reciprocity of love.

I agree, but you have just made a symbol out of an image, assigning meaning too soon. Let us concern ourselves for the moment only with the sense impressions we receive from the image, the sight of the "circular smile" being "tossed from lover to lover."

When identifying symbols in Thomas, be careful. He does not use the literary symbol as do, let us say, Van Doren or Jarrell. I doubt if Thomas had any definite idea, even when he had completed each poem, of what each image was supposed to represent. Hemingway's intention to make "real" things is in sharp contrast with Thomas' desire to create images which could include everything, hence resist any attempts to assign to them specific references. The gunner in Jarrell's poem, for instance, symbolizes modern man, but Thomas rarely uses such a concrete image in any of his poetry.

Certainly I would agree that the "circular smile tossed from lover to lover" could symbolize the reciprocity of love, but if you stop here, what do you make of the poet's rejection of the woman? And which one did the tossing, he or she? Could Thomas be commenting sardonically on what his relationship with the woman lacked, or is he perhaps implying something else entirely? Don't try to pin down Thomas; it won't work.

Look only at the image for now; later you may make as many associations as you wish. Return to page 359, reread stanza 2, and try again.

[*from page 360*]

YOUR ANSWER: I don't particularly like this poem.

All right. You have a right to your opinion, but I should prefer that your attitude was not a result of laziness, prejudice, conceit, or ignorance. Justified dislike is useful; without it, no improvement would be possible.

If your dislike is justifiable to you, if you would be willing to argue the point with someone else, then I have no quarrel. But if you have expressed displeasure only because you do not understand, then I suggest a rather abrupt reappraisal, perhaps not only with regard to this poem, but in other areas as well.

You may either skip the rest of the poem entirely, going on to page 372, or return to page 342 and start again with a more open mind, or, if understanding has descended suddenly upon you, return to page 360, reread the poem, and select another answer.

[*from page 359*]

YOUR ANSWER: I sense that he may be describing the act of blowing a kiss.

I think so. A "circular smile" perfectly describes the puckering of the lips; then the kiss is "tossed." Why? To throw a kiss, you must be apart from your "lover," and the act also represents the final good-by, or slang-inspired "kiss-off." After this, the "golden ball spins out of the skies." How final — and how sad.

The last four lines seem to show a sobering and slowing down. Notice how the meter lags after the repeated phrase "Not from this anger." The poet appears to have exorcised his rage and become drained of emotion. He is now making his vow for the everlasting future. "This," he says grimly, "is what shall forever be." Don't miss the implied humor.

Read the last four lines again.

> Not from this anger after
> Refusal struck like a bell under water
> Shall her smile breed that mouth, behind the mirror,
> That burns along my eyes.

Repeating both the "struck" image (this time implying the speed and permeating quality of an underwater sound) and the idea of birth or bearing away, the poet makes a pronouncement. What is it?

He will never see the woman again. **page 357**

He will not allow even the thought of the woman to make him angry. **page 372**

He will never think of the woman again. **page 379**

[*from page 376 or 390*]

YOUR ANSWER: Leda is the mother of Castor and Pollux.

Right. If you know this, then you must also know what other child resulted from Leda's union with Zeus, who assaulted her in the form of a swan. If you guessed, then go back to page 390 and find out.

Realizing that the swan is Zeus, the greatest of the Olympian gods, reread the poem, looking for the effects shown by Yeats of this union of spirit with a mortal being.

Leda and the Swan

A sudden blow: the great wings beating still
Above the staggering girl, her thighs caressed
By the dark webs, her nape caught in his bill,
He holds her helpless breast upon his breast.

How can those terrified vague fingers push
The feathered glory from her loosening thighs?
And how can body, laid in that white rush,
But feel the strange heart beating where it lies?

A shudder in the loins engenders there
The broken wall, the burning roof and tower
And Agamemnon dead.
                                        Being so caught up,
So mastered by the brute blood of the air,
Did she put on his knowledge with his power
Before the indifferent beak could let her drop?

Historically, what does Yeats describe as the result of Zeus' rape of Leda?

The death of Agamemnon. **page 361**

I can't find the reference. **page 377**

I don't know. **page 380**

The fall of Troy. **page 382**

[*from page 383*]

YOUR ANSWER: No. Also, it is impossible to discuss why a poem was written.

But we are not discussing why the poem was written. We are attempting to correlate what the poem says and what it sounds like. Thank you for remembering one of my earlier comments; I haven't changed my mind at all, but here we have a different case entirely.

Remembering that the poem begins with true rhyme and moves slowly to a slender example of consonance, reread the poem for theme.

Leda and the Swan

A sudden blow: the great wings beating still
Above the staggering girl, her thighs caressed
By the dark webs, her nape caught in his bill,
He holds her helpless breast upon his breast.

How can those terrified vague fingers push
The feathered glory from her loosening thighs?
And how can body, laid in that white rush,
But feel the strange heart beating where it lies?

A shudder in the loins engenders there
The broken wall, the burning roof and tower
And Agamemnon dead.
Being so caught up,
So mastered by the brute blood of the air,
Did she put on his knowledge with his power
Before the indifferent beak could let her drop?

What does the poem say?

Nothing at all. It asks a question. **page 381**

The relationship between cause and effect is important to consider. **page 384**

Sexual love is of vital concern to contemporary society. **page 386**

[*from page 376*]

YOUR ANSWER: Leda is the mother of Zeus.

Offhand, I might say you were guessing. Please don't, except as a last resort.

Either use your intelligence to find the answers or admit your ignorance, but don't take wild guesses.

Turn to page 390.

[*from page 368*]

YOUR ANSWER: He will not allow even the thought of the woman to make him angry.

This appears the most logical supposition, although both of the other answers are partly correct. The thought of her smile, perhaps at the moment of refusal, has infuriated him, and literally the sight in the mirror of his mouth, twisted in hatred, could be what "burns along his eyes." Along? The smile is etched on his eyes, burning. He vows that this will never happen again. Could the smile be *her* smile? Reread the poem and decide.

I like to sum up this one possible interpretation by saying that the poem is a magnificent, rolling, roaring, rollicking expression of sexual sour grapes, and I think Thomas knew it.

Now let me destroy everything I have said so far. Reread the poem, considering that Adam is speaking about his reaction to Eve's having eaten the apple. Apply the thought expressed in *Psalms* cii: 15 — "As for a man, his days are as grass: as a flower of the field, so he flourisheth." Add to this *Isaiah* xl: 6 — "All flesh is grass, and all the goodliness thereof is as the flower of the field." I would love to know how you make out.

I have saved the next poem until last because it contains examples of everything we have discussed so far: it is suggestive to emotion as well as intellect, it appeals to the layman as well as the scholar, and, finally, it is one of the finest short poems in the English language. I expect many of you to disagree violently.

Please go on to page 373.

[*from page 372*]

Before we look at the poem, I would like to introduce one final term, the *literary allusion*. You understand what a symbol is, how it is simultaneously itself and something else. Diagrammed, the symbol looks like this:

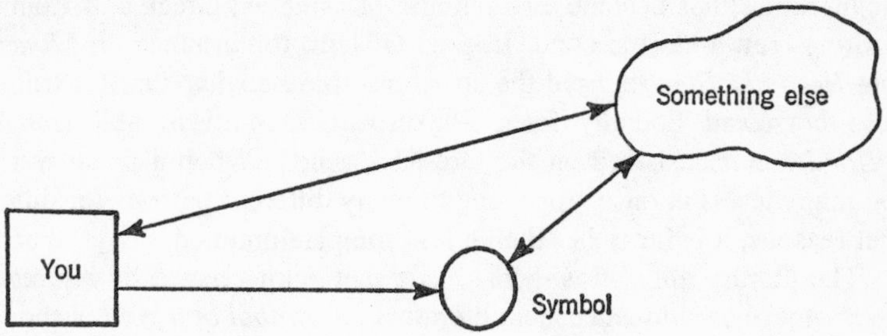

A tree can thus symbolize life; the color black, death. But what if you alter the diagram like this:

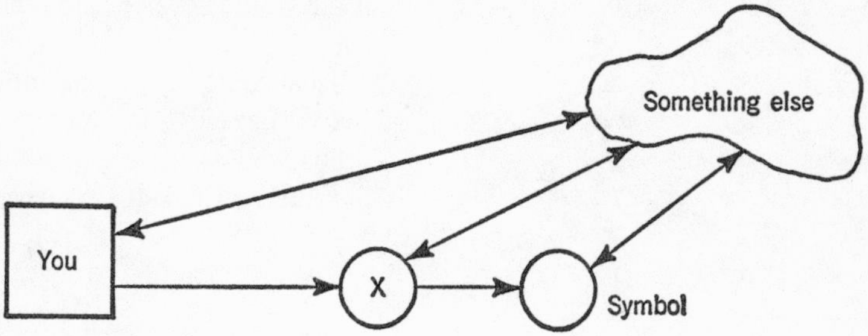

The (X) represents an element of a work of art used to allude to a previously accepted symbol. Take a tree, for instance. What if a poet, writing of a tree, uses it not only to symbolize life but also to represent Eden's particular tree of the Knowledge of Good and Evil? Similarly, a man standing with his arms held straight out may allude to the cross on which Christ died, a cross which itself is a symbol of suffering. The literary allusion is nothing more than a symbol once removed, or, if you will, a symbol of a previously used symbol.

Please go on to page 374.

[*from page 373*]

The literary allusion has become an important part of contemporary literature. Attempting to create as much meaning in as small a space as possible, modern writers with increasing frequency refer again and again within their works to elements of the past. The Bible, considered as literature, has become a storehouse of symbols; Greek and Roman writings run a close second. Eugene O'Neill, for instance, in *Mourning Becomes Electra*, used the structure of Aeschylus' Orestes trilogy and borrowed liberally from Shakespeare's *Macbeth* and *Hamlet* (*Hamlet* is itself based on the Orestes legend). When a poem works on many levels at once, appealing to many different persons for different reasons, it is far richer than a less complex creation.

The literary allusion is defined as a metaphor created by reference to a symbol used in antecedent literature. *A symbol of a symbol* should do nicely.

Now go on to page 375.

[*from page 374*]

William Butler Yeats is thought by many persons to be the greatest poet since Shakespeare. He has certainly produced as many outstanding poems as anyone in the contemporary period. This is one of his best.

Leda and the Swan

A sudden blow: the great wings beating still
Above the staggering girl, her thighs caressed
By the dark webs, her nape caught in his bill,
He holds her helpless breast upon his breast.

How can those terrified vague fingers push
The feathered glory from her loosening thighs?
And how can body, laid in that white rush,
But feel the strange heart beating where it lies?

A shudder in the loins engenders there
The broken wall, the burning roof and tower
And Agamemnon dead.
Being so caught up,
So mastered by the brute blood of the air,
Did she put on his knowledge with his power
Before the indifferent beak could let her drop?

All you need to understand this poem is knowledge of the allusions from Homer, Greek mythology, Biblical history, and Yeats's private cyclical theory outlined in his book *A Vision*. Or do you need all this? Understanding is one thing, appreciation another. You can feel the power of this poem even without complete understanding. Read it again. A woman is assaulted, "mastered by the brute blood of the air" who is shown to be indifferent and powerful. But is he completely indifferent? Note the last line:

Before the indifferent beak *could* let her drop.

Please go on to page 376.

[*from page 375*]

Not *would* let her drop. We will examine structure later, but let us begin by attempting to explicate the poem. I will not require you to use any outside materials unless you want to; just select the answer "I don't know" every time. But I suggest, if you do not know the answer to a factual question, that you look it up. Start with the dictionary, then go to an encyclopedia, then try to find some works in which the allusions are discussed. A classical dictionary would help, as would any general reference work on Greek mythology. The Bible will come into the picture later. If you want to do the work on your own, you can check your results against the wrong answer pages to follow.

All right? First of all, who is Leda?

The mother of Castor and Pollux. **page 369**

The mother of Zeus. **page 371**

I don't know. **page 390**

[*from page 369*]

YOUR ANSWER: I can't find the reference to the result of Zeus' rape of Leda.

Congratulations, you tried. Often a source is hard to pin down, and only through exhaustive searching can the precise information be located.

When attempting to find literary source material, start with the obvious reference, in this case Leda, but do not expect to find the answer to every question you may have from the first piece of material you read. For instance, the *American College Dictionary* provides the following information about her:

> Le-da, n. *Gk. Myth.* the mother by Zeus of Helen, Clytemnestra, Castor and Pollux.

End of information, telling you nothing about Yeats's purpose in using this mythical woman. But are there not more possibilities suggested by this brief dictionary definition? What about Helen, Castor, Pollux, or Clytemnestra? Some sources say that Clytemnestra was not a direct descendant of Zeus, but a true daughter of Leda and her husband, Tyndareus.

Look up each of the names included in the Leda reference, preferably in an encyclopedia, but a dictionary will do for a start. Try to discover what bearing these figures have on Agamemnon (look him up, too). Many of you will learn that you understood all along but did not make the proper associations.

Finally, see if you can find out where all of this information came from in the first place, what the reference to *Gk. Myth.* means. Who created the myth in the first place? Where can you read more about it? This process is one of the great rewards of reading, for one small bit of knowledge often creates the desire for more, and before you know it, you are an authority on something. When you have followed my suggestions and are either informed or thoroughly disgusted, return to page 369 and try again.

[*from page 383 or 384*]

YOUR ANSWER: Yes. The disruption of rhyme coincides with the creation of disorder within the poem.

Right. What appears at first to be nothing more than a well-written descriptive sonnet is actually a discussion of the meaning of history. I want to make certain that you see how cleverly Yeats accomplishes this. Reread the poem, isolating the three questions which Yeats asks in stanzas 2 and 3.

Leda and the Swan

A sudden blow: the great wings beating still
Above the staggering girl, her thighs caressed
By the dark webs, her nape caught in his bill,
He holds her helpless breast upon his breast.

How can those terrified vague fingers push
The feathered glory from her loosening thighs?
And how can body, laid in that white rush,
But feel the strange heart beating where it lies?

A shudder in the loins engenders there
The broken wall, the burning roof and tower
And Agamemnon dead.
Being so caught up,
So mastered by the brute blood of the air,
Did she put on his knowledge with his power
Before the indifferent beak could let her drop?

Now, answer the three questions, in order.

They can't; it must; yes. **page 385**

They can't; it must; no. **page 387**

They can't; it must; I don't know. **page 391**

I'm confused. **page 392**

[*from page 368*]

YOUR ANSWER: He will never think of the woman again.

But what if he should? Then what? Wouldn't his reaction be much the same as the poet's in "A Woman Too Well Remembered," where we saw the "I" admitting that "When . . . I think of her, other faces fade"? For the "I" of Thomas' poem, what would remembrance produce? Probably anger all over again, *if* you see him vowing only never to think of her again.

Haven't you made similar promises: "I will never have another cigarette . . . another drink . . . tell another white lie"? What happened? Some of you succeeded, but many of you amended each respective statement thus: "But if I do . . . at least I won't do it so *often*."

I do not think Thomas has created so angry a man that all common sense has been lost. Perhaps he will think of her again, but the poem has shown a change in his attitude toward her as his rage wears off. In effect, the poet does think of her again when he writes the poem about his former anger.

Return to page 368, reread the last four lines, and try again.

[*from page 369*]

YOUR ANSWER: I don't know what results from Zeus' rape of Leda.

Here is the section of the poem we are concerned with:

A shudder in the loins engenders there
The broken wall, the burning roof and tower
And Agamemnon dead.

Three lines, eighteen words, and Yeats has presented an important element of the world's history as seen in Greek legend.

The broken wall, the burning roof and tower, and the death of Agamemnon all refer to the Trojan War. The broken wall alludes specifically to the wall surrounding Troy, broken down by the Trojans themselves to drag in the giant horse left by the scheming Greeks (certainly you know this story). What happened? Greeks hidden inside the horse emerged at night, opened the gates to their comrades, and together the two bands sacked Troy, creating the scene described as the "burning roof and tower." The roof may be a direct reference to that of the palace on which Aeneas stood watching the destruction, and the tower could be one of many in the city.

And Agamemnon? Try looking this man up. Almost all reference works carry the necessary information about him, and you should have no difficulty tying everything together. Whether you are successful or not, go on to page 382.

[*from page 370 or 389*]

YOUR ANSWER: The poem says nothing at all. It asks a question.

This is shallow thinking. I cannot help feeling you don't really want to understand poetry.

Let me ask this. If you are proved wrong, how do you feel? Resentful? Angry? Or are you perhaps one of the gracious people who are actually thankful to have errors mentioned to them?

If you are one of the latter, then we can talk. Your approach to poetry is wrong because you are likely to miss something important. By refusing at least to attempt an understanding of poetry (and this does not mean merely scanning a line or two here and there), you cut yourself off from your own age, whether or not you happen to like what you read. No one can afford the luxury of intentional ignorance — not today. End of sermon.

If you are just being facetious about the whole thing, then you should realize that facetiousness usually follows that nervous, embarrassed laughter we often emit when either caught doing something we should not be doing, or have had our lack of preparation exposed for the world to see.

Either way, I think you should reconsider. Return to page 389 (or if you came from page 370, return there) and try again.

[*from page 369 or 380*]

YOUR ANSWER: The fall of Troy results from Zeus' rape of Leda.

Right. The "burning roof and tower" refer to the sacking of Troy by the victorious Greeks, culminating the ten-year Trojan War which began when Helen, wife of Menelaus, was abducted by Paris, a Trojan. Who was Helen? Of course, the daughter of Leda and Zeus.

So far, so good, but what about Agamemnon? Some mythologies maintain that Leda produced four children, Castor, Pollux, Helen, and Clytemnestra. You should have found in some reference work by now that Clytemnestra was Agamemnon's adulterous wife, who, together with Aegisthus, killed Agamemnon upon his return from Troy. The Trojan War, and "Agamemnon dead."

The rape of Leda by Zeus becomes a symbol of cause. Leda, from her union with Zeus, gave birth to Helen, who in turn was responsible for the Trojan War.

Let's attempt to see how a poem considering an ancient subject can have a bearing on contemporary thought. Read the poem again, this time with an eye to general structure.

Leda and the Swan

A sudden blow: the great wings beating still
Above the staggered girl, her thighs caressed
By the dark webs, her nape caught in his bill,
He holds her helpless breast upon his breast.

How can those terrified vague fingers push
The feathered glory from her loosening thighs?
And how can body, laid in that white rush,
But feel the strange heart beating where it lies?

A shudder in the loins engenders there
The broken wall, the burning roof and tower
And Agamemnon dead.
Being so caught up,
So mastered by the brute blood of the air,
Did she put on his knowledge with his power
Before the indifferent beak could let her drop?

Please go on to page 383.

[*from page 382*]

If you did not recognize this as a sonnet, shame on you. Look again before proceeding.

Although this is a sonnet, it is like none we have seen so far. Notice the rhyme scheme:

Stanza 1 — abab

Stanza 2 — cdc+d (the consonance between "push" and "rush")

Stanza 3 — efgefg+ (consonance again, this time between "up" and "drop")

You should recognize the progression. The first stanza contains perfect rhyme; the second introduces consonance, but between words which look almost alike; the last stanza finishes with a slant rhyme held together by a single letter. Is this progression intentional?

No. Also, it is impossible to discuss why a poem was written. **page 370**

Yes. The disruption of rhyme coincides with the creation of disorder within the poem. **page 378**

Yes. This is a frequent device of Yeats's. **page 388**

[*from page 370 or 389*]

YOUR ANSWER: The relationship between cause and effect is important to consider.

Certainly. The key to this as a theme is seen in the final lines when the poet asks:

> Did she put on his knowledge with his power
> Before the indifferent beak could let her drop?

The cause of the Trojan War? Zeus, of course. And the effect? Everything which followed. What the poem asks is for us to relate cause and effect in terms of Leda's possible understanding of the consequences. Is all history a result of indifference, or is there some form of knowledge which guides the events of time? Is it possible for a human being to understand?

Yeats concludes with a question which is intentionally unanswerable, and we are offered a choice much like what Bowers called naming "for lack of name." If we answer, "Of course, God directs all things," then we might be overly hasty, because the poem concerns a time and subject which existed in pre-Christian times.

What seemed to be a definite act, rape, has suddenly produced an unanswerable question. Was Zeus actually indifferent, or was his assault of Leda, an action which produced the ultimate disorder of war, part of his predetermined plan? Does this poem discuss an ordered plan which creates disorder . . . now you see, don't you? Order has the same relationship to true rhyme that disorder has to slant rhyme, and Yeats has shown a consistent progression in both sound and sense. And yes, he does this often, but each time for a specific purpose within a particular poem.

You should now be able to see the intention behind the rhyme, so go on to page 378.

[*from page 378*]

YOUR ANSWER: They can't; it must; yes.

I envy you. What you have just done is solve one of the most pressing problems of all time, the relationship between first cause and ultimate effect. By answering the question "Did she put on his knowledge with his power" in the affirmative you have said that Leda, shown here to be somewhat like Van Doren's "mother of life," knew what she had done and what the significance to the world would be. You have shown also that you believe it possible to transfer qualities of spirit as well as flesh through sexual union, also implying that Leda was herself responsible for the Trojan War.

You didn't mean all this? Most of it? Some of it? No matter; your answer has demonstrated the range of meaning which a poem can offer different readers. You supplied the meaning; the poem only suggested a theme, here seen as a question which appears unanswerable.

The poem has forced you to apprehend, think, contrast, evaluate, and conclude. You have exemplified the intellectual process.

Don't let it worry you that I may disagree with everything you say. The conclusion you have arrived at is your own, and if you believe it, don't waver from it. I prefer to leave the final question unanswered, thus allowing it to be asked over and over again, and in each of my attempts to formulate my own belief, I learn something.

As a final favor, accept an "I don't know" answer, and go on to page 391.

[*from page 370 or 389*]

YOUR ANSWER: Sexual love is of vital concern to contemporary society.

No doubt it is, but this is not the question here. You will rarely see a twentieth-century poet using the need for physical love as a theme. As a subject, yes, as we have seen, but few poets feel the need to justify its existence.

You should pay more attention to the poem itself. What does it say? What bearing does an act as definite as rape have to do with the Trojan War and all succeeding history? Yeats uses sexual love as a metaphor of history. Although the occasion for the poem is unquestionably erotic, the subject is philosophical — the nature of cause and effect. Consider Yeats's final question closely. Can you answer it? Do you know whether Leda put on Zeus' "knowledge with his power"? Did she understand what she was about to be at least partially responsible for? Or did she have any responsibility at all, seeing as she was taken by force?

Keep these questions in mind, return to page 389 (or if you came from page 370, return there) reread the poem, and select another answer.

[*from page 378*]

YOUR ANSWER: They can't; it must; no.

This is an interesting conclusion, and I hope you realize what you have just said. By stating that Leda did *not* "put on his knowledge with his power" you are absolving her of all responsibility for ensuing events. You imply that she probably did not recognize this swan as any different from any other swan.

And here, in contrast to some of the other assumptions I may have induced you to make, your belief is valid because it results directly from the poem itself. The poem suggested a theme, seen here as a question which shows the need for an answer; you supplied the meaning of the poem.

You have been forced to apprehend, think, contrast, evaluate, and conclude. You have thus exemplified the intellectual process.

Don't waver from your belief if you can continue to justify its existence. But allow me the right to leave the final question unanswered, because I like to see it asked over and over again, and in each of my attempts to formulate my own belief, I learn something.

As a final favor, accept an "I don't know" answer and go on to page 391.

[*from page 383*]

YOUR ANSWER: Yes. This is a frequent device of Yeats's.

True, it is, but how does this technique affect this poem? You remind me very much of the student who hopes he will never be called upon in class, but just in case he is, he has a few stock answers ready, responses which he knows are true and all-encompassing. After answering the first question, he prays that the instructor will be fooled and call on someone else for the next question.

Whoever told you (or perhaps you guessed) that Yeats often intentionally disrupted rhyme is correct. Now what?

Why not apply your knowledge to this poem and see why Yeats does it here?

Let's begin. Keeping in mind the progression from true to slant rhyme, reread the poem for theme.

Please go on to page 389.

[*from page 388*]

Leda and the Swan

A sudden blow: the great wings beating still
Above the staggering girl, her thighs caressed
By the dark webs, her nape caught in his bill,
He holds her helpless breast upon his breast.

How can those terrified vague fingers push
The feathered glory from her loosening thighs?
And how can body, laid in that white rush,
But feel the strange heart beating where it lies?

A shudder in the loins engenders there
The broken wall, the burning roof and tower
And Agamemnon dead.
                                        Being so caught up,
So mastered by the brute blood of the air,
Did she put on his knowledge with his power
Before the indifferent beak could let her drop?

What does the poem say?

Nothing at all. It asks a question. **page 381**

The relationship between cause and effect is important to consider. **page 384**

Sexual love is of vital concern to contemporary society. **page 386**

[*from page 371 or 376*]

YOUR ANSWER: I don't know.

If you have a dictionary or encyclopedia available, why not try it out? You still have a chance to discover something on your own.

If not, here is the source. When you understand it, you will have been introduced not only to the literary allusion but to a bit of Greek history as well.

Leda, the wife of Tyndareus, king of Sparta, was assaulted by Zeus, who had taken the form of a swan. Zeus, as you probably are aware, was the principal of the Greek gods who reigned from Mount Olympus. Following the assault, Leda produced two eggs, the first of which contained the Greek heroes Castor and Pollux, the second of which became Helen, later the wife of Menelaus. Some mythologies also identify Clytemnestra as another child.

It is Helen who concerns Yeats here. Keeping her in mind, go on to page 369 and continue.

[*from page 378, 385, or 387*]

YOUR ANSWER: They couldn't; it must; I don't know.

I don't know, either.

The girl's fingers were powerless against the advances of a god, and her body, "laid in that white rush," must have felt the "strange heart beating." ("White rush" describes not only the ground on which she lies but also the swan who has rushed upon her.) Finally, the poet asks if Leda "put on his knowledge with his power." Did she? Did she realize her effect on history? Was she aware that because of a single physical act, the world would be unalterably changed? Does anyone realize the significance of one apparently isolated action? Is it possible through physical union to transfer more than flesh? Did Zeus have knowledge of the tragic war to follow, and yet remain indifferent? Yeats presents the rape, and Zeus' indifference, as a metaphor of history, cause and effect, and predetermination. Is there some plan which is not known to man but which determines his future? Is it possible for man to discover his destiny?

Do you know the answers to any or all of these questions, each of which is suggested directly by the poem? Are you certain? Can you prove your points?

Should we go more deeply into this poem? Should we consider the application of Yeats's personal theory of cyclical change (his third such system, by the way)? Should we reread, seeing how other expressed beliefs fit? (For instance, how did the Holy Ghost appear to Mary to reveal the coming birth of Christ? As white "feathered glory," a dove? Did Mary put on "his knowledge with his power"?)

Is this poem and, for that matter, every poem we have discussed in this book worth rereading again and again and again?

Yes. **page 393**

[*from page 378*]

YOUR ANSWER: I'm confused.

I don't wonder. We have rushed through this poem, but there is not enough space to discuss everything I would like to. Let me for the moment expand the question which has confused you. Here are the three questions referred to earlier:

> How can those terrified vague fingers push
> The feathered glory from her loosening thighs?
>
> And how can body, laid in that white rush,
> But feel the strange heart beating where it lies?
>
> Did she put on his knowledge with his power
> Before the indifferent beak could let her drop?

You were asked to answer each question for yourself, and the list of possible answers, arranged in order, appears at the bottom of the page. Notice that the first two questions are rhetorical. The final answer, however, is left up to you.

Return to page 378, reread the questions in context, and try again.

[*from page 391*]

YOUR ANSWER: Every poem we have discussed is worth rereading again and again and again.

Yes, but unfortunately we can no longer continue our discussion. We have moved from the alphabet to Greek history, considered life, death, love, reality, art, society, pain, war, existence, and God; I have made you angry, and you by association have made me furious by your refusal to accept what I offer as truth. But as I have said often, I applaud your disagreement as long as you are certain of what you think and are willing to justify it.

This book has been only an introduction to twentieth-century poetry. If it has helped you to become one tiny bit more aware, it has succeeded in the same way a poem succeeds when you let it.

APPENDIX

Guide for Further Reading

This appendix is designed for those who wish to read more poetry but are uncertain where to begin. The first five books constitute a basic library; the books by the individual poets represent either their most recent or their most representative works.

I

Anthologies and Reference Works

Allen, Donald M., *The New American Poetry, 1945-1960* (New York: The Grove Press, 1960). This paperback anthology contains more than 200 poems, many of which are published here for the first time, and is especially valuable for its section "Statements on Poetics," which provides insight into the thinking and theories of post-World War II American poets.

Brooks, Cleanth, and Robert Penn Warren, *Understanding Poetry*, 3rd ed. (New York: Holt, Rinehart and Winston, 1960). For years the standard poetry textbook for many colleges and universities, this book contains extensive critical analyses of 200 poems, as well as a supplement of 43 modern poems by virtually every important contemporary American and British poet.

Cecil, David, and Allen Tate, *Modern Verse in English, 1900-1950* (New York: The Macmillan Company, 1958). More than a mere anthology, this book offers compact critical introductions on both British and American poetry as well as biographical information on each poet. It contains selected poems of 120 modern poets.

Drew, Elizabeth, *Poetry: A Modern Guide to Its Understanding and Enjoyment* (New York: Dell, 1959). One of the Laurel Poetry Series, this inexpensive book discusses the poetic process and traces such major subjects as time, death, and love through all periods of British and American literature.

Thrall, Hibbard and Holman, *A Handbook to Literature* (New York: Odyssey, 1960). An essential for any interested reader, this handbook contains discussions of almost every literary term, movement, genre, style, and school since the beginnings of literature. Invaluable.

II

Biographical and Bibliographical Information

Wystan Hugh Auden (1907-) moved to the United States from England in 1939. He won the 1948 Pulitzer Prize for his long, didactic verse play *The Age of Anxiety*. In a style varying from singsong to free verse, many of his poems show his disillusioned idealism and his hatred of war. Recommended from *Collected Poems* (1945) are "O Where Are You Going," "The Unknown Citizen," "In Memory of W. B. Yeats," and "September 1, 1939."

Edgar Bowers (1924-), originally from Georgia, now teaches at the University of California at Santa Barbara. His heavy, Miltonic style often makes his poems, which treat religious, historical, and commonplace subjects, seem more difficult than they really are. Particularly interesting from his first collection, *The Form of Loss* (1956), are "The Wise Men," "Amor vincit omnia," "Two Poems on the Catholic Bavarians," "The Prince," and "Palm Sunday."

Stephen Crane (1871-1900), perhaps best known for his novel *The Red Badge of Courage*, died when only 30 years old. A forerunner of the Imagists, he prefers in his brilliant, short poems not to discuss but to indict war, Puritanism, and modern culture. Once read, his poetry will never be forgotten. All of his few poems are good; if the *Collected Poems* (1930) is not available, the Rinehart Edition of *Selected Prose and Poetry* (1950) contains examples of his poetry as well as some excellent short stories.

E. E. Cummings (1894-) is the son of a Boston educator and minister. His unique style, at first called only "precious rhetoric" and "scrambled syntax," has had a noted influence on younger poets. Regardless of their occasional overdependence on ingenuity, his poems are always delightful to read for their fresh, often exciting presentation of familiar, sometimes trite subjects. From *Poems 1923-1954* (1954) are suggested: "POEM, OR BEAUTY HURTS MR. VINAL," "the Cambridge ladies who live in furnished souls," "la guerre," and "a man who had fallen among thieves."

J. V. Cunningham (1911-) has lived in Maryland, Colorado, California, Hawaii, and Virginia, and is now chairman of the English Department at Brandeis University. His publisher, Alan Swallow, attributes to him "the fury of a first class mind." Rarely writing poems longer than 15 lines, Cunningham is the unchallenged master of the contemporary epigram. With equal craft he translates Latin poetry and satirizes modern morals. His latest collection, *The Exclusions of a Rhyme* (1960), contains such memorable poems as "Montana Pastoral," "Ripeness Is All," "The Metaphysical Amorist," "Ars Amoris," and many sparkling epigrams.

Peter Kane Dufault (1923-   ) writes primarily of personal experiences gleaned from his kaleidoscopic life as combat airman, laborer, guitarist, lobbyist, newspaperman, actor, and dramatist. Whether about an aerial battle or a subway scene, his lyrics reflect the perspicacity with which Dufault appraises modern existence. Experimental, undisciplined, often obscure, his poems testify to an unabashed love of sensuous experience. His two volumes of verse, *Angel of Accidence* (1954) and *Music for Some Stringed Instrument* (1957), are characterized by "The President Orders Construction of the Hydrogen Bomb," "Views in a Bar," "Tour de Force," "Crow Calls," and "After a Night Flight."

Lawrence Ferlinghetti (1919-   ), a New Yorker by birth, calls himself neither "dead nor a junkie." Feeling that the Beat Generation is "as phony as a four-dollar piece of lettuce," he has produced two remarkable short collections, *Pictures of the Gone World* (1955) and *A Coney Island of the Mind* (1958). His barbs are directed not so much at the futility of modern existence as at those people who make happiness, love, and peace impossible in today's world. Of particular interest are his recordings for *Fantasy: Tentative Description of a Dinner Given to Promote the Impeachment of President Eisenhower* and *Poetry Readings in the Cellar*.

Robert Frost (1875-   ), dean of American poetry, wrote for twenty years before British publication led to American and world-wide acclaim. Although not a college graduate, he has taught and lectured extensively, has received many honorary degrees, and has been awarded the Pulitzer Prize four times. Rarely didactic, his poems capture the rhythm and idiom of common speech. He presents a simple rural scene as a subject for philosophical inquiry and is equally effective with the short lyric or the introspective dramatic monologue. Readers of his *Complete Poems* (1949) will be especially delighted by "Mending Wall," "The Death of the Hired Man," "After Apple-picking," "Birches," and "Stopping by Woods on a Snowy Evening."

Robert Graves (1895-   ) offers in his *Collected Poems* (1961) a fascinating study of the development of a major modern poet. Sticky, sentimental, and imitative, his early poems soon are overshadowed by what Graves calls a movement toward "punctilious and intuitive realism." His main subject is modern love, and it is interesting to watch his progression from the early "Reproach" and "Love in Barrenness" treatment to the brilliant, often sardonic, discussions in "Established Lovers," "The Succubus," and "Ulysses."

Thomas Hardy (1840-1928), who continually wrote of a "world where one so often hungers . . . for friendship," is perhaps better known for his nineteenth-century novels than for his twentieth-century poetry. His long dramatic poem, *The Dynasts* (1909), established him as a poet; his later lyrics, many of which further develop the "capricious fatalism" of his fiction, are usually bitter, occasionally hilarious. Of particular note in his *Collected Poems* (1954) are "The Voice," "The Ruined Maid," "Channel Firing," and "The Man He Killed."

Gerard Manley Hopkins (1844-1889), unpublished until 1918, belongs in the contemporary period for his influence more than his style. His sensuous love of God is always apparent, but as a Jesuit he had to write most of his poems in secret because of an unsympethetic superior. He shows his dissatisfaction with the bare, bleak existence of nineteenth-century seminaries through brilliant imagery and vibrantly rhythmic innovations. The best of his *Poems* (1948) are "The Windhover," "The Starlight Night," "Pied Beauty," and "The Leaden Echo and the Golden Echo."

Randall Jarrell (1914-   ) is representative of the questioning, introspective, often disillusioned twentieth-century poet. His early poems, many of which concern childhood, reflect his continuous doubt of reality, truth, and love. His war poems, like those of Wilfred Owen, are among his best, containing impressionistic imagery and carefully controlled bitterness. His constant plea for individuality in spite of modern mechanization characterizes his post-World War II poetry. In *Selected Poems* (1955) he includes valuable explanatory notes for such poems as: "A Girl in a Library," "The Black Swan," "The Dead Wingman," and "Come to the Stone. . . ." His latest volume, *The Woman at the Washington Zoo*, contains excellent translations of contemporary European poets.

Amy Lowell (1874-1925), like so many other modern poets, was first influenced by the nineteenth-century Romantics. Her initial collection, *A Dome of Many-Colored Glass* (1912), published when she was 38, showed her dependence upon John Keats. Soon, however, influenced by Ezra Pound, she became the American leader of the Imagist movement, and her subsequent free verse is noted for its colorful, often confused images. *What's O'Clock* (1925) received a Pulitzer Prize, awarded posthumously. *Selected Poems* (1928) contains some of her more notable poems: "Patterns," "Solitaire," "The Taxi," and "The Sisters."

Wilfred Owen's death in 1918 when he was but 25 exemplifies the horror of war, the subject of most of his good poems. Like Amy Lowell, he first imitated Keats, but his experiences in World War I quickly created his direct, sardonic, often brutally ironic hatred of man's inhumanity toward man. Written at the front under fire, his war poems are perhaps the best of all time. The 1933 edition of his poems (with a revealing memoir by Edmund Blunden) contains many potentially magnificent fragments, as well as "Dulce et Decorum Est," "Exposure," "Strange Meeting," and "Anthem for Doomed Youth."

Carl Sandburg (1878-   ) was once considered a twentieth-century Walt Whitman, for Sandburg's rollicking, slangy, unrefined lyrics often suggest the "barbaric yawp" of his predecessor. Unknown until 1914, the then 36-year-old newspaperman began his sustained attempt to use poetry to reproduce American sounds, sights, and attitudes. Although often violent, his verses are marked occasionally by extreme tenderness. He was awarded the Pulitzer Prize in 1940 for his biography, *Abraham Lincoln: The War Years*. His *Complete Poems* (1950) contains "Chicago," "Grass," "Jazz Fantasia," "Early Lynching," and his famous "Fog."

Louis Simpson (1923-   ) exemplifies the contemporary poet who is uncertain of his attitudes toward modern society and its beliefs. Many of his poems reflect his experiences while traveling in Europe on fellowships; others comment upon man's inability to differentiate between love and lust, the real and the imaginary. Often written in a slangy style, his poems (regularly published in the *New Yorker*) show consistent irony, occasional sarcasm. His first book, *The Arrivestes* (1949) was followed shortly by *Good News of Death*. His latest, *A Dream of Governors* (1959), contains the intriguing long narrative poem, "The Runner," as well as the bitter "To the Western World" and the delightful "The Custom of the World."

Dylan Thomas (1914-1953) has been called the "Ideal Romantic Poet" because of his frequent use of drugs and liquor and his unwillingness to tolerate any artistic, social, or moral conventions not of his own making. His extravagant, pulsating, sensual poetry is often incomprehensible, always dazzling, best when read aloud. His *Collected Poems* (1952) includes "I See the Boys of Summer," "The force that through the green fuse drives the flower," "Fern Hill," and "In Memory of Ann Jones."

Mark Van Doren (1894-   ), scholar, critic, lecturer, teacher, is similar to Robert Frost in his frequent consideration of commonplace rural scenes. Most of his lyrics, however, are shorter and often more precise than Frost's. He has written plays, short stories, and essays, edited many anthologies, taught literature, and reviewed motion pictures. His *Collected Poems* (1939) won a Pulitzer Prize. His brief poems are his best. Recommended are "Civil War" and "Young Woman at a Window."

John Hall Wheelock (1886-   ) is one of the many modern poets with two professions, in his case poetry and publishing. He has been associated with Charles Scribner's Sons since 1911, the year he published his first volume of verse. Often sentimental, filled with verbiage, and unsustained, his poems usually exhibit extreme sensibility but lack polish. His *Poems, Old and New* (1956) contains such occasionally excellent poems as "Bomac," "Afternoon; Amagansett Beach," and "Night Thoughts in Age."

William Butler Yeats (1865-1939), an Anglo-Irishman, was a patriot, mystic, prophet, and above all a dedicated artist. He attempted to make his poetry express not only his theories of history and reality but also his determination that art could provide stability for a world in flux. His poems, plays, and essays progress from his youthful idolization of the past, through hard, deliberately idiomatic commentaries on society, to imaginative, perfectly constructed works which continuously justify their own existence. His *Collected Poems* (1959) introduces the reader to such masterpieces as "The Lake Isle of Innisfree," "Adam's Curse," "September 1913," "The Second Coming," "Among School Children," and "Lapis Lazuli."

INDEX